One Dog at a Time

Saving the Strays of Helmand
An Inspiring True Story

Pen Farthing

EBURY
PRESS

3 5 7 9 10 8 6 4 2

This edition published 2010
First published in 2009 by Ebury Press, an imprint of Ebury Publishing
A Random House Group company

The Random House Group Limited Reg. No. 954009

Addresses for companies within the Random House Group can be
found at www.randomhouse.co.uk

A CIP catalogue record for this book is available from
the British Library

The Random House Group Limited supports The Forest Stewardship
Council (FSC), the leading international forest certification organisation.
All our titles that are printed on Greenpeace approved FSC certified
paper carry the FSC logo. Our paper procurement policy can be found at
www.rbooks.co.uk/environment

Printed and bound in Great Britain by
CPI Cox & Wyman, Reading, RG1 8EX

ISBN 9780091928810

To buy books by your favourite authors and register for offers visit
www.rbooks.co.uk

Contents

Prologue

'Sergeant, I thought you might want to do something about this.'

Mase, the young Royal Marine who had called me on the radio to join him in his sand-bagged sentry post, was pointing towards the barbed-wire road block. It was about 100 yards north of our isolated compound in the Afghan outpost of Now Zad.

Thick with rolls of gleaming, new wire, the obstacle was designed to prevent a suicide bomber driving directly into the compound's thick mud walls. Today, however, it had only succeeded in stopping something else – a small, white, terrified-looking dog.

Straight away I saw it had a wire noose tied around its neck. I had seen dogs tied up like that before out here in Afghanistan. This one had obviously broken free from whatever it had been tied to and tried to run through our makeshift barrier, but the trailing strand of wire from the noose had caught fast on the barbed wire. The more it struggled to break free, the tighter the noose became. The dog was slowly killing itself.

'Bollocks,' I said to myself.

The 100 yards that separated me from the dog was in no-man's-land. Definitely no place to pretend to be a member of the RSPCA.

The obstacle was situated across the only 'real' road in this area of Helmand province, a single strip of tarmac that ran north to south for over 400 metres. At one time the shops that ran along this road had sold fruit, vegetables, watches, shoes, medicines, even music tapes. Not so long ago their wares would have been spilling out on to the road tempting passers-by.

Now, however, there was no one to be seen, and the fronts of the stores were a mess of twisted metal and broken wood; their walls decorated with bullet holes. No place to take a stroll, even if you were carrying the world's largest white flag. Aside from the threat of rifle fire, the network of alleyways that led off the road was notorious as a hiding place for local Taliban fighters. We had even named one of the alleyways 'RPG alley', after the rocket-propelled grenades that they fired at us.

As I scanned the scene now, I knew that the Taliban could be hiding in any one of these buildings just waiting for one of us to pop out of the compound.

I closed my eyes, wondering why this was happening to me.

Deep down I knew that I should just tell Mase to carry on with his sentry duty and ignore the dog. I knew others in my position wouldn't even give the animal a second thought. They would leave it to die of starvation or stand by while it strangled itself to death. Hell, some might even use it as target practice.

But I knew I couldn't just walk away. Especially, given what had happened in the four months or so since I'd arrived in Helmand province.

I opened my eyes and turned my attention back to the white dog.

It had stopped struggling and had resigned itself to lying on the ground, panting heavily from the exertion of trying to break free.

I explained my plan to Mase, although there wasn't much of one. I removed my webbing and radio and placed them down on the floor of the sand-bagged sentry post, or 'sangar' as we called them. I took out an extra magazine of ammunition and shoved it in my combat trousers pocket, just in case.

The plan was simple. The front of the sangar had a narrow slit that the sentry looked through, which was big enough for a man to slide through sideways. I would squeeze out through the slit, down to the edge of the roof on which the sangar was perched, then jump four feet down to the top of the sand-filled 'HESCO block' that protected the base of the building, and then drop off the side of that on to the tarmac road.

I waved at the sentry in the next sangar along. He waved back.

I pointed my weapon through the slit first and then followed it with my body.

Mase scanned the deserted street for any signs of bad guys. I hadn't really thought about what I would do if the Taliban decided to attack. I knew I should be able to climb back up into the sentry post extremely quickly. Hopefully even quicker if I was being shot at.

I looked north and south along the street one more time. Everything was eerily quiet.

'Laters,' I said to Mase as I dropped down on to the HESCO block.

I had done some fairly stupid things during the course of my life. As my feet hit the tarmac road I thought that this might be the stupidest yet.

My heart was racing. I took a deep breath. 'Try not to get shot, idiot boy, or you won't be much use to anybody, let alone the dog,' I scolded myself.

All my attention was focused on the ruined shops ahead. There were a thousand shadows inside the rubble-strewn buildings, which meant a thousand dark places for an enemy to hide. But everything seemed as it should have been.

'Yeah, for now,' I muttered to myself.

I didn't have all day. I took one last look through my

weapon sight and moved towards the dog, the muzzle of my rifle moving with me as I scanned the area. I ran at a crouch up the centre of the tarmac road. The dog was only about 70 yards ahead now. It seemed to have resigned itself to being caught in the wire, but as I got closer it started to fight to free itself again, obviously panicking that I might try to hurt it.

'Chill, dog, I'm on your side,' I called out as I arrived.

I was conscious of talking too loudly, but the dog struggling against the wire obstacle was making enough noise as it was. With the metallic clattering of the barbed-wire strands knocking against the upright struts, everybody within a mile would know what I was doing.

'Help me out here little fella, I don't want the Taliban to know I am here, all right?'

I didn't have the time to go for the softly, softly approach.

I let my rifle hang by my side as I pulled out my Leatherman and reached into the coils of barbed wire as far as I could. I wasn't too bothered about the dog trying to bite me. I had my jacket and leather combat gloves on. It wasn't as if it was that big anyway. Its filthy white coat covered a lean under-nourished body. Its frightened eyes kept me in check as the wire cutter tool sliced through the thin strands of wire at the first attempt.

The dog was still pulling madly away from me as the strand broke. In an instant it shot away through the other side of the obstacle without even a second thought. As it ran the wire loop was still hanging around its neck, but I hoped that it would eventually work loose.

'No problem, buddy,' I said, watching it go.

I looked around quickly, suddenly aware of how exposed I was. Standing in the middle of a deserted Afghan street in the Taliban heartland was not a good idea.

As swiftly as I could, I walked backwards towards the sentry post, keeping an eye on the road all the way.

'Nice one, Sarge,' Mase said as I rolled head first on to the floor of the sangar.

I realised I was breathing heavily; the fast climb back up had been more physical than I had thought it would be. As I looked back along the road I smiled to myself. The dog was nowhere to be seen.

'Let's keep this one quiet, eh?' I said as I dusted myself down.

'Keep what quiet?' Mase smiled.

I gave him the thumbs up, grabbed my webbing, and headed towards the ladder back down into the compound.

As I climbed down, the impact of what I'd just done hit me.

Things were seriously getting out of hand. How the hell had I managed to become personally responsible for the welfare of seemingly every stray dog in Helmand?

CHAPTER ONE

No Going Back

Six months earlier

As I reached up high with my left hand, the tiny grit-covered edge my fingers grasped didn't really feel that solid. Even if it was strong enough, I didn't think I could hold my full body weight on just the fingertips of my left hand.

I looked down again at the small wire that I had placed in the rock face two feet below me, as protection should I fall off. The wire was connected to a piece of solid aluminium I'd jammed into a half-inch-wide crack in the rock face and clipped on to the rope that was tied securely into my climbing harness. It didn't look big enough to stop a falling 13-stone marine. But I knew it would.

As I weighed up my next move, I knew that there was no going back once I left the secure hand- and footholds I was finely balanced on at the moment. Once I committed to my left hand I would have to push upwards and go for the top of the rock wall. It was all or nothing.

I was preparing myself to make the move when I heard a voice shouting up at me from 50 feet below.

'Get up there, climbing ninja. It gets dark in a few hours.'

I looked down nervously, followed the way-too-thin-looking climbing rope as it snaked its way back down the steep rock wall, and saw Lisa at the end of it. She was staring up at me with her normal encouraging smile while holding the device that would lock the rope and stop me hitting the ground, should I fall.

That's the problem with being married to a Wren, I thought. They have the same sense of humour as Royal Marines; they are, like us, firm believers in encouragement through taking the mick.

'Lisa – I am trying to figure out the moves. Do you mind?' I shouted back.

'It looks easy – just reach for the left-hand hold and go,' she replied, matter-of-factly, as if it was the easiest thing in the world. And then Beamer Boy, our completely daft springer spaniel, started barking up in my direction. It was his familiar 'get up there so I can run around some more' bark.

That only set off Fizz, our Rottweiler, who, like Beamer, was tied to the base of an oak tree. Soon the pair of them were joining in a chorus of barking encouragement.

'OK, everybody shut up. I'm going,' I said, closing my eyes and taking a deep breath as I turned back to face the rock, my nose only centimetres from the sharp granite.

Without really thinking I launched myself upwards. My left hand gripped the hold, I smeared my feet against the cool granite rock face and pushed upwards, reaching for the 'thank God holds' at the top of the climb. I pulled my body clear of the edge, rolled on to the open ledge that signalled the finish of the climb and looked down to where Lisa, Beamer Boy and Fizz Dog were standing.

Lisa was looking up at me with an expression that said: I told you it was easy, why didn't you do that half an hour ago? The dogs were hopping around excitedly because they knew their tied-to-a-tree duty was almost over and we would soon be on the move.

It really was good to be on summer leave.

For the last four months all I had done was eat, sleep and

breathe the preparations for my six-month tour to Afghanistan and the day I would be thrust into the fight against the Taliban. With the 20 or so young lads who made up 5 Troop of Kilo Company 42 Commando Royal Marines I had spent my days and nights on exercise all over the country, with little or no time for a personal life. We'd spent endless hours on the wet miserable rifle ranges in the north-east. We'd also endured long days in the vast rolling countryside of the Thetford Army training areas, taking part in Afghan-based scenarios designed to help us deal with potential situations we might face once out there.

At times it was hard and eye-opening but the lads had taken it all in their stride. I had watched them mature into Royal Marines with pride.

After all the hard work we'd put in, I should have been excited by the prospect of going to Afghanistan.

It was, after all, what I'd dreamed of as a kid back in my home town on the south-east coast of England, where all my mates and I wanted to do was play at soldiers down in the marshes. Back then we would set up make-believe ambushes in the woods behind my nan's house, using water bombs as our ammunition, dreaming of the day we would be in a heli-copter on an SAS-style mission to kill the bad guys. Now, it was going to be for real.

But with the daily reports of the constant battles from the army units we were due to replace I was beginning to have niggling doubts. What if we weren't ready? What if I forgot what to do?

Since starting my leave, however, I had tried really hard to concentrate on having three weeks of non-marine time. The dogs had played their part in helping me; they were a great way of getting my mind off things. Fizz and Beamer Boy were a great pair of companions and loved going on Dartmoor for walks, which worked out well, given my passion for rock climbing on its testing granite tors.

Fizz was your typical Rottweiler, with her distinctive

black-and-tan coat and docked tail. Now aged six, she had come to us as a puppy from a breeder in Manchester. Lisa had picked the most active-looking of the nine or so fluff-balls we'd found scampering around the floor next to their worn-out-looking mum. For Lisa it was love at first sight and to this day Fizz is still Lisa's dog.

We'd had our fair share of abuse from passers-by over the years, people who didn't have a clue as to the difference between a sausage dog and a St Bernard, but were convinced none the less that all Rottweilers belonged to the devil. But I was adamant then and still am now that it's the way you bring a Rottweiler up that counts. Apart from the times when she was indulging her passion for chasing cats or squirrels, Fizz was the softest dog on the planet. Although, it has to be said, if someone was aggressive towards her she would snap back at them, which I thought she had every right to do. If somebody punched me I would punch them back. Of course, I still wouldn't leave Fizz alone with just anybody and we normally kept her on a lead.

Beamer, our black-and-white springer, was just hyper, so hyper in fact it sometimes got really annoying. But you couldn't ever blame him for that. His passion was for anything that was wet and dirty. For instance, he loved nothing more than floating around in the smelliest cattle trough he could find, with only his head and eyes showing above the water. He would normally do this, of course, when we were out on a long walk, didn't have any towels in the van to dry him and when we had a long journey home. We had got him from an animal rescue centre in Somerset. After buying Fizz we'd decided that if we got another dog it would be a rescue; there were far too many of them that needed good homes. Picking Beamer up from the centre I knew we had made a good decision. I don't think his fluffed-up tail has ever stopped wagging since. Our only regret that afternoon in the rescue kennel was seeing row after row of other dogs, wagging their tails, barking away, just wanting to be loved. If we could have we'd have taken them all with us. We were just heartbroken at having to leave them in their runs.

We'd had to lie slightly to the people at the animal rescue home before being allowed to take Beamer. They'd wanted us to prove that the dogs would be living in a stable home, that Lisa and I would not spend too much time travelling between our various work venues and that Beamer would spend no more than four hours or so on his own every day.

Our way of life in the military meant that we did everything but stay at home. But we also knew that Beamer would adapt just as Fizz had and that they would both have a fantastic lifestyle. In fact, I doubt that many dogs would refuse the lifestyle that our two hounds now enjoyed.

A couple of years on and the pair were now absolutely inseparable. We couldn't even take one of them to the vet on its own, they both had to go, which always amused the vet. It was the same if I was in camp in Plymouth for the day. The two of them would have to come with me, as if they were afraid one of them would miss out on the fun. It was amazing how many well-hard marines would knock feebly on the door of the gym asking to be let in when Fizz was propped against the see-through glass door, on self-appointed sentry watch. I would just shake my head and tell them not to be so scared. They always looked visibly relieved when they opened the door and tentatively walked past Fizz, who didn't even bat an eyelid.

Both dogs loved travelling, too. All I had to do was ask who wanted to go for a drive and both would immediately tear down the garden path towards our waiting van. They would sit on the rear seat and stare out of the window at the passing countryside for hours on end. The previous summer, en route to a climbing trip to the Alps, Fizz had happily propped herself up against the rear side window for nine hours.

I had met Lisa ten years earlier in North Wales. She had just passed her course to become a Physical Training

Instructor for the Navy and was studying at the Military centre where I worked as a rock-climbing instructor for the marines.

We had got on well and stayed in touch but it had taken a lucky phone call to get our romance going the following year. By chance we realised that we were both going to be in the same place one weekend, and from there the relationship that was to be my life soon began.

We had a lot in common from the start. My friends were already Lisa's friends, and I could joke around with her mates and feel comfortable around them. Lisa was a Navy footballer and armchair Man. U. fan and I was a climber. Part of the deal when we married was that I had to get into football and she had to 'get' climbing.

It wasn't too difficult for me. My passion for football had peaked as a youngster when I watched Ipswich, the team of my youth, beat Manchester United 6–0 at Portman Road back in 1978. It couldn't get better than that, especially as both my dad and brother were Man. U. fans. But Lisa fulfilled her side of the bargain too.

Piling the dogs into the van and walking on the moors to find a rock to climb was now our weekend ritual. As long as we always made it home for *Match of the Day* in the evening then Lisa was happy. Our relationship was – and still is – built on trust and we didn't harbour any secrets from each other. I still find it slightly amusing that, out of most of our friends who are married, Lisa and I are the only ones who have a joint bank account.

By the time I'd finished the day's climb, the sun was dipping over the eastern edge of Dartmoor. We jumped in the van and headed in search of a country pub, which we soon found down a quiet country lane on the Cornwall–Devon border. The dogs sat happily under our table in the beer garden, as good as gold as they waited for the leftovers from our lasagne and chips. This was probably the closest I got to doing nothing so I relished the hour or so we spent there.

Lisa and I sat chatting. As was often the case, we fantasised a little about where we would buy a house when we left the forces. Mid-Wales was the clear favourite. We fancied a smallholding near the mountains where we could run a small B&B, I could offer rock climbing and mountaineering coaching and the dogs would have loads of free space to run around.

But lately America had been coming a close second. I wasn't sure my potential outdoor business could make us enough money to compete with the ever-increasing cost of living in the UK.

As the evening closed in, we talked about other, more mundane and everyday things too. But every now and again I would stare into space and my mind would turn to Afghanistan and what was to come.

I had no idea how life-changing it would be.

As I sat in the small shack, the northerly wind was hammering the rain against the wall of the corrugated-iron shelter. At times, it was beating hard enough to almost drown out the firing from the range nearby.

On the battery-powered radio in the corner, BBC Radio Five Live was having a special debate on British troops in Afghanistan. It felt surreal listening to the presenters talk about the place in which I would be serving in less than a week.

The picture being painted by the debate was not good.

The lead item on the hourly news that day had been about the identity of the young Royal Welsh Fusilier who had been killed the day before. There was also an update on the crash a few days earlier of an RAF Nimrod just outside Kandahar – all 14 servicemen on board had been killed, including one Royal Marine.

In recent weeks I'd absorbed lots of reports of this kind, not just on the radio but also in newspapers. In particular, there had been a lot of in-depth reports from the parachute regiment we were due to replace at the end of their deployment, many of them focused on life in the so-called 'safe houses' that they were occupying in the more remote regions. Precisely what was 'safe' about a mud compound that was surrounded by religious fundamentalists with guns who wanted to kill everybody inside I had yet to understand.

The reports also explained how the Taliban were trying to wear down the lads by limiting their sleep pattern to a few hours per day. They said the threat from incoming mortars and heavy machine-gun fire was constant. There were also reports on the lack of food and water they were experiencing because of the problems with supply lines. It didn't sound a fun place to visit.

I knew I'd joined the marines for all this but at the moment I couldn't fire up any enthusiasm for it. I was worrying about other things. I knew that Lisa, along with probably every other family member and loved one connected to the lads about to deploy, would be reading the papers and listening to the radio too. From the detailed intelligence reports we got back at camp, I also knew things out there were even worse than the media reports suggested.

All the secret excitement I had felt about going to Afghanistan had gone. Inwardly I felt anxious and slightly scared. I loved life, I wanted to spend my time with Lisa and the dogs exploring the hills without a care in the world, but it was too late for that now. We were leaving in three days. The possibility of being killed was now very real.

I knew time would stop while I was out in Afghanistan. There would be no dwelling on things, no wondering about life back home, no more taking the dogs to work with me or sitting in the pub with Lisa or planning our weekend to fit some climbing in. I would have to become totally focused on the job at hand. No privacy, no rest, no respite from the constant threat of being dropped right in the middle of some real nasty shit.

Added to that, I was now responsible for 20 lads and I knew I had to get on with it and concentrate on getting them

– and me – back in one piece. No distractions; just get the job done.

As I looked around at the lads that made up 5 Troop they too were hanging on every word that came from the radio. Some of them were more or less straight out of training, one even from only the previous week. The youngest of them was just 18, nearly 20 years younger than me. I felt too old for this shit, but that, I suppose, was the whole point of being a troop sergeant; I had the experience to look after these youngsters. After 32 weeks of what everyone tells us is the hardest military training in the world, I felt fairly confident they would produce the goods when we needed it.

But again I had my niggling worries. Are they really ready? Will they really cope with life on the front line?

Scanning their young faces again as they listened to the radio, I began to see the apprehension spreading across them. Not good. Only one thing for it, I decided, and stood up.

I knew we still had another 40 minutes before it would be our turn to practise our last sessions of live firing on the wet peat bogs outside. But a quick half an hour of troop fitness training wouldn't go amiss in the meantime, I reckoned.

'Right, outside everyone, time for some morale-boosting exercise,' I shouted.

As I pulled on my waterproof camouflage jacket, I didn't see too much movement; in fact, only one of my marines had made a move to go outside.

'Any time today, ladies,' I said in a louder voice.

'But it's raining, Sergeant,' Tim, one of my keenest and youngest marines, piped up.

'Well, I'm sure the Taliban will understand and let us shelter indoors when it rains out there,' I replied in my most sarcastic of sergeant voices.

'But it doesn't rain in Afghanistan, does it?' said another marine.

I shook my head in disbelief.

'I guess geography is not your strong point then?' I looked once more around the room. 'Move it, NOW.'

Saying goodbye is never easy. Saying goodbye and not knowing when you will be back is the worst feeling in the world.

I looked at Lisa and knew she was holding back the tears. I didn't think my attempts at the steely commando face were working too well either.

'Pack it in or you'll have me crying in a minute,' I said, trying to smile, but it didn't make either of us feel any better.

Even Fizz and Beamer knew something was up. They somehow sensed that the packed bags outside meant I was going away. Neither of them raced to get their leads as they normally did when I opened the front door. Both just sat upright in their beds looking at me. I bent down and shook both their heads in turn.

'Fizz Dog – you are in charge, be good – no chasing squirrels, all right?'

She just continued to look at me with her sad big brown eyes, a confused expression on her face.

'I hate this,' I said, shaking my head and holding Lisa for the last time.

I held her for not nearly long enough. I kissed her quickly as tears rolled down her face, and turned straight for the door. I walked out into the early-September morning without looking back.

CHAPTER TWO

Covert Operations

As the last echoes of the explosion faded, the view from my vantage point seemed unchanged. Apart, that was, from the smoke that was rising, mushroom-like, into the early-morning sky.

Down below me nothing was moving in the tightly packed alleys, compounds and basic mud dwellings of the town. Not even the usual morning birdsong broke the silence. As I had been finding out lately, incoming mortar rounds tended to have that effect. Like the rest of the locals, the Afghan birdlife hid away when the firing started and emerged again only when it stopped. It would be a while before they returned to their favourite perches in the sparse line of trees to the north of the mud-walled district compound (DC), that myself and the 53 marines of Kilo Company now called home.

It was only two weeks since we had arrived in the small market town of Now Zad. During the short time we had been here the Taliban had managed to keep us occupied nearly every day.

They tended to hit us with their mortars first thing in the morning or about half an hour before it got dark at night. The Taliban weren't stupid; they knew we would be able to home in on the muzzle flashes from their weapons at night with ease. They used the dark to move around the woods instead.

Taliban Central, the expanse of woods where they felt safest, was on the other side of a large *wadi* – a riverbed that's dry save for when it rains – that the locals used as a road during the dry season. We, naturally, had named it the Taliban Motorway. Apparently, even the might of the Russian Army had not been able to penetrate the woods and tame the Mujahedeen resistance, which was not a great confidence booster if it was true.

As the last of the smoke from the mortar round impact faded, I scanned the far distance with my weapon sighting system but could see no fleeting movements that might give the bad guys away.

At first sight Now Zad looked exactly like a scene straight out of Monty Python's *Life of Brian*. Nothing had changed in hundreds of years. There was no electricity and sanitation was non-existent. The ever-present dust lined the inside of our nostrils and mouths and stuck to everything we owned. The stink of human waste was bad, especially on the sunnier days we were still getting in the run-up to winter.

The surrounding landscape was, it had to be said, spectacular.

To the south the flat expanse of the Afghan desert plain stretched into the distance, barren and uninhabited apart from the nomadic goat herdsmen who somehow eked out a living in this unforgiving place. But five or six kilometres to the west, north and east of the town the mountains rose suddenly from the desert floor. To the north a sharp, dome-shaped peak called Narum Kuk ran from west to east, overshadowed by the vast ranges of the Zar Kuh Kuhe Mazdurak Mountains in the far distance.

The only greenery for miles was found close to the mountains. An abundance of trees and small hardy bushes grew along the line of the Taliban Motorway stretching away to the north-east. The plants and shrubs owed their survival to the winter rains from the mountains that thundered unpredictably down the deep-sided *wadis*. As we were finding out, the town had been plagued by some of the worst fighting seen since the coalition forces removed the Taliban from power. Sitting at the head of the Sangin Valley, Now Zad was a transit stop for the Taliban to resupply as they headed west towards two other important strategic locations, the main dam at Kajacki and the market town of Sangin, both of which – like us – were taking their fair share of punishment. Our attackers were probably using us as target practice while they were passing through to one of these two locations, I guessed.

There was no guarantee that any of the roads in or out could be safely travelled, so the only way in had been by helicopter and that had been a major operation. The army regiment we'd replaced had been holding this isolated outpost from the Taliban for more than 100 days. They had arrived, like everyone else, believing the politicians who said they were on a peace-keeping mission that would last for three years and would not require them to fire a single round.

The Paras had left Afghanistan after putting down around 87,000 rounds of ammunition and with little, militarily speaking, to show for it. Despite having suffered around 250 casualties, the Taliban were still there, still hell-bent on disrupting the efforts of the ISAF to stabilise the country and allow rebuilding to take place. I was hoping that would not be the case with us; I was hoping we would fare a little better.

'You think they have finished with the alarm call? I had just picked up my breakfast, the bastards,' Hutch – one of my more experienced section corporals – muttered, without once coming off of aim from behind the GPMG machine gun propped up on the sandbags in front of him.

Sure enough, when I looked in the back of the sangar I saw bacon and beans deposited all over the lower sides of the rear sandbags. Hutch's breakfast had landed there when he had hastily taken cover.

'Yeah, maybe,' I said. 'Don't they normally fire three in a row though? That was only two.'

Hutch said nothing.

'Anyway, you could do with losing a few pounds. They're doing you a favour.'

Back in Plymouth Hutch was one of those who went to the gym to stay in shape, not get in shape. Married with kids, he was as keen as they came for a young corporal marine, although I imagined his wife would probably have been happier if he had taken a different career path.

I kept scanning the woods but there was no sign of the mortar crew. Where the hell were the little buggers? I soon had my answer.

'Hill to all stations – incoming,' a voice screamed through my headset, signalling that the lads in the observation post on the hill above the town had noticed the giveaway puff of smoke in the distance.

'Heads down, here we go again,' I yelled down into the compound beneath me, where the lads who were off watch had gathered to see what all the excitement had been about. 'Incoming. Get under cover now.'

They looked up at me with glum resignation in their eyes before turning and running back to the safety of the old police cells we were using for our accommodation.

The slowly growing howl of an incoming mortar as it arches across the sky sounds good only in movies. Right now it was scary as hell, not least because it was a complete lottery as to where it would land.

Luckily for us this mortar crew didn't seem that competent.

I heard an explosion behind me, well away from our compound, and looked up once more to survey the damage to the once thriving town. Not that it would've mattered had it hit another building near us. There were no people living within 200 metres of our compound; it was just too dangerous. The buildings closest to us along the main bazaar road were just rubble, with nothing but piles of twisted metal and snapped wood where doors and shop fronts once stood, their contents long since ransacked.

There were people still living in the northern part of the town, but we hadn't patrolled that far away from the compound yet so we didn't know how many were there. Given the devastation the constant battles had caused, many of the locals in this southern part of town had done the only sensible thing, packing their bags and moving further south until it was over.

Their decision seemed even wiser now as the lads on the hill opened up with the heavy machine guns in the direction of the mortar firing point. That one lucky spot of the smoke from the mortar tube had been enough. They had obviously found the enemy.

In the sangar it was almost impossible to hear anything over the 'thud thud thud' of the 50-calibre machine gun firing over our heads.

'Hey fatty, guess we miss breakfast again,' I yelled over to Hutch.

This time he turned his head towards me, his eyes alive with adrenalin, and gave me the finger before resuming his fire position.

We had flown direct from the UK to Camp Bastion, the main British concentration in Afghanistan, just over a month ago. The vast camp, named after the first British soldier to be killed in the conflict, sat in the middle of the Helmand desert surrounded by miles of nothing. There was no tarmac road, only the dusty worn tracks that led there through an unforgiving desert.

Bastion was the biggest tented camp of its kind. Impressively, it was built by the Royal Engineers in 2006 in about 12 weeks. More than 4,000 British servicemen and women currently called it home.

Most of the camp was made up of row after row of identical tented walkways. Trying to find the Expeditionary Forces Institute (EFI) shop that sold cans of fizzy drink and chocolate bars was a mission in itself. Quite why the EFI sold swimming goggles when there was no hint of a swimming pool for over one thousand miles was a question I never got answered.

Temperatures of 100 degrees Fahrenheit were not uncommon in the midday Afghan sun. To quote Robin Williams in the film *Good Morning, Vietnam*, it was 'hot, damn hot, crotch-pot cooking hot'. Just walking around Bastion meant that sweat stains grew under the armpits of my combat shirt and I couldn't begin to imagine what it would be like when I had to run around the desert with full kit. At least I wouldn't have to worry about putting any weight on out here, I'd told myself.

Apart from the heat, the worst thing about Afghanistan during those first days was the dust: it was everywhere, absolutely everywhere. It was in our sleeping bags, on our hands, under our nails, sometimes in our food or clogging the mouthpieces of our water bottles and, especially annoyingly, lining the inside of our combat helmets.

During the brief few days we had spent at Bastion the dust had become a really irritating part of our everyday life. I didn't have to tell the lads to clean their weapons daily, they just did it. But as soon as we ventured outside the accommodation tents, their work was undone. Within moments small gusts of wind deposited fine layers of dust on the newly cleaned metal, which stuck to the rifle oil like superglue.

It was even worse when we went out on to the open ground where we practised our drills. There the dust clouds would rip across the desert plain like monster tidal waves gathering speed as they charged towards us. When we got back inside our faces would be caked in the stuff, the dust stuck to our sweat like a beauty parlour-style mudpack that you'd pay a fortune for on the High Street. The only dust-free area was where our combat goggles had protected our eyes.

On the only free evening we'd had I'd watched the sun go down from the top of the bulletproof HESCO protection blocks that formed the perimeter of the camp. Sitting there with my thoughts I'd seen the final Chinook flight of the night swooping in low from the east, straight across the fading face of the sun. The Chinook flew over the main landing site and headed straight for the emergency landing site by the fully equipped field hospital, which told me somebody was in a bad way. The scene would not have been out of place in an episode of *M*A*S*H*, which I'd watched as a kid.

Any thoughts we'd had of getting comfortable at Camp Bastion were very quickly knocked on the head. During Kilo Company's six-month tour we would spend less than four weeks in the tented city. The rest of the time would be in the 'real' Afghanistan, a very different place.

After being given only a few days to acclimatise we had been sent to the small market town of Gereshk where any thoughts of being broken in gently were quickly dispelled. Our first patrol had resulted in a firefight with the Taliban.

We'd passed through the old town of Gereshk for a rendezvous with the Afghan National Police, or ANP, who guarded the large, Chinese-built dam that gave the town its strategic importance. During our conversations with the ANP they'd pointed to a group of men standing on a nearby hillside. They told us they were Taliban but we couldn't get involved, and no shots had been fired. But as we'd made our way back up into the town the men on the hillside started firing mortars and small arms fire at the Afghans and us. So we'd had no choice but to engage them.

For a brief while we'd been caught in the middle of the Taliban engagement, with our rear exposed to a potential attack. It had taken the rockets from a Harrier fighter jet our OC had called in to finish the encounter. It had been a sobering moment for most of us, a realisation that training was well and truly over.

With two weeks of patrolling under our belts we had then been sent back to Bastion to prepare for deployment to the 'safe' house in the town of Now Zad, where we'd be based for at least the next two months. The 'safe' house was where I was standing now, looking warily out from behind the sandbags of the sentry post for any sign of another incoming mortar.

I had just been about to sit down to a tasteless lunch of military brown biscuits accompanied by something that had come out of a tin labelled 'meat patty' when the call came over the radio for me to visit the small operations room that we had set up as the headquarters of the compound. After eating the same thing for lunch for the last few days I was grateful for the excuse to slot the biscuits back into their green packet. I trotted over and stuck my head in the door.

'You rang Boss?' I said as I looked around the corner of the room, which was crammed full, even with just four people stood in there.

As it turned out the boss, who was the Officer Commanding Kilo Company, was busy on the radio.

The signaller gave me a wave and I waved back while the boss finished his conversation then replaced the spare headset that was connected to the main sangar and hill radio network.

'Your department I think, Sergeant. The hill is reporting that the Afghan National Police are outside the gate. Firstly I haven't given them permission to be there and secondly they are abusing a tied-up dog.' He knew all about my dogs, having stepped over Fizz on numerous occasions to get into the gym back at our base in Plymouth.

'Check it out and get them back inside and be diplomatic!'

'No problems Boss – on my way.'

I ran back over to my grot to get rigged up as even a quick stroll outside required full body armour and equipment. I couldn't go out single-handed, so along with Hutch I grabbed Dave, another one of our more experienced corporals.

Dave had earned the right to be a section corporal after completing his Junior Command Course prior to us deploying to Afghanistan. It was a job he relished. He loved nothing more than getting on with the job of being a Royal Marine and then partying afterwards with the ladies, or so he liked to boast anyway – most of the lads would testify that Dave's chatting-up techniques left a lot to be desired. From talking to him in the sangars, I knew Dave had grown up with dogs and, like me, had a soft spot for them.

We geared up as I hurriedly explained the situation and made our way around to the west gate. With my headset now attached to my left ear I could hear the hill watchkeeper talking urgently to the main building watchkeeper.

'0 this is Hill. The lads say that the ANP are getting quite nasty with that dog. What do you want us to do? Over.'

'Hill this is 0. Wait out and keep an eye on 20C who is making his way out there. Over.' As troop sergeant 20C – pronounced 'Two Zero Charlie' – was my call sign.

'0 this is Hill. Roger. Hope he gives them a good kicking. Out.'

I told Hutch and Dave that we had the hill playing over-watch but we still covered each other religiously as we headed out of the compound. Hutch knelt to provide semi-cover behind a mud wall at the corner of the alleyway that led from the gate as Dave and I ran across the small patch of open ground to the front. Dave then went to ground to adopt a good fire position while Hutch caught up and we both moved on to the next piece of cover.

Even though we were two streets away we could hear the sounds of a very angry dog barking.

I didn't really have a plan.

The ANP had been tasked by the Karzai Government to bring stability back into Afghanistan, but the truth was they were poorly paid and not very well trained. They weren't very popular with the locals either. For their protection the ANP shared our compound, which infuriated the local people – we had had complaints that at times the ANP had threatened them for money and food, allegedly, but we had no way of proving it.

As we made our way forward, I knew I had to remain professional; after all we were here to save the people of Afghanistan, not the dog population. I had to play it cool. I couldn't create an incident between us and the ANP, who were supposedly on our side. But there was no way I was going to tolerate animal cruelty. Especially not while I had a big gun.

We moved patrol-like along the edges of the alleys lined with mud walls until we broke out into a clearing. Hutch took up a position covering the scenario in front of us.

As I continued forwards Dave walked by my side. This again was something we'd learned in Afghan training, an all-important part of the politics in this part of the world. Having a leader walking side by side with a bodyguard conveyed confidence; it was a small show of strength.

Twenty feet away, in the middle of the open ground, was a white pickup truck. Sitting on top of it was the ANP commander, dressed in his long flowing olive-green robes. His second in command was standing in the back of the truck bed with an RPG launcher balanced on one shoulder. As I moved into the open ground, their eyes followed me unemotionally.

I soon saw what had been causing the commotion. On the open ground in front of them both, two of the commander's young sidekicks were pulling on opposite sides of the biggest dog that I had ever seen. The white-and-grey-haired giant was at least four feet high and had a head the size of a grizzly bear, with teeth to match. Its lips were curled up in one of those 'get near me so I can rip your head off' snarls.

Straight away I noticed that the dog had been relieved of its ears. I had read about this practice. It was a sign that the dog was used for one of Afghanistan's most popular sports – dogfighting.

I had Googled Afghanistan and its culture prior to the deployment. Dogfighting had been one of the more distressing aspects that I had found. It was a centuries-old tradition, commonplace among the tribal clans. Owning a victorious dog could bring an owner a great deal of money and respect among his peers.

The images on the Internet had not been pleasant. It wasn't anything a pet owner would want to be involved with. The large-breed dogs had no choice but to attack each other – resulting in a bloody frenzy. It was fight or, potentially, die. The dogs would have their ears and tail removed with a knife – without any anaesthetic – so that no superficial wounds would be inflicted as the result of a torn ear or tail and the fights could then last longer. Dogs were in abundant supply in Afghanistan and extremely far down on the welfare list. (Although to be fair, human life wasn't exactly that far up it.)

The irony of all this was that when the Taliban came to power, not only had women been banned from all forms of education, but they also banned dogfighting as they deemed it un-Islamic. With the Coalition Forces removing the Taliban from power in Kabul in 2001, the void in Government had allowed the back-street spectator sport to flourish once more. One step forward, two steps back.

As I watched the dog, its frustration at being tied up was plain to see. Looking at it with no ears was just too much. I'd been ready to free the dog before, but I was even more determined to do so now.

The young police were having a hard time trying to hold on to the dog, which was bucking like a bronco at a rodeo. They had braided together some narrow-gauge wire to form a long dog leash, which had been wrapped around the dog's neck and back legs. This meant that the dog couldn't move either forwards or back, and the more it struggled to break free the tighter the strands of wire twisted around themselves, which only made the dog even angrier.

I wasn't quite sure what I'd do if the dog actually got free. I didn't think it would understand I was here to help it, so I took a step back as casually as I could.

'*Salaamu alaikum*,' I said, directing my greeting towards

the commander. We had been told during our pre-deployment training that it was customary to speak to the Elder first during any conversation.

Appreciating this, he replied in kind then nodded at the youngest lad who was the only one of the police detachment who spoke any English.

'Why are you out here?' he asked me, casually thumbing the trigger on his Kalashnikov fully automated rifle, something our lads wouldn't even consider doing. The rifle looked way too big for him to handle properly in the first place, but life was very different here.

'Tell the commander he needs to come back into the compound,' I said. 'You left the compound without permission and the lads on the hill nearly confused you with the Taliban.'

The last bit was a lie but I thought it might bring a swift solution to the situation.

After a brief exchange in Pashtu the young lad explained that the commander wanted to enter the Regional Dogfighting Championships to be held in Lashkar Gar in a few weeks' time.

'He wants this dog to be his champion,' he said, nodding at the big beast, which was getting even more agitated as we stood there.

OK, no quick solution then.

'And where does the commander think he is going to keep the dog until then?' I asked.

As the boy translated my words back to his boss, I was conscious of the fact that we were out in the open. Our movements were clearly visible to anybody looking this way from within Taliban Central. As if to remind me of the potential danger, I could hear the hill relaying our progress to the operations room through my headset. I figured that my boss was also listening in on developments.

'Get them in the compound, 20C,' a voice said over the radio.

I looked around at Hutch, who just looked back at me

with raised eyebrows. He also motioned towards Taliban Central in the woods to the east. I knew what he meant.

I decided to speed things along.

'Tell the commander that our commander will not allow a dog like that into our compound,' I told the boy, 'but I know where he can keep it.'

It was clear that the dog had had bad experiences around humans and I wasn't going to take the risk of it mauling one of our lads by taking it into the DC. At the same time, I doubted somehow that the ANP would cage it properly even if they did look after it, so I needed a temporary 'kennel' and the wrecked building that stood in the middle of the ruined compound next to ours was ideal for the moment.

'We need to move now,' I said, pointing in the direction of safety.

The debate that then ensued between the commander and the young lad seemed rather one-way. But at the end of it the commander jumped off the roof of the vehicle and got into the driver's seat without looking at me. 'He will keep the dog outside the compound,' the young boy explained, shouldering his Kalashnikov and making it seem like the commander had come up with the idea himself.

'OK, I can live with that,' I said, signalling to the hill that we were about to move back.

We escorted the ANP back to the compound in an unlikely looking convoy. Dave led the way followed by the truck then the young police boys, dragging behind them the dog which, by now, seemed to have given up resisting. Hutch and I covered the rear of our little circus.

The fact that I had formed a cunning plan to free the dog must have been written all over my face because as we walked Hutch kept looking at me curiously.

I gave him the 'I'll tell you in a minute' look back.

'You sure the boss is happy with this, Sarge?' Hutch asked as we geared up in the evening light.

He knew I hated him calling me Sarge. Only the army used that slang and marines are desperately fierce about the fact that we are not part of the army.

'Kind of,' I replied.

'What do you mean, kind of?' Hutch said, looking at me with mock concern. 'Kind of means he doesn't know, doesn't it?'

'He said deal with it. So I am dealing with it,' I nodded, smiling back and handing him the Leatherman. 'Here, I think you might need that.'

When we'd arrived back in the DC, I'd updated the boss on the situation with the dog. He'd told me to deal with it but not to upset the ANP if I could help it. He hadn't wanted to know what I had in mind.

The cool air of early evening sent a shiver down my spine. It was getting a lot colder a lot faster at sundown.

I pulled my jacket collar up around my neck and walked over to join Hutch and a lad called Pete, who had volunteered to help us out during the three hours when he was meant to be sleeping. Without saying much we climbed on to the roof of the old cells that formed the back wall of our compound. The roof had been painted white to reflect the heat, which gave it the air of having been built with real materials instead of straw and mud. Not that tonight, with only a slight moon in the sky, you could really tell what colour it was.

We used the darkness as we had been trained to, and ran at a crouch along the parapet on the edge of the roof through the shadows cast by the light from the low moon.

The ANP lived in a small unkempt building towards the rear gate of our compound.

Annoyingly they would always come out to investigate the clanging noise that meant the entry gate was being opened. For us to free the dog we needed them to be unaware of what we were up to. So that meant we couldn't go through the gate but would have to drop down the rear wall.

As we reached the lowest part of the wall, we could see the

small, ruined building that we'd watched the ANP lock the dog in. It was pitch-black but I knew that it contained a very big, tied-up, angry dog, although by now I hoped he had calmed down a bit.

Once down the wall we would have to cover about 40 feet to where the dog was being held. I looked over towards the ANP building. The door was firmly shut. The soft glow from the window through the dirty curtains meant they were preoccupied, probably smoking marijuana as they did most nights. That was fine by me.

We lowered the small aluminium assault ladder down the side of the 15-foot wall. It wasn't quite long enough to reach the ground, so we had brought some rope to lower and secure the ladder in case it slipped.

We had nothing to tie it to on the mud roof so either Hutch or Pete would have to hold the rope for the first man down, which, of course, would be me. It was my plan, after all.

By lowering my legs over the wall and hanging on to the top of the parapet I could just reach the top rung of the ladder with my feet. But it wasn't easy. I could not look down to see where my feet were in relation to the rungs and to make matters worse my rifle swung around and the muzzle stabbed me in the crook of my knee. I clenched my teeth as the short sharp pain caught me by surprise. As if all this wasn't enough, the weight of my body armour was doing its best to push me away from the wall.

Somehow, however, I managed to lower myself on to the ladder. Slowly padding down the wall with my hands, I located each rung to descend. As I inched my way down to earth I hoped that the bottom of the ladder wouldn't slip away from the wall. That would definitely hurt. It wasn't exactly rock climbing but the ridiculousness of the situation made me smile.

I looked up to see that Hutch was grinning down at me.

'Are you holding the bloody rope?' I whispered up to him.

'Oh shit, sorry.'

Once on the ground I held the bottom of the ladder for Hutch as he climbed down. Pete was going to stay and keep our option of climbing back up the ladder open, should the need arise.

'Let's go.'

Before leaving our compound I had spoken to the sentries currently on watch in the sangars so they knew we were out. I had no plans to get shot by my own lads.

With weapons at the ready we ran at a crouch across the open ground. The angry dog heard us before we had covered even half the distance.

'So much for being commando-like,' I whispered over to Hutch as we ran in the dark.

The animal sounded like it was going berserk. We reached the front side of the building and quickly scanned the surrounding area. Nothing but bits of rubble lay in all directions.

The dog was shut in what was left of the ruined building. It was battering its body against the very old wooden door like something out of a horror movie.

'How are we going to get it out?' Hutch whispered, rather unnecessarily.

By now the whole of Now Zad probably knew something was up. Noise at night always sounds louder and carries further, especially when you are trying to rescue an angry Afghan fighting dog.

'Guess we just let it out?' I said.

I couldn't see his face as we were in the darkest part of the shadows but I knew Hutch well enough to know that he was probably not happy with the thought of an angry bear-sized dog running loose while we stood there. But then, come to think of it, neither was I.

'Ready?'

I didn't wait for the reply.

I kicked the door as hard as I could. The old lock was no

match for the force of a solid kick and with a splintering crack the door swung inwards to be replaced by a dark shape of snarling angriness.

'Run.'

I didn't have to say it as Hutch was way ahead of me.

We ran round the side of the building, totally forgetting we had automatic weapons and grenades on us. It was only when we came to a halt and caught our breath that we realised the dog hadn't chased us. We slowly regained our composure in the shadows. Even in the dark I knew that Hutch was giving me one of his trademark ironic looks. It sounded like the dog was still in the building. I nudged Hutch and we crept back around to have a look.

We couldn't see what was restraining it, but whatever it was it had left the dog mobile enough to attack us if we got close. Presumably the wire I had seen tied to its back legs and neck earlier that day was still in place. I quickly came to the conclusion that there was no way we could get into the room to actually untie it.

No plan survives first contact, we are told time and time again. And this one, it would seem, was no exception. Luckily, I had a contingency for something like this. I reached into my pocket and pulled out the sausage I had lifted from our primitive galley before we came out.

'Plan B,' I said to Hutch, who just nodded. I realised he was poised to run again. He had a point; we didn't actually know if the dog would be able to break its bindings as it thrashed around furiously.

I threw the sausage at the ground, landing it precisely underneath the monster dog's head. He stopped struggling at once and sniffed the air. After a few seconds of searching the dust with his nose he gathered the sausage up in one go. I don't think he even chewed it.

I pushed Hutch backwards as we moved back along the edge of the wall.

'Now we wait, I guess?' he asked.

I nodded.

'How long do you think?'

I had no idea really. I had asked the doctor back in the compound for enough Valium to knock out an adult person and then some. He had guessed straight away what it was for. The Taliban had left us alone today so the incident with the dog and the ANP had been the talk of the compound. The sausage was the only way I could get the dog to digest the Valium.

We sat chatting in whispers about everything and anything while we waited for the dog to grow sleepy. The radio headset kept me up to date with the goings on in the compound, although thankfully for once it was fairly quiet. Every now and then one of the sangars would give the pre-arranged code word that they could still see me through their night sight. Each time I gave them the thumbs up back in the dark.

Finally after what seemed like ages, but was probably no more than an hour, there was no sound coming from beast dog. It was actually spookily quiet.

We moved back around to the door this time to see the dog lying down across the threshold of the doorway on all fours. The big snarling head had been transformed into a tranquil face that actually seemed quite approachable. The dog's eyes were still open though and it was breathing in a regular low-sounding humph. When I reached forward and it didn't attempt to go for me, I patted its head with my gloved hand. It seemed to breathe a sigh of relief. I had brought some more non-drugged sausages with me and fed them to him one at a time. He chewed them, more slowly this time.

I sat like this for nearly thirty minutes as Hutch struggled to cut the wire with the Leatherman. The ANP had done a good job. The wire was twisted on itself at least four times and wound around the dog's middle, its neck and hind legs to ensure it wouldn't be going anywhere. I had no idea how they would have got in the room to untie it when the time came to travel to the dogfight.

We'd been there for the best part of 30 minutes when finally Hutch cut through the remaining piece of wire.

'That was an epic,' he said, as he stood up.

I patted the dog's head one last time and moved back out of the building and into the open ground. We then watched as the dog pushed itself to its feet, wobbly at first but growing in steadiness as it moved in the opposite direction back to join the pack that we knew prowled the perimeter of this camp during the cold of the night.

We didn't need to say it but we both knew that the dog could've gone for us at any time while we were cutting the wire.

But he hadn't.

We safely made it to the base of the wall. Hutch climbed the ladder first while I held it. But when I followed him up, climbing until I was balanced on the top of the final rung, I found I still couldn't reach the top of the wall. The bottom of the ladder must have sunk in the mud. I looked around for handholds in the wall above me but there were none. I then grabbed the rope with one hand to find nobody had hold of it at the other end.

'Pen – hurry up, they are coming.'

'Who's coming?' I said in a loud whisper as I tried to balance on the top rung of the ladder.

'The Afghan sentry,' came the urgent reply.

'Damn.'

Our compound was also home to a detachment of the Afghan National Army. We hadn't seen them much; they kept themselves to themselves. But they did have a duty to patrol the rear gate every now and again, a minor detail I had forgotten. I wanted to avoid explaining to the Afghans why we were climbing up a wall in their part of the compound in the middle of the night if at all possible.

I reached down to grab my commando dagger from the

front loops of my body armour. I carried the dagger, mainly for symbolic reasons, and I hadn't ever expected to use it in action until now. With a stabbing motion I drove it into the hardened mud like an ice axe. It held and I launched myself upwards, pulling on the dagger as my feet kicked uselessly against the smooth wall. Tantalisingly I was almost at the top.

That was the good news. The bad news was that I was supporting not just my body weight but also the weight of my gear. Something was going to give, whether it was my fingers or the crumbling mud of the wall around the dagger.

'Grab my hand, for God's sake,' I half-screamed at the two marines standing uselessly just centimetres above me.

To my relief I looked up to see the straining face of Pete as he wrapped both his hands around my right wrist and pulled hard. As I inched upwards, I also noticed the puzzled face of an ANA sentry looking down at me.

Hutch stood off in the shadows giggling as I was pulled, rag-doll-like, over the top of the wall and on to the safety of the roof of the rear building.

'Some lookout you are, Pete,' I said as I regained my breath and stood up. 'Thought you said they were coming. Not that they were already here.'

The ANA said something that we couldn't understand.

I just patted the confused guard on the shoulder and headed towards the end of the roof and the other ladder that led back down to our compound.

A few minutes later and I was safely inside my mosquito net. I fell asleep with a smile on my face, not even for a second realising the impact the night's events would have on my future life.

CHAPTER THREE

The Dogs of Now Zad

We had only been in Now Zad for just over a week but already it felt like a lifetime.

Our relentless routine, which consisted mainly of being rotated on sentry duty around the sangars and staring at the same panoramic Afghan backdrop for hours on end, was broken up only by the occasional short patrol to check out the alleyways and buildings in the immediate vicinity of the compound.

If truth be known the main highlight of the day for the lads was zipping themselves up in what they called their 'time accelerators' – their sleeping bags. Not that a full night's sleep was ever forthcoming given the demands of the sentry roster.

Most ordinary people would find it hard to understand, but incoming Taliban mortars and small-arms fire were often the only excitement of our otherwise dull days.

The eight-man Gurkha detachment that had accompanied us when we arrived in Now Zad specialised in engineering work. Although we had marines who could undertake that job, they had been tasked elsewhere. The Gurkhas were extremely hard-working and as soon as they had arrived under the command of their corporal, who spoke to us in broken English, they had worked relentlessly in making the DC more secure and liveable. It normally takes a lot to impress a Royal Marine when it comes to the army (Royal Marines are actually part of the Royal Navy and therefore not part of the army). But the Gurkha detachment commanded our immediate respect.

The Afghan architects who had designed our mud-walled compound belonged to another age, a time long before the British had ever ventured this far into Afghanistan. They had seen the need for only one entrance to our remote compound, which they had built along the eastern wall.

As a result, it didn't take a genius to work out how we got in and out of the compound during our patrols, especially as the Taliban had called the place home themselves until only a few years ago. The current gate was also directly opposite what the soldiers of the Air Borne Brigade who occupied the compound before us had come to know as RPG alley. The hastily repaired holes in the wall either side of the gate bore testimony to the RPG rounds that had been launched at them during their stay. Luckily for us, the alley had not lived up to its name so far during our time in Now Zad.

So within a few days of our arrival the OC had decided that a second entrance should be opened up along another section of the outer compound wall. A new gate would at least keep the Taliban guessing for a while, he figured.

The Gurkhas had been only too happy to oblige.

The Gurkha corporal had quickly calculated the size of the hole that needed to be blown in the wall and then taped explosive charges to short wooden planks that his team nailed to the designated spots on the wall. Those who were not on duty watched from a safe distance as the Gurkha in charge of the detonation team calmly lit the fuse with a windproof match then walked away, seemingly without a care in the world.

The resulting explosion took our breath away. The shock wave echoed around the compound. When the dust settled and the air cleared it revealed several Gurkhas congratulating themselves and a jagged gap in the three-foot-thick wall that you could now drive a wagon through.

The entrance had been completed by two enormous metal gates, hinged on to a pair of massive upright support posts driven into either side of the jagged hole in the wall. Four large brackets had been welded on to the gates to hold the solid steel bar that prevented the gates from opening. The bar felt like it weighed a ton and, ideally, it took two marines to lift it into place. On your own it was a real challenge.

The way the new metal-panelled gates creaked as they were opened and the bar clunked when it was dropped into place reminded me of a Hammer House of Horrors movie. You almost expected to see Count Dracula standing with his arms crossed waiting to come in when you opened the gate.

Although we had halved the odds of getting hit at patrol time, we had quickly created a new problem: Now Zad's stray dogs were now able to breach our defences, through the one-foot gap that had been left between the desert floor and the bottom of the new gates. It was enough for a determined dog to squeeze through, and every now and again a few hungry pack members would venture into the compound to see what was on offer.

The large pack was hard to miss, especially during the dark hours as they roamed the town and perimeter of the compound. There were dozens of them, of all types of breed of dog. Some were long-haired, others short-haired. There were big mastiff-type hounds and smaller dogs that looked like a cross between a greyhound and a springer. All had one thing in common: they looked bedraggled and unfed. None wore collars so I assumed they were all strays.

The pack was generally quiet during the day; the heat saw to that. But as we slowly crept through the month of November and the sun dipped below the mountains to the west and the cool air flowed in from the north, the pack would form for its nightly manoeuvres.

From my post in the northern sangar I would watch as a pack of at least 50 dogs flowed along the base of the compound wall on the hunt for scraps of food. Through the night sights I would follow the white heat outlines as they snapped, licked, tussled, barked and sniffed each other as they went.

I figured the dropping temperature was what kept them moving. There were times when their constant howling and barking sounded as if they were pleading with the moon to shed some heat from its brilliant white glow.

The dogs knew our compound was the only source of food within their neighbourhood. The 'burns pit' for burning our rubbish was just outside the rear gate. Several times I watched amazed as the bravest – or maybe the hungriest – of the dogs scavenged through the smouldering remains looking for that one morsel of food that had not succumbed to the fire.

One night, amid the quiet and stillness of the deserted town, I found myself watching a young dog. He was a scrawny but agile youngster with long floppy ears. The way his long tail waved madly through the air as he trotted playfully along, you would never have known he was involved in a desperate life-or-death search for food. He seemed like a dog without a care in the world.

Watching the skinny dog bounce along jumping at his own shadow I suddenly thought of Beamer and the never-ending wag of his tail as he ran round and round in circles going nowhere in particular.

I knew the dogs were a health hazard – there was no doubting that – but I figured at night they were actually on our side. If the Taliban ever attempted to get close to the wall the pack would, I was sure, give the game away by immediately investigating the new smell on their patch.

I certainly didn't relish the thought of the pack checking me out while I lay in a ditch trying to remain hidden.

When the dogs entered the compound by crawling under the gate they would always go for the rubbish bags that we stored by the rear gate prior to being dumped in the burns pit at first light. The early-morning sun would reveal torn empty ration pack wrappers and other rubbish scattered around the rear gate where the dogs and the occasional cat had discarded them.

I could handle picking up rubbish but clearing up the assorted piles of dog crap that was clearly evident among the torn bin bags was not what I had in mind as my first job of the day.

One morning as I headed out to clear up from the pack's latest forage into the compound, I was shocked to find a dead dog lying by the bin bags. It looked like an old St Bernard-mix, and its coat was matted and dusty. I assumed it had died of old age; it didn't have any obvious wounds. I couldn't leave it lying in the midday sun to decompose but I couldn't just pick it up either. So I'd tied a piece of old rope around its body and then dragged it out to the burns pit.

I tried not to feel sorry for it as I pulled it along the ground. It must have had a good innings to survive to the age it had out here. I wasn't sure how the dog had managed to crawl under the gate – it looked too big. But as I got closer to the closed gate I noticed that an industrious dog had burrowed into the dust and dirt to make a small ditch. I realised I needed to solve the problem of the gate as soon as I could.

When I'd finished disposing of the old dog, I grabbed a shovel and cleared a trench that ran the length of the under-side of the gate about a foot deep and half a foot wide. I then filled the trench with a collection of large rocks that lay outside the compound walls.

It wasn't that much of a chore. I'd been getting frustrated not being able to do proper PT every day so I relished the opportunity for a workout. I arranged the rocks in the trench as close together as I could then I replaced the dirt I'd removed to cover them. By the time I'd done this I'd raised the level of the ground so that there was now no more than a six-inch space under the gate, too narrow for even the skin-niest and most determined dog to force its way in.

My exertions had attracted several younger dogs to see what food was on offer and one of them had slipped through the open gate. When I had admired my handiwork it was hard to coax the stray back to the gate. The offer of an open bacon and beans meal pouch did the trick. The dog was young and was soon waiting patiently at the gate to go out as if I was taking him for a walk. As I opened the gate a few dogs were still hanging around in hope. I made a fuss of them as they rolled around in the dust and, once more, couldn't help but think of Beamer and Fizz back home. These dogs were just like any other playful dogs the world over.

I placed the remainder of the food on the ground in small piles. The smell was too overwhelming for them and they soon broke off from my attentions, making a beeline for the free food. I took advantage of the distraction to slip back in and close the now dog-proof gate.

I felt bad locking them out but it was for their own good and anyway what else could I do? It didn't help the dogs but at least my bin bags were safe.

The shouts, cheers and excited screams were getting louder by the second as I approached the end of the alleyway. I looked across to where Dave stood surveying the entrance to another alley opening to our left. He gave me a confused look and shook his head. He too had no idea what was going on around the corner.

Normally, no locals strayed this close to the compound, especially not in large numbers. There was nothing for them around here any more. What the hell are we going to find here, I wondered.

I was leading a short clearance patrol to make sure the Taliban were not sneaking up on the compound via the narrow alleyways. The late-afternoon sun was particularly hot and after only ten minutes of walking I was sweating profusely under my body armour. I was looking forward to getting back into our small sanctuary and cooling off when

I'd heard the crowd noise but now all thoughts of rest were gone.

A telegraph pole that had probably once supplied one of the only phonelines in Now Zad had somehow fallen over and was leaning precariously against the mud wall ahead of me. I would have to duck under it to look around the corner if I didn't want to make myself a prime target by standing in the middle of the alley. The only thing holding it in place was a length of telegraph wire. Any sudden movement and it looked as if it would fall further. I had no choice, however. I needed to see around the corner, so I ducked under the telegraph pole trying not to catch the radio antenna that protruded from my backpack as I crouched low.

Looking down the alleyway I saw a knot of around 15 Afghans formed in a circle in the largest of the alleys that approached our compound from the west. With their distinct dark green tatty camouflage uniforms I could see that most were ANA and the rest were made up of the ANP that shared our compound. They were wearing the light blue flowing robes that they wore only on 'official business'.

They had obviously left the compound without permission as I hadn't been warned in the patrol brief to look out for any friendlies. As we hadn't been out that long they must have left only recently. They had clearly left their common sense back in the compound too, because none of them was carrying a weapon. Not the smartest of ideas in Now Zad.

I was motioning for Dave to join me when I suddenly heard frenzied barking coming from where the crowd was gathered. I looked back and saw the crowd of Afghans was now jeering and shouting louder than ever. Then, as the men moved around excitedly, I caught a glimpse of two very angry dogs inside the closed circle.

I realised immediately what I was witnessing. 'Fucking hell,' I muttered.

It had been bad enough seeing the ANP dog being restrained a week or so earlier.

I had never imagined they would hold a dogfight here in Now Zad as well.

I saw one dog hit the dirt alley floor with a sickening thud. Its larger opponent landed next to it. Its jaws were spread wide to attack the dog that attempted to pick itself up from the littered alley floor. Teeth clashed as both dogs went for each other's throat, their one main weak point, as both dogs had bloodied stumps where their ears had once been.

It takes a lot to rattle me. I had learned a long time ago to walk away from a fight. But it's an entirely different matter when it comes to witnessing animal cruelty. Animals can't stand up for themselves. I had seen enough. I had come to Afghanistan to help people get back on their feet, not promote this kind of barbaric behaviour. After the episode with the ANP dog I was not about to take the diplomatic approach again.

Without a second thought I started moving in the direction of the screaming throng. I could now see that one of the dogs was definitely bigger than the other. The larger one was a huge dog as big as a mastiff, the other more like an Alsatian. Through the silhouettes of the Afghans stood huddled in the circle, I could make out that most of the spectators were using long, solid sticks to push and beat the dogs. The scene that was playing out in front of me was far worse than any I had viewed on the Internet.

I try my best to respect and understand other cultures before I pass judgement, but these dogs were given no choice: fight or be beaten. I snapped.

The Afghans were so engrossed in the spectacle that they hadn't noticed my approach. The dogs were lunging at each other now. The larger dog had the upper hand and easily overpowered the smaller one, knocking it to the ground. The smaller dog clearly looked winded as its larger opponent, jaws wide ready for the inevitable attack, charged forward. The Afghans were shouting louder.

I burst through the circle with such force that two of the ANA soldiers just managed to catch themselves with their hands before they hit the floor face first.

'What the hell is going on?' I screamed as I emerged into the middle of the circle.

It was probably pointless. I had no translator. But I hoped the anger in my voice would cross the language barrier.

As one the men turned in my direction, the wide-eyed hatred immediately evident on their tanned faces. The distraction gave the two dogs their chance. They both bolted through the gap I had created and ran off.

The Afghans now surged towards me shouting angrily. I had no idea what they were saying although I guessed they were pretty annoyed that I had disrupted their sport.

They stopped just a few yards from me to allow the most senior Afghan policeman present to step forward. He pushed me in the chest as he spat incomprehensible words in my direction. I was close enough to taste the stench of his breath. I needed some space.

'Back off buddy,' I said, using the palm of my free left hand to shove him back for all I was worth.

He tripped over his own feet and landed in a heap on the floor, the dust from the floor of the alley creating a small plume either side of him. Any other time it would have been comical but I wasn't laughing. I had also just upset the rules of diplomacy, as I had just decked their commander, but I wasn't thinking straight.

'Don't touch me again,' I said, pointing my forefinger at him and raising my rifle from its position at my right side.

I had a horrible feeling that this was about to get nasty.

The Afghans were shouting and screaming as they pushed towards me, pointing in the direction that the dogs had fled. I stepped back to create some distance between me and the crowd as the policeman picked himself up. As I did so, I realised I was being forced back against the wall of the alley. I screamed obscenities at the police commander, who was yelling what I assumed were obscenities back at me.

I was thinking that there was no way I could get out of this situation when all of a sudden Dave pushed into the throng to stand alongside me. 'Nice one, Pen,' he said. 'Time to leave.' He grabbed my arm and led me back towards the patrol.

I could see our lads had closed ranks into the alley. The Afghans soon cottoned on to the fact that, rather than securing the area around us as they would normally be doing, the patrol was facing them.

The lads didn't need to raise their weapons; the assembled Afghans got the message loud and clear but remained staring at us, faces twisted in anger. Dave motioned for the lead marine to start moving away from the mini-riot I had just started.

As we moved off, I looked back towards the Afghans, and especially the policeman who had just pushed me in the chest. He stood motionless but as vocal as before, his curses and shouting resonating around the alley walls. The temptation to go back and smash him into tomorrow was unbelievably strong. I was shaking with rage.

I wanted to go back into the crowd but Dave had sensed what I was thinking and continued to drag me away, into the safety of the departing patrol. Before I rounded the corner I turned once more and pointed at them and then in the direction of the compound. They knew what I meant. I wasn't going to just stand by and watch the dogs fight. No matter what somebody else's culture allowed.

The derelict building stood towards the western end of our compound, across a large open area away from any of the occupied buildings. The ANP sometimes used it for cooking, usually when they had missed the opportunity, for whatever reason, to prepare their meal during daylight hours. Cooking at night in the open air would provide the Taliban with an opportunity too good to miss.

The building was in a poor state. It had no windows or doors and the stench of waste wafting from the main door was extremely unpleasant. Dust poured continuously from the cracked and unpainted walls.

Since Kilo Company had arrived in the compound we had given the building only a cursory glance. I'd decided to take a closer look today partly because it offered the prospect of some shade from the blazing midday sun.

The temperature dropped a few degrees as soon as I crossed the threshold into the main hall. The cool air was a welcome relief now, but the Afghan winter was fast approaching. I didn't hold much hope that the thick mud walls would hold much heat. Not that we had heating systems anyway.

The hallway was small with two doorless openings that led off either side into larger rooms. Each room had one small window that allowed the thinnest of shards of brilliant afternoon sun into the room. As I scanned the room I couldn't make out much detail.

I pulled my torch from its housing on my webbing belt and put it to use.

There was no furniture, just the odd dirty cooking utensil and discarded food wrappers, nothing of any value left on the floor.

I noticed, though, some old paper lying on the floor with five or more shaped blocks lying on top of each other. Out of curiosity I bent down to take a closer look. I picked one up. The object was hardened mud roughly shaped into a square tile, but at least ten times as thick as the conventional wall tile I was used to back home. In the middle of the tile was an imprint of four long leaves radiating outwards as if to form the points of a compass. I turned the heavy tile over in my hand. Why would anybody take so much time and effort to fashion this instead of concentrating on the more important issues of the day, I asked myself? Survival seemed to be a hard enough job.

I walked another three steps into the gloom. On my left, hidden from the main doorway, was a small alcove. On closer inspection it revealed itself as a doorway to a smaller store-room.

Secretly a part of me was hoping that this old building would reveal something of the compound's past, although somebody, I was sure, would have been through this building long before me.

I wasn't expecting the low menacing growl that came from the back of the small room though. That caught me totally off guard.

I lowered the beam towards the floor and the source of the growl. Two large red eyes were reflected in the torch beam. Another growl from the dark and the eyes didn't turn away.

I took a step back and allowed the torch beam to fill the room. As it did so I saw a dog, curled up in the corner of the storeroom. I recognised it immediately. It was the Alsatian-looking dog from the dogfight I had witnessed in the alley a couple of days earlier.

'Oh shit,' I said. It seemed appropriate.

The dog growled again but didn't move.

What the hell was he doing in here and, more to the point, who let him in? I asked myself. My dog-proof gate was working well.

'The ANP let you in here, didn't they?' I said to the dog in a low whisper. As it was a fairly good-sized dog it had just enough space on the dirty dust-covered floor to curl up tightly. Its rear legs were cocked to one side tight against its body.

He lifted his head towards the light from the torch to check out the intruder who had disturbed his simple retreat. I could see that the dog had the face of an Alsatian except where the big brown ears should have been. There he had two stumps. The right-hand one was still covered in dried blood. His back was covered in short light brown hair, but his front legs halfway up to the knee joint were covered in white hair, as if he was wearing socks.

The dog just stared at me.

'Okay, so I am not on the menu,' I said to him, a sense of relief washing over me.

Food is the language of all animals. 'Fancy some cardboard biscuits?' I asked him as I lowered the torch to the ground so the dog could clearly see me. I crouched down and reached into my top pocket for the biscuits that I carried around with me at all times. The term 'biscuits' was a loose description; they really did look and taste like stale cardboard. But we had all learned that with the Taliban liable to attack at any time, you didn't want to get stuck in a sangar for hours on end with nothing to snack on, even if you did need to drink a litre of water with each bite.

I reached my left hand out towards the dog, holding the biscuit between my forefinger and thumb, just in case I was suddenly back on the menu. I had seen his teeth in action. I didn't fancy a viewing close up.

He growled again. It was a deep rumbling sound, like some nightmarish beast that had just woken up. I flinched. I reached a little further forward, but still a good foot away from the dog.

'Nice and easy, Pen,' I muttered to myself as I reached closer. I was hoping its bark was worse than its bite.

'Good boy, I'm not going to hurt you,' I said softly. 'They taste nice – really!'

I flicked the brown biscuit towards the dog's nose. This time he flinched. He looked at the biscuit and then sniffed it suspiciously. I doubt he had ever come across biscuits before in Now Zad. He moved his head and attempted to pick the biscuit up with his teeth.

'Good boy – more of them where that came from.'

I was glad to see the dog was more interested in the biscuits than in me.

I pulled another one from the green packet and pushed it

towards the dog, but as my hand got close to where the first biscuit had landed he gave a snappy bark and lunged his big head forward without warning.

I reacted too quickly and shot backwards, landing on my backside.

The dog hadn't moved its body, just his head. The message was crystal-clear though.

'Okay. I get it, your space. That's fine Mr Angry Dog,' I said, flipping the biscuit at him and standing up slowly.

The dog didn't bother sniffing the treat this time. Instead he strained his neck forward until he could grab the biscuit with his teeth and slowly started to chew.

'All right buddy, I'll get you some water. You'll need it after eating them.'

I knew I couldn't leave the dog to his own devices within the compound. I didn't want to think about what the ANP had planned for the poor bugger.

But with the compound now dog-proof, he wouldn't be able to leave even if he wanted to. I was going to have to get the dog out. But common sense already told me that I wasn't going to attempt anything until he trusted me. I certainly wasn't going to try to drag him outside.

I backed out of the storeroom and into the bright glare of the mid-afternoon sunshine. I walked over to the water storage area and picked up one of the jerry cans, designated for washing water. It felt a quarter full. Back in the building I had noticed a large silver bowl lying on the floor in the room that the ANP sometimes used for their cooking. It had been used on an open flame in the past and whatever had been cooked in it was baked to the inside. The outside was charred black from the naked flame.

I gave it a quick rinse around and wiped as much of the old baked food from the inside of the bowl as I could just using my fingers. I filled it as full as possible with water and carried it carefully back into the gloom where the grumpy dog was lying. He was exactly as I had left him. This time I was a little more cautious as I placed the bowl down. I wasn't ending up on my arse again.

The dog didn't move. I nudged the bowl forward. No growls.

'Good lad, see: I'm on your side,' I said in the friendliest voice I could muster.

Checking my watch I realised I didn't have much time left before the orders brief at 1600 hours so I emptied the remainder of the biscuit packet by the bowl. 'Later buddy – enjoy the biscuits.'

I left him chewing happily on the biscuits, a question turning over and over in my mind as I walked to the briefing. How was I going to get an Afghan fighting dog out of the building without losing an arm?

I was dreaming of home when the bleeping of my watch alarm snapped me awake.

It was 0130 hours, time to start the day again. I had zipped myself into my sleeping bag only two hours before. As I unzipped the bag I felt the chill of the cool night air and quickly dressed in my fleece and pulled my boots on. Fortunately, it was only a short walk across the compound to reach the relative warmth of the ops room and the radio watch that beckoned.

As I walked across the small open area of ground I noticed a lone figure sitting oblivious to the cold, bathed in the glow of the silvery moon. It was the fighting dog, the shape of his earless head silhouetted distinctively against the mud wall behind him. I stopped to look at him for a moment. Without warning he pushed off his rear legs with an unsteady jerk and wandered towards me.

For a second I thought about running, but I told myself not to be stupid and stood still as the dog approached. The dog moved up alongside me, its head brushed against my legs as he sniffed my combat trousers.

I realised I was holding my breath.

I reached my right hand down towards the dog's head. It suddenly struck me that he had probably never been stroked before. But it was too late and my hand was next to his muzzle.

I kept my hand extended to let the dog sniff it. He inhaled deeply a few times, made a small 'Ophmm' noise then unexpectedly sat down next to me.

I pushed my luck. I gently stroked him on the head, making sure I avoided what was left of his ears. He didn't flinch but pushed his head back against my hand. I rubbed his head harder, giving him a good scratch. As I did so he let out a low growling noise, but this time much softer and definitely less aggressive than anything I had heard from him in his hideaway. It reminded me of the little growls of appreciation that Fizz or Beamer would make, so I guessed I was doing okay.

I looked at my watch again: 0156 hours. I was due to be relieving Dutchy, the other troop sergeant, on the radio in just a few minutes' time. I guessed he wouldn't mind if I was a little late and anyway he was probably still in the middle of a game of poker with the signaller on the other radio, although they played only for boiled sweets. I doubted if we had more than $200 between us in the compound. Money was no longer part of our daily lives.

I stood in the bright glow of the Afghan moonlight for a few more moments, sharing the cool night air with the dog as he enjoyed being made a fuss of for the first time in his very lonely and unloved life.

CHAPTER FOUR

The Dog Warden

The next few days passed slowly; nothing was happening on the Taliban front and our patrolling had been restricted due to a lack of air support. Other operations in Helmand province were taking priority.

The downtime had provided us with an opportunity to make some improvements to our very basic facilities. Today we were building the shower area.

With no running water in Now Zad, or indeed most places in Helmand, we had come equipped with solar showers, large black plastic water bottles that, once filled, were laid out in the sun to absorb the heat for a few hours. They were then hung up on something strong enough to support them, allowing two men to grab a quick shower while the bag emptied via a small tap with a sprinkler head.

They actually worked quite well. The few, brief seconds of warm water they provided even allowed time for a shave with the disposable razors that we had to bring with us. They were supposed to be 'single use' blades but we all used them for several days in a row as we didn't have an unlimited supply. Walking to the shop to buy a new razor wasn't a luxury available to us. Maintaining the unit's strict 'no beards' policy could literally be a pain.

We started off by digging an irrigation ditch to channel the water away from the shower so that it didn't pool outside our accommodation. Instead the water would flow into the small garden that the ANP tended regularly. I'd asked once what type of plants they wanted to grow there. The happy smiles and imaginary puffs of a pretend cigarette they answered with told me all I needed to know.

With the ditch dug, the lads found some old canvas material on the scrap pile. Tied to the supports for the solar showers, it made quite an effective screen.

Showering with your comrades is no big deal, but the ANP were much more private in that respect. They found it highly amusing that we were prepared to stand together naked under a small bag of water. The screen would mean that they would not have to watch and we would no longer risk causing offence to their sensibilities.

The shower was looking good and almost finished so I delegated the rest of the job to one of the lance corporals. I wanted to go and check on the fighting dog.

He was still hiding away in the dilapidated building during the day, emerging at night to prowl by the back gate, where he would root around the pile of bin bags looking for food. I wasn't sure whether the ANP knew he was there or not, but I guessed they must have been the ones to let him into the compound.

The few times I'd tried to prevent him from ripping open the bags and spreading the used wrappers on the ground of the compound he'd given me a menacing growl. To save the remainder of my bags – and my arms – I'd thrown him an open ration pouch instead.

Away from the bin bags, however, his attitude was very different. If he hadn't seen me before that night, when I headed over to man the radio he would bound over to me at an alarming rate. I guessed he weighed about 30 kilograms, more than enough to put me on my backside again if he wanted to.

I had been a little apprehensive at first. It was confusing to see him like this when he was so unapproachable over at the bin bags. But after about the third time it happened, I realised he was actually happy to see me. And to tell the truth I was happy to see him.

Because of our limited patrols, Kilo Company had not had much of an opportunity to interact with the locals of Now Zad. I guessed the dog represented, for now at least, my Afghan hearts and minds operation.

I found the dog sitting on the dried mud platform outside his hiding place. As usual he sucked up the attention and biscuits I lavished on him. There was now a definite trust between us and, in the bright daylight, I managed to take a closer look at him.

The right side of his face just below his eye carried three deep scars. I figured they must have been inflicted during a previous dogfight. He actually looked to have been quite lucky not to have lost his right eye.

I took the opportunity to check out his bloodied ear as I fed him some biscuits. It was looking bad. I couldn't just leave it as flies were always hovering around it and I didn't want it to get infested or infected. I used my free hand to massage some antiseptic cream I'd brought along across his ear. I braced myself in case the scarred dog didn't appreciate my efforts, but he just continued to munch on the biscuits from my left hand, not paying the slightest attention to the gentle rubbing.

I wondered how many fights he had been made to take part in. I felt sorry for him and the other dogs that were on the other side of the compound walls, constantly scavenging for scraps. This was no kind of life. But what could I do to help him and the thousands of other dogs across Afghanistan?

Back in the UK I could call the RSPCA and a horde of volunteers would appear as if by magic. Here I was a million miles from anywhere. The possibility that I could do anything other than feed him biscuits was nil.

I felt despair at my inability to bring about change. But I couldn't just walk away. My problem now was that the dog with no friends and I were actually becoming mates.

*

It was good to hear Lisa's voice even if it was 2 a.m. and she might as well have been on the other side of the moon.

It was finally my turn to phone home on the one satellite phone we had for our company. I suppose we should have been glad we had been given a phone in the first place, but one phone between 60 of us made it slightly difficult to get much use from the weekly phone cards that allowed 20 minutes of talk time. The constant recharging of the one battery pack was also a major source of annoyance. Finding the time was another problem, especially with the five-hour time difference between us and the UK.

I wasn't that interested in politics but I always shook my head in mock amusement when politicians would announce that they had improved the welfare of squaddies in combat zones. Extra Internet terminals or added welfare minutes was great back in the main bases, but it made next to no difference to our lives in the forward operating bases. We had been told that Tony Blair had recently visited Afghanistan as a morale-boosting exercise for the armed forces. From where I stood and looked around the compound it was clear that nobody gave two hoots as to whether Tony Blair had visited or not. It made no difference to us. We would have been more impressed if they had given us a share of the money it cost to get him here. That would have boosted morale.

At least Lisa was in the services too and was used to the difficulties of staying in touch. When she had served on board HMS *Manchester* a few years previously, as part of an anti-drug-smuggling operation to the Caribbean (I guess I joined the wrong part of the Navy), we had grown to accept the infrequent single-page emails and early-morning calls as a part of life. We each knew what the other was facing and so didn't really have to talk about it.

This wasn't the case for some of the other lads though and many of them struggled to convince their loved ones back home that they really could not call on demand. More than a few 'Dear John' letters were in circulation back at Bastion.

Being in the military, Lisa also knew I was not able to talk openly on an unsecure phoneline. We had been told that the main military powers in the area would probably be trying to monitor all calls. If truth be told, I wasn't that bothered that some bored signaller in a shack was listening to me discussing Fizz and Beamer and what was going on in the world of the HMS *Raleigh* PT department.

I waited until we had almost run out of things to talk about when I mentioned the fighting dog. I spent a few minutes explaining how I had found him and how I had witnessed the dogfight.

I heard the sigh on the other end of the line.

'Honey – you are not bringing home a dog from Afghanistan,' Lisa said. She didn't sound annoyed, just practical. I couldn't blame her.

'I know, but I have to do something for him. He's got no ears, Lisa. There must be some form of animal welfare organisation in Afghanistan.' I realised I was almost pleading now.

'And then what?'

'Well, they will rehome him I suppose?'

It suddenly dawned on me that I really hadn't thought this through properly at all. Who would want to rehome an Afghan fighting dog?

'All right, I'll look, see what I can find,' Lisa replied, more to keep me quiet than anything else.

'Love you, honey,' I said. I meant it.

'You are a nightmare, but love you too,' Lisa said. 'Stay safe.'

I pressed the button to end the call just before the beeps sounded.

I hated saying goodbye.

*

With Lisa now hopefully on the case looking for an animal welfare organisation, I had to make the fighting dog's residence in the compound a little more formal. That at least meant building the dog a small enclosed run. I still didn't understand his temperament fully, so I couldn't risk him wandering free around the compound, just in case he decided to have a go at any of my lads. I was also concerned in case the ANP tried to use him for a fight again.

Before I did any of that, however, I would have to inform the OC of my plan. After all, it was his compound.

I waited until the next morning meeting of the officers and SNCOs. I cornered him as he left the room, before he walked into the ops room.

'Boss, can we have a chat?' I asked.

The boss was a tall lean figure who always took the opportunity to remind us that he supported the Scottish football team, seeing as the Euro Championships had been playing just before we deployed. We didn't hold that against him. He was softly spoken and it took a lot to rattle him. I thought he was a very approachable officer and I enjoyed working for him. He listened to the advice his two sergeants gave him and, at times, acted upon it.

I got straight to the point. He knew I had been pretty hacked off after the encounter with the ANP at the dogfight. I was gambling on the sympathy vote. As I described discovering the dog in the outbuilding and my plan to have him sent to a rescue he just nodded. I lied slightly and said Lisa had already found an animal welfare organisation that was willing to take him.

'We're just trying to organise the transport,' I said.

Throughout the boss remained quiet, with a slightly wry smile on his lips.

He didn't say 'yes' but he didn't say 'no' either, which I assumed was the permission I needed to crack on with my rescue plan.

I made my way to the door, smiling slowly to myself.

'So what are you calling him then, Sergeant Farthing?'

I stopped and turned to face him. He still had the wry smile on his face but he was also looking up towards the ceiling and shaking his head.

'Good point, Boss, I don't have a name. I'll get back to you on that.'

As I emerged from the ops room on my way to the lads' compound I pondered over some names for the now legally resident dog.

Bullet? No. Royal? Perhaps not; the military angle didn't sound good. What about AB? After all, the biscuits that he loved so much were properly called 'AB biscuits', although I had no idea why.

I found Dave with the rest of his off-duty section, gathered around the wooden table that had become the focal point for the daily moaning sessions. Currently, the main grievance was the government's so-called deployment bonus, which involved servicemen receiving a tax rebate on the tax they have paid on their wages during their six-month deployment. You'd think that this would make us all happy, but the sting in the tail is that the amount of tax rebate is calculated on the pay band of the lower ranks. As most of us are in the salary bands above that the actual amount of tax rebate or 'deployment bonus' is nowhere near the amount of tax that we pay during a six-month tour in a war zone. It was something we could moan about for hours.

'So how did it go?' Dave asked as I joined them. He was three weeks into growing a incredibly dodgy gringo moustache and was engrossed in a magazine with several pictures of topless women festooned across its front cover. Dave had been over to feed the dog a few times. For all his good intentions, however, all he had received in return was an extremely menacing bark and growl as he bent down to feed him.

'Yeah, good. The boss seemed okay with the idea. Put it this way: he didn't say no,' I replied. 'He did ask what we were going to call the dog though – any ideas?'

'What about Commando?' Dave offered, even though he still had one eye on his magazine.

'Yeah, something like that, or maybe Bootneck?'

'Bootneck' was the slang term sometimes used to describe Royal Marines.

Dan, one of the lads sat at the table, lowered his own lads' mag.

'How about Nowzad?' he said, looking towards me and Dave.

We had Dave's full attention now and he put his magazine down.

'The town is battle-scarred, right?' Dan continued, justifying his choice of name. 'Well, so is the fighting dog, no ears, scars on his face.'

The lad had a good point. Nowzad sounded good and it had meaning.

'Well done young Dan,' I smiled. 'Have a night off duties.'

'Really?' he said, looking well chuffed with himself.

'No,' I said, bringing him down to earth with a crash. 'If I had the manpower yes, but I haven't, so maybe next time.'

As I walked off I looked back at the marine. 'I'd wait until I am out of earshot before you call me a tosser,' I said.

It looked like a good spot. The building had long ago lost its roof and one of its walls. With a little imagination and the application of some of the DIY skills that Lisa kept telling me I didn't have, I could fence off the three remaining walls and make a run for Nowzad.

I looked at him tied to a metal stake behind me. He was lying in the shade panting heavily as the midday sun beat down. Mad dogs and Englishmen, I thought. Although maybe it was only me who was slightly mad.

I had at least two hours before I needed to be on watch. The letter-writing session I had planned would have to wait until later. I figured I had just enough time to build a dog run. Not that I had ever built one before.

I had collected some of the old bent and twisted HESCO fencing that had been discarded by the engineers and had asked a couple of the lads to help me straighten it out. Eight foot of it would serve as an ideal fence to seal off the remaining three sides of the derelict building. I figured that by using a large metal coil I could even make a hinged gate so I could get in and out of the run to feed Nowzad.

There was just one problem though: the open floor of the building was covered in small piles of human crap. The ANP refused to use our toilet platform and so this apparently was one of the areas they used. It was everywhere. There was even a pile on a small ledge at waist height that had once served as a window. I had no idea how they had managed to get up there to squat.

Luckily for me I was the current Kilo Company expert in burning shit. Every Saturday we would go through the ritual of removing the toilet platform and burning the waste to stop the thousands of black flies gathering there. It was one of my responsibilities as a sergeant, although I had still to find that mentioned in any recruiting brochure. The best way to get rid of it was by mixing petrol and diesel together and letting the fuel soak into the shit for a while. For some strange reason throwing in the match gave me an immense feeling of satisfaction. It is amazing what keeps you interested when boredom is knocking on the door.

Our fuel container was full at the moment with numerous cans of petrol and diesel. I carried one of each back across to the run.

It was getting hotter, making the smell even worse. It was bad. I put my sunglasses on and pulled my sweat scarf up around my nose and mouth.

'You'd better appreciate this, lofty,' I said, looking at Nowzad, snoozing in the shade. I noticed two large flat sand-coloured flies appear through the short crisp coat of hair on his back and then disappear. I had tried to get them off him before but the little buggers were too quick. I would have to deal with them later.

I struck the match and threw it from a safe distance. The resulting whooomph as the mix of fuel ignited only managed to rouse Nowzad from his sleep for a second or two.

Nowzad didn't so much as bat an eyelid as I built his new home during the next half hour or so.

The burnt crap scooped up easily with the shovel. It wasn't a glamorous job to say the least. I dumped it in a black bin bag and took it for the second roasting of the day at the burns pit. Although I wore a scarf across my mouth I tried my best not to breathe as I toiled away.

The HESCO fencing easily fitted into place once I had driven home two 'borrowed' metal stakes that would normally have been used to support defensive barbed wire. They would hold the fencing upright and in place, sealing the open end of the run. The hinged section was just big enough for me to squeeze through and worked perfectly as a gate.

By now curiosity had tempted a few of my off-duty troop over to see what was keeping me so busy. Most knew of my plan to attempt to get Nowzad to a rescue centre. Some of the lads had seemed genuinely supportive; a few others had thought I was completely nuts. I didn't mind. It kept me busy and I felt I was at least doing something positive.

However, I didn't have an answer when one marine asked where Nowzad was going to hide the next time we got mortared. I didn't want to admit that I hadn't actually thought of an overhead protective cover for him. But I didn't have time to think about that now. It would have to wait.

After two hours of hard work I left a rather confused-looking Nowzad in his newly built run and headed off to the radio.

The duty dragged as it always did when the Taliban weren't playing. This whole week had been quiet. The radio crackled into life as a marine carried out a radio check but that was it.

Our only patrol to the north-west of Now Zad a few days earlier had returned with news of a requested ceasefire from the town's elders they had met en route. It made sense as our intelligence had suggested that the Taliban were lacking heavy weapons in this area and the news of a wanted cease-fire confirmed it. The town's elders were being backed into a corner, I imagined. They insisted that we be confined to patrols around the DC, which meant then that the Taliban would be able to resupply unhindered. But we had to let the elders negotiate for themselves at the *shuras*, or local meet-ings, held with the Taliban leaders. If diplomacy didn't work then we would have to get involved. I didn't hold out much hope for debate to win the day.

Currently the elders didn't want us to leave the compound for a patrol as they felt this could be perceived as hostile action on our behalf and give the Taliban the excuse they wanted to start attacking again. It was annoying that we had to play the game.

I walked back across the silent compound when the duty finally finished, because I needed to get some personal admin under way, but halfway towards our living compound I decided to check on Nowzad and see how he liked his new home.

I stood open-mouthed when I saw what had happened to the run. I had left it with just the gridded fencing in place, but Nowzad was now lying in the shade under part of a desert camouflage net. What really took me by surprise though was the fact that a quarter of the run was now taken up by Nowzad's very own mortar shelter. It was two foot high and had walls made of filled sandbags and a piece of plywood covered in a layer of sandbags for the roof. A small entrance facing away from the vulnerable fenced end of the run was Nowzad's way in and out. I smiled to myself and nodded approvingly.

I knew how much the lads hated filling sandbags – I can't have been the only one with a soft spot for the big dog. As I admired their handiwork, I only hoped Nowzad wouldn't need it.

The evening scran queue was waiting patiently and the lads were full of jovial banter and gossip from the sangars. For such a small group we managed to create some monster rumours. The latest one was that Gordon Ramsey was coming to cook for us at Christmas.

Our young chef emerged and placed two pots of steaming hot chicken curry on the fold-away table that acted as a serving counter. As we'd been discovering these past few days, the fresh-faced lad had been volunteered to train as a chef. Sadly he had only paid attention to part of the course as he only really knew how to cook a curry.

No sooner had he put the food down than the sky above our heads simultaneously burst into thousands of red streaks as tracer rounds from the hill raced eastwards. The Taliban were obviously back in town.

We didn't need to scream 'Stand to!' But both I and the other troop sergeant reacted together anyway, yelling at the queue of marines to disperse. Most were already on their way.

'What the hell am I meant to do with this now?' the chef yelled, just audible above the 'boom boom' of the .50 calibres firing overhead. Out of frustration he threw his serving spoon into the yard, just missing my head as I grabbed my weapon and body armour from the doorway

'Put it in the fridge, we'll be back later,' I yelled as I charged off.

I just caught his reply as I raced out of the living section of the compound towards my position in the northern sangar.

'But Sergeant, we don't have a bloody fridge …'

*

The explosions were probably only 700 metres away. The blinding split-second flashes as our mortars hit their targets lit up the surrounding buildings as if they had been caught in the white flash of a camera.

I heard over the radio that the hill was taking accurate incoming small arms fire. The Taliban were obviously making up for the quiet of the last few days. The OC ordered our sangars into action and between us we directed fire back towards the enemy position. The sangar to the east of me reported small arms fire being directed at them, too. It was clear that we wouldn't be eating curry any time soon.

The hill intensified its bombardment of the enemy position but was now split between two reported firing points. The company sergeant major was directing our own mortars within the compound to put up illuminating rounds to help the machine gunners pinpoint their targets.

The noise was deafening. The sky was ablaze with tracer rounds going both ways. We scanned the darkened ground to our front, mindful that it could be a diversion to allow the Taliban to get in closer.

I thought of Nowzad and hoped he would be okay. I was shit-scared myself, so I had no doubts a caged, already nervous ex-fighting dog would also be terrified. I was even more glad and grateful that the lads had built him that mortar shelter. I hoped he would be safe in there. The pack of dogs outside the walls was certainly nowhere to be seen.

As the noise intensified I had to push my headset to my ear to hear the shouted messages over the radio between the hill and our compound. The OC had declared a TIC (troops in contact), which meant that back at Camp Bastion the HQ staff would now focus on our situation and that meant going to the top of the list for any available fast jets that were on call. In other words some heavy ordnance would soon be dropped on any positions we had identified as Taliban.

'0A this is Hill, widow maker ETA figures 5 over.' It

always amused me that one of the fast jet pilots called himself the widow maker.

'0A, roger, give me the one-minute heads up, out.'

To any non-military person listening in to the radio conversation it would sound like gobbledygook. To us though, it was a short, sharp conversation that conveyed key information. I now knew that in five minutes the big bangs would really kick in.

I tried to ignore my thoughts of Nowzad in his run. I had a responsibility to the lads I was commanding. I felt guilty that I couldn't tell him it would be okay and lead him away from this madness. But I couldn't do anything about it; my hands were tied.

Our translator was eavesdropping on the Taliban as they sent radio messages to each other. They didn't seem to be that bothered by the amount of ordnance being sent their way. I had a sneaky feeling they would be in a minute or so.

'All stations this is 0A, stand by – 30 seconds to impact.'

The hill had already stopped the mortar barrage to allow the F18 to come in low, ready to drop two 500-pound bombs on the identified targets.

For a split second everything went quiet as we all waited for the impact. The two flashes were blinding. For a moment even the mountains in the far distance were lit up against the perfect black night sky.

Then the force from the blast arrived.

A wave of air radiated outwards from ground zero. It hit our position with an audible oomph that caused the wooden sangar roof to shake.

'Bloody hell,' said my GPMG gunner, crouched in the sangar next to me.

The noise was next to hit us and the boom vibrated around the mountains as it faded to nothing.

'Cease all firing,' I yelled along the line of my sangar while we waited for the hill to survey the scene and report in.

The translator had been quiet for a while, normally a sign we had hit the right spot. Not that I wanted to be responsible for someone's death, but the Taliban had been given more than enough chances to settle their disputes around the debating table. And, more importantly, they had started firing first.

Everything was still, quiet. Now Zad was dark again. The air smelt of gunfire, but nothing moved. Two illuminating flares were fired towards the last-known enemy position. They burst into two brilliant floating lights that slowly sank earthward under their parachutes. The shadows danced on the ground as the flares moved with the wind.

'0A this is Hill, negative movement at the firing points, over.'

'Hill, 0A roger, keep eyes on. Over.'

For the next half hour or so we sat quietly in the dark waiting to make sure the Taliban we had fired upon were indeed dead. I desperately wanted to check on Nowzad, but I couldn't risk the Taliban kicking off again while I wasn't where I should be. Beyond our sangar the darkness was all-encompassing. If anybody was out there then they had had enough. The only chatter on our radio was confirming that all of our call signs were okay. Nobody had been injured.

The OC broke the silence over the net.

'All stations this is 0A, chatter received. And I quote: "All okay. That was close. Meet back at house." 0A out.'

We all started laughing. After nearly an hour and a half while there had been a constant exchange of fire we had only managed to scare them into going home.

'How the hell did they survive that?' Dave asked from his position in the left-hand firing point of the sangar. 'No way could anybody get out of that, the jammy bastards.'

Dave was right: it was unbelievable.

I waited another five minutes and then climbed out of the sangar. I still had all the radios on and could hear the hill reporting that nothing was to be seen in the two target areas.

I jogged round to Nowzad's run.

All seemed as it should. The gridded fence was still in place with the old rope to secure the gate as I had left it. I quickly untied it and squeezed into the run, using my fingers to shield the torch light as I waved the beam across the floor. I didn't want to be responsible for giving the Taliban a target.

Nowzad must have been petrified; he didn't come out to see me. Normally I would see his blackish muzzle with its prominent white streak poking out of his shelter. He would then emerge eagerly anticipating the unlimited supply of biscuits that I would bring with me.

But not tonight. There was not a sign of him.

'Nowzad, come on bud, where are you?' I crouched down calling out his name as softly as I could.

With still no sign of him I walked towards the back of the run looking for the opening to the mortar shelter. I knelt down and shone the torch carefully into the shelter. It was empty as well.

I stood straight up and double-checked around the run in case I had missed Nowzad curled up in a corner. There was nothing there. I hurried over to the gate again. Had I missed something? It was done up when I got here, wasn't it? Surely my mind was playing tricks. I tried to remember if I'd definitely had to untie the gate as I entered.

It hadn't been forced open. I closed it to make sure it wasn't bent and sure enough it closed forming a smooth seal against the metal picket.

I scanned along the bottom of the run's only fence. I had purposely dug it a half a foot or so into the ground so that Nowzad wouldn't be able to dig his way out. The ground was still undisturbed, so he hadn't got out that way.

The only other way of escape was over the top of the fence. But that was at least five foot high. I was sure Nowzad didn't have the physical ability to clear it. I looked at it again; he couldn't jump that high, could he?

Not that it mattered now anyway. Nowzad was gone.

The off-duty lads had been required to spend the battle hidden away in their small cells. Some had actually relished the opportunity for some enforced shut-eye; there was not a lot they could do so why waste the opportunity? Most were now coming out to form the queue that was snaking towards the barely warm curry that was still sitting where we'd left it. The chef hadn't bothered to move it during the entire battle.

Although I was apprehensive about Nowzad I was also anxious about the lads. Nowzad still didn't get on too well with strangers and the last thing I needed was him deciding to bite somebody as, scared and desperate, he roamed around the compound. This would have sealed his fate immediately.

How would he have reacted if the lads had tried to catch him? I just hoped he hadn't done anything that we would both regret. Of all the dogs that I had watched roaming outside I had chosen to keep the fighting dog in the compound, although to be fair, hadn't he chosen me? I quickened my pace as I realised I needed to find him; after all I couldn't abandon him now.

As my mind went into overdrive, I was brought back to the compound by Dan, the lad who had given Nowzad his name, whom I just avoided bumping into as he ran out of the small mud archway that formed the entrance to the living area.

'Sergeant, come and have a look at this,' he spoke quickly. He looked slightly bewildered, his eyes wide.

'What Dan? I'm looking for Nowzad,' I replied. 'Have you seen him?'

'It is Nowzad.'

'What?'

I followed him over to one of the old cell doorways. The glow from a small candle on a high home-made shelf partially lit the cramped room.

'He's in here,' Dan said, pointing to one of the three military-issue beds that were squeezed into the small space.

I crouched down and looked under the bed. Sure enough, there was Nowzad, curled up in a small ball, legs tucked under his body, eyes wide and looking at directly at me. I reached under the bed and rubbed the soft stump of his right ear.

'What happened?'

'Halfway through the contact he just barged into the room,' Dan explained. 'We all shat ourselves wondering what he was going to do, but then he just looked at us and squeezed under the bed.'

I gave Dan a slightly disbelieving look.

'Yeah, he did, and we haven't been able to get him out since, not even with food.'

Nowzad had never been over this side of the compound, yet he had found his way to safety, just one room away from where I slept. I was fairly sure he'd have forced his way in there if my door had not been closed while I was in the sangar.

I coaxed him out with his favourite biscuits as he crawled out from under the bed. He even let Dan stroke his head as I led him out the door.

We must have looked an odd couple as we walked back across the darkened compound, one fully laden soldier holding out biscuit after biscuit for a dog with no ears.

'It's okay, mate, the fireworks are over now.' I patted his head, which was just level with my knee as I led him back towards his run.

As we approached his makeshift home I marvelled at how he had managed to jump the fence. That could be the only explanation for his escape. As I opened the gate Nowzad pushed past my leg to get back in the run. I looked at the fence again and then at Nowzad. 'How did you clear that fence, bud?' Nowzad was no springer spaniel and I just couldn't picture him scaling the fence like a spider dog.

CHAPTER FIVE

Rocket-Propelled Grenade

I was in the middle of carrying out my morning rounds, when I noticed a marine with a faded-yellow truck over by Nowzad's run. I knew it was John – he was the only person who drove a vehicle within the compound. Although he was only a young marine, he had shown he was keen and reliable and had been given the task of coordinating and gathering all of our intelligence reports. Unfortunately he had also been volunteered for dropping off each day's allocation of washing and drinking water to the sangars. Rather than delivering the jerry cans around by hand, John had used his initiative and taken to using the old Toyota pickup truck we had inherited from the ANA when we took over the compound for the daily water deliveries. It made the job a lot easier.

'All right, mate, how's the water boy today?' I said mockingly, as I approached the run.

'Doing just great, cheers Sergeant,' he replied, his dark hair already growing down around his ears. The regimental sergeant major would have had a fit had he been here.

'I brought Nowzad this,' he said, holding out an old red satin cushion decorated with a faded gold leaf design that, had it been clean, would not have been out of place on a settee back home.

'Where did you get that from?'

'Found it loafing,' he replied with a knowing smile.

I smiled back. I wasn't going to ask too many questions. Nowzad was about to be given his first ever dog bed.

I opened the gate and walked over to Nowzad's normal spot under the cam net. As soon as I placed the cushion down Nowzad sniffed it suspiciously a few times before stepping on to it and then plonking himself down into a tight ball.

'Good choice, John. I think he likes it.'

We left Nowzad to spend the remainder of the day curled up on his cushion, watching a very slow world go by through the fencing of his run.

A few of the lads were now regularly visiting Nowzad during their downtime. I figured they enjoyed the normality of feeding him biscuits even though they took care to stay on the safe side of the run. Nowzad still didn't let anybody but me get near him without letting out an evil-sounding growl and none were brave enough to find out if he meant it or not.

Keeping him in the run would be safer for everybody. So far he hadn't attempted to jump the fence again and I reckoned he wouldn't until the next firefight we were drawn into. All of the lads knew to avoid him if he was out. I'd thought about getting him a collar but I would have to wait for Lisa to post one to me.

To be truthful I was still slightly wary of him and wasn't sure how much he actually trusted me. He might still bite me if I attempted to tie anything around his neck. Added to this, I was always keeping an eye out in case the ANP decided to try and use him for another fight even though they had been warned by the OC that those sorts of activities would not be tolerated within our compound.

Nowzad looked chilled enough about being left in his run but whenever I entered to feed him, he would try to squeeze out of the gate. He made it every now and again, haring off on a tour of the entire inner perimeter of the compound, sniffing, scratching and marking his territory as I tried to coax him back in. Food was usually the key to persuading him back into the run. An open bag of pork and dumplings wafted under his nose worked every time.

Since my conversation with Lisa, I'd been wondering whether my cunning plan to save Nowzad was a good idea or not. At the moment I was leaning towards the latter.

Who was going to want to rehome a former fighting dog? How could they, even if they wanted to? Nowzad knew no house rules, he hadn't been socialised. But he was quiet enough during the day – surely I could spend what few minutes I had each day at least trying to socialise him? After all, he hadn't exactly been well treated in his experiences with humans so far, had he? So he deserved a shot at a decent dog's life. Deep down, though, I knew Nowzad would be a nightmare for any prospective owners.

I delayed making any decisions; I would wait and see what Lisa found out. Maybe I just wasn't brave enough to face up to reality. It was the coward's way of delaying the inevitable.

The onset of winter was becoming more apparent; it was getting a lot cooler in the evenings and we guessed that it wasn't far off hitting zero degrees during the early hours of the morning. I was now pulling on my duvet jacket more or less as soon as the sun dropped below the western compound wall.

I had been in Afghanistan a little over seven weeks and we were entering the Rest and Recuperation period, the time when the lads were allowed to go back home to the UK for ten days. With a few lads already back home, sentry duties were coming around quicker than ever for those of us who were left behind. Even the chef and our mechanic were coming along to make up the numbers on patrol, although they didn't mind getting out and about.

We would patrol through the deserted labyrinth of open alleyways that were littered with rubbish and rubble, always staying within the immediate vicinity of the compound. We were still waiting patiently for the elders to attempt a peaceful settlement with the local Taliban commander.

We normally arrived back in the DC having failed to meet a single local, which was disappointing for me. I wanted to try and interact with the people of Afghanistan. I had to admit my attempts to forge a relationship with the ANP had failed miserably, although I laid the blame completely at their feet. I couldn't pretend I felt anything but animosity towards them after witnessing their treatment of Nowzad and the other fighting dog.

But there were other, ordinary Afghans out there. From the northern sangars we would watch the still populated part of northern Now Zad during the daytime. There, far enough away from the compound to remain safe from any fallout from our battles with the Taliban, locals, looking like small ants in the distance, would go about their daily business. Lone figures would appear from one alley and then disappear down another. Fathers and sons would stroll together, their white turbans standing out against the dull yellow of everything around them, as I struggled to imagine what their daily lives entailed. I really did want to help these people but being part of ISAF would always prevent me from finding out what it was really like to be a part of their society. I had read somewhere that the United Nations put the average life expectancy of an Afghanistan national at only 43 years old and that over a third of Afghan women died during pregnancy. All this could be prevented through education, one of the things the Taliban detested.

But I wasn't sure that one person alone was going to make much difference. By joining the Royal Marines, making a difference was what I had come to Afghanistan to do and at the moment I felt fairly useless. I guess I had to think that we were just a small piece of the new tapestry that depicted Afghanistan's rebirth.

I had picked up the 0200 watch again and by 0140 was dressed and walking across the quiet deserted compound. The alarm was set 20 minutes earlier these days to allow me time to let Nowzad out.

With nobody about at this early hour, I could let him have the run of the compound. He would spend the first few minutes chasing me around, always trying to prod me with his right front paw. I enjoyed running around with him in the mini-dust cloud that formed around us. For those rare minutes he would be like any other socialised dog the world over and for me all thoughts of being in the most dangerous place on earth vanished. We were just a man and his dog, enjoying each other's company and having fun.

I had been informed during the late-night scheduled radio report with the main Unit HQ back in Camp Bastion that two of my lads, who had been sent to bolster the troops temporarily in the nearby town of Kajacki, had been seriously injured when their Land Rover crashed. The Taliban had not been involved. It was just an accident.

None of us wanted to be injured but, if the fates decided otherwise, then I knew that we would all prefer to suffer our injuries as a result of a fierce battle, preferably as the hero of the moment, than as the result of a stupid vehicle accident.

The news had set me thinking back to early September. I remembered standing in a rugby club back in Plymouth with my troop on our last night out on the town before we deployed. I had gathered the lads around in a huddle, all of us holding full pints of beer.

'Here's to kicking the Taliban arse and *all* of us coming home war heroes,' I'd shouted as we toasted each other with a clash of pint glasses, spilling beer down our arms in the process. It sounded a cliché but these were my young lads and it seemed the right thing to do at the time. But now I wished I hadn't said it. Maybe I had tempted fate.

The limited information we had received over the radio about the two lads didn't sound good and it would be a while before a full report made its way to us. For now, everything was just speculation.

I wondered if I had been there whether I could have

prevented it. But I hadn't been in Kajacki, I was in Now Zad, and common sense told me it was too late for that now, what was done was done.

There was nothing I could do until more information came in. I needed a few minutes to decide how to break the news to the rest of the troop. Seeing Nowzad would give me space to think.

The night was bitterly cold. As I walked over to Nowzad's run I pulled up the collar on my jacket.

A movement in the shadows to my left stopped me in my tracks.

The figure in the darkness, whatever it was, stopped too.

I took a step forward but the crescent moon was only a small slither of light in the night sky and I couldn't make out any details in the shadows. Until, that is, I suddenly saw it running at me.

'What are you doing out?' I said, assuming that the dark shape was Nowzad. It was probably only a matter of time again before he escaped.

But as it moved in closer I saw that it wasn't Nowzad. It was another dog, too thin and leggy to be him.

The dog didn't seem able to run in a straight line, it darted from one side to the other, as it crossed the 30 yards between us in a series of zigzags. He threw himself down on the dusty ground in front of me, his legs splayed out, two glistening beady eyes eagerly watching me. He wasn't a fighting dog. For a start he wasn't big enough, and he was still in possession of a pair of long, floppy ears.

The memory of the time I'd watched the skinny young dog play through the viewfinder of the night sight suddenly came back to me. The way the dog had moved that night was identical to the movements of the dog that now sat in front of me. 'I've seen you before, haven't I?'

I reached my right hand out. The dog immediately spun twice on the spot, kicking up a dust cloud. When I took a step towards him, the dog charged full pace towards me, before at the last moment twisting 90 degrees to the left and charging off around the snatch wagon that was parked by the rear gate.

'Playful little bugger aren't you?'

I walked around to the front of the sand-coloured snatch wagon. The windows of the vehicle wore protective metal grilles, a relic of the Northern Ireland days of Orange marches and protests.

The dog's long thin snout appeared from under the wagon. As quick as a flash he shot out and ran around me before diving back under the wagon again. A moment later he was out again, charging at me then stopping short and then quickly heading off to the side. He reminded me of Beamer, back home.

'Mad as a bag of rabbits,' I said to myself. 'So how have you got in?' I asked the mad little dog.

I looked towards the gate. I shook my head and smiled. Little bugger. The dog had dug his way between two of the big rocks I had buried in the trench, leaving just enough of a gap to slip underneath.

I chased the erratic dog around the parked wagon for a minute. He played me a dummy move and sent me to the right as he turned and went left, always keeping just in front of me.

The young dog was clearly enjoying the interaction, his legs never quite seeming to work in unison but always managing to get him where he wanted to go. As the dog played, all around the wagon slowly dispersing dust clouds hung in the air. I looked at my watch. I'd been playing with the dog for nearly ten minutes. I was using up Nowzad's free time.

'Sorry buddy – got to go and see one of your pals.'

As I walked over to Nowzad's run, the small dog followed.

Without really thinking, I let Nowzad out. He charged out and headed straight for the small dog, who had suddenly stopped in his tracks, frozen to the spot.

'Oh shit, carnage,' I thought out loud.

For a moment I told myself I had made a huge mistake letting Nowzad loose within sight of another male dog. He was a veteran fighting dog, after all. But, to my relief, another of his basic, canine instincts kicked in.

When Nowzad came to a halt next to the other dog he simply started sniffing the new arrival in the compound. Rather than running away, the smaller dog simply sniffed back. Amazingly they were playing together within moments.

I let them play for a minute or two then waited for Nowzad to go for his evening wee, hovering with the plastic bag I had ready to scoop the small pile he usually deposited by the rear gate.

As usual, Nowzad didn't want to go back into his run when playtime ended – I couldn't blame him really as he didn't get that much time outside – and the small dog just sat watching me chase Nowzad round and round in circles. After a good struggle I managed to coax and push him back through the gate to the run.

With the gate locked and a very unhappy Nowzad on the other side, I turned round to the young dog that was still waiting patiently.

'You get a reprieve,' I told him. 'I haven't got time to get you out the gate now.'

I was already late. Dutchy was cool about me sorting Nowzad out but I couldn't push my luck.

I walked away from the young dog but as I looked over my shoulder I saw it was following me. I stopped and suddenly jumped towards it. Just as I thought, it still wanted to play. It spun around twice on the spot, shot off in a random direction, did a mini-lap of the area and then flopped back down in front of me with its legs splayed open again.

When I got to the ops room door I turned around again to see the dog was still merrily following me. 'Sorry buddy you can't come in here,' I said, opening and closing the door quickly behind me.

I put the headset on to be greeted by the normal chat on the radios as the lads checked in from the sangars and the hill. Dutchy was keen to get some 'rack' time so we hardly spoke as he headed off to bed.

I radio checked everybody to help pass the time. It also made sure the lads were awake.

The ops room was housed in an old storeroom with no windows. In the background all you could hear was the permanent, dull growling of the compound's small diesel generator, powering the three small lamps that illuminated the room. The only furniture was a couple of folding tables, one of which was stacked precariously with the radio equipment that kept us in touch with the outside world.

The simple whitewashed walls were adorned with different-scale maps of Now Zad and the surrounding area. There was also a lone tatty picture of a stunning blonde who seemed to be smiling directly at you no matter which angle you looked at her from. She was, however, the one token distraction in an otherwise focused military operations centre.

I read the log. It corresponded with Dutchy's briefing. It was a dull read. Things had been quiet since the air attack on the Taliban position. Maybe it really had been too close for their comfort. Since then we'd been just waiting for them to attack again, but they hadn't. Instead we'd spent the past week ticking off the days on our home-made calendars, enduring our stagnant schedule of duties and sleeping and eating. But even eating was becoming routine; the one choice hotpot curry that the chef made every night was becoming much too predictable. Our sessions in the time accelerators were becoming ever more appealing.

Tonight my mind was already working on how quickly I could get back across the compound and snatch an hour of sleep when my duty was over. I sat with Jimmy the radio operator but we hardly spoke. Both of us kept our heads down in our books. I was currently reading envious tales of mountaineering daring in Mick Fowler's *On Thin Ice*. Jimmy and I had discussed everything that we could over the last three weeks, but with no regular supply of newspapers we didn't have anything new to say.

I was still quietly dreading breaking the news about the two injured lads to the troop at first light. I didn't read many pages of my book.

The 'Doc' was my relief. He was a naval doctor who was still coming to terms with the fact that the sea was nowhere near our current location. I had to wake him twice to get him out of his sleeping bag when my shift was almost up. At least I didn't have to walk far. The Doc slept outside the makeshift medical room that was situated in the same building as the ops centre. I don't think 'going on watch' had been part of the sales pitch when he signed up for medical service.

'Anything to report, Sergeant?' he asked while still trying to rub the sleep out of his eyes.

'Nope – all is quiet. The air plan for the day is coming in at 0600. The boss wants a shake at the same time.'

We would know then whether or not we had air cover for the patrol that was planned to the south of the compound. I pushed myself up from the small folding chair I was sat in. My back hurt. Sitting for hours in a folding chair was not good. I had put some boiling water on for a tea to take with me. Jimmy the signaller still had another hour.

'Later Jimmy,' I said as I flicked him a mock salute as I finished stirring my tea.

'Yeah, enjoy your bed, Sergeant,' he replied without looking up from his book.

I patted the Doc on the back as I handed him the battered headset as he took my place in the chair.

I opened the outer door from the ops room building as the beautiful tint of the new morning sun was breaking over the easterly wall of the compound. The skies were a fantastic swirl of red clouds forming around the perfect mountains that surrounded us to the north. A beautiful part of the day;

shame I rarely saw it back home, normally the double duvet would hold me fast until the last possible moment.

The unexpected lump at my feet almost tripped me over. I looked down just in time to see the small playful dog curled up in a ball right in front of the door. I could barely believe he was there.

As soon as I bent down to stroke him he jumped up and adopted his playful, legs-splayed stance. Instantly he was wide awake.

'Am I your new friend then?' I teased him. 'Have you waited all this time for me to come out?'

The dog just looked at me with its head cocked to the left. With the early-morning sun rising steadily I could see him much better now. He was a skinnier version of Nowzad, with long legs, a light brown tan coat and a darker muzzle. And of course he still had his ears.

I fished a biscuit out of my pocket. 'I'll have to stock up again at this rate,' I thought as I gingerly fed him one of the few remaining that I had.

I knew he couldn't stay. 'Sorry buddy but you will have to leave the compound – I can't let the boss see you running around,' I told him.

It took me the best part of an hour to finally coax him out of the compound. The young dog just assumed it was a brilliant game we were playing. By the time he was safely out of the gate I was covered in a thin layer of dust. It was almost breakfast time as well. The time accelerator would have to wait. I had to go and find my troop, who would be getting sorted for breakfast.

It was time to give them the facts about what had happened in Kajacki – or as much of them as we knew – before the rumour mill went into overdrive. I managed to locate my section corporals, who were just waking up or coming off guard. I explained the situation, fending off the exacting questions that they hit me with.

'Fellas, we don't know why they drove off the cliff all

right? Look, until we know more, we have to just be grateful that Tom and Matt are still alive. As soon as I know more I will let you guys know. Spread the word to our lads so they don't start listening to rumours.'

During my stint in the breakfast queue I learnt from the signaller that the planned patrol had been canned. The air cover was being diverted to more pressing ops in the south again.

I used the time to check the lads were on top of their admin. It was two days to go to the next resupply flight. I was looking forward to receiving mail from Lisa. The rest of the day dragged. We made small talk among ourselves and I managed to handwash most of my clothes. The day ended quietly and without fanfare.

The early-morning watch came all too soon as I found myself walking across the compound through the ANP garden.

I noticed the small skinny mischievous dog again. It was sat waiting for me. I had overslept and had only 15 minutes to let Nowzad run around. I waved at the dog and reached in my pocket for some of the cardboard biscuits. I knelt down and held one out. The dog looked at me and slowly crept forward to sniff the treat. It gently took the biscuit out of my hand then immediately darted off in a zigzag run for fifteen feet before throwing itself to the ground and munching on the biscuit as if its life depended on it.

I thought back to the first time I had seen a rocket-propelled grenade (RPG) fired in anger at us back in Gereshk. The missile has no guidance system and flies in a random line in the general direction it was pointed. The way this little dog ran reminded me of it.

'RPG. That's a good name,' I said to myself.

I opened the gate for Nowzad and he charged out to see his friend. They played between the dust clouds that were kicked up as they leapt at each other. The younger-looking dog was always faster than Nowzad as they chased each other round and round in circles.

I walked over to the rear gate. The filled-in gap was dug away again. The little bugger really did want to get in.

I looked at the two of them playing together, a fighting dog and a skinny youngster. Neither was aggressive; if anything Nowzad was the submissive one.

I knelt down and extended a biscuit in each hand. I called Nowzad. Both dogs stopped their play fighting and ran towards me, Nowzad trotting over in a straight line, little RPG in a random zigzagging motion.

As the pair of them munched on their biscuits I made my mind up immediately. Little RPG was going to be given the same chance as Nowzad. If I was trying to rescue one I might as well make it two. It would save me having to fill the trench under the gate each morning.

I chuckled to myself. Lisa would want to kill me. But then again the Taliban were trying to do that already so what did it matter? RPG joined my improvised dog pound.

The satellite phone took two attempts to connect; I listened to the long drawn-out tones as electronic circuits beyond my comprehension coupled with a grey cordless phone that sat on our kitchen work surface in Cornwall.

I was dying to hear Lisa's voice. I didn't have to wait long.

'Hello,' said a tired voice far too many miles away.

'Hi honey, how you doing?' my voice hopefully conveying the excitement I felt about speaking to her again. It had been over a week.

The conversation swayed between my days of doing nothing and Lisa's busy days in the gym with the Royal Navy's new recruits.

I waited until there was a pause in conversation and then went for broke. I told her about the skinny dog I had named RPG.

'Lisa, if we are going to try rescuing one dog then why not two?' I asked – or maybe it sounded more like pleading.

She didn't sound that chuffed. I tried to reason with her.

'If I find a rescue, what are you going to do then. Who in their right mind is going to take an ex-fighting dog?' She voiced what I had been thinking all along. 'Look Pen...'

I cut her off. 'Somebody will,' I pleaded. 'I can't leave him here to be abused any more Lisa,' I replied, suddenly fully aware both of her lack of progress in finding a rescue centre and of the absurdity of the situation. It was like trying to rescue a dog from the middle of the Somme during the First World War. 'C'mon Lisa, you have access to the Internet, I don't. Can you please just have a look; there must be something out there?'

'I am looking but there isn't anything. I'll search again tonight when I get home, all right?' She sounded annoyed. I suppose I couldn't blame her. It wasn't like she had nothing to do.

'Thanks honey, it is just annoying as I can't do anything myself. I need you to look for me,' I replied, trying to sound chilled.

With nothing more to discuss the phone call came to a natural end. Lisa reassured me that she would do her best to find a centre, if one existed that was.

There must be somewhere in Afghanistan that would take them?

The lack of patrolling was severely depressing everyone. It wasn't that we craved action, we just wanted to do something, anything.

Even though all the living quarters and mini-compounds of the DC were fairly close together, there were some days when I didn't actually see some of the lads. If they weren't needed on duty or they didn't have any admin to crack on with, they just disappeared into their own little world.

My little world was now the dogs. It gave me a few minutes of respite from an otherwise fairly grim existence.

The constant threat of incoming mortars and the very real chance of getting shot was with us even when we were sleeping, but the two Afghan strays didn't seem to have a care in the world. It was just a shame the rest of the world couldn't get along as well as these two did.

I was amazed that they had become buddies so quickly, especially since the first time I had seen them play together I had thought RPG was a goner.

RPG had initiated the playtime by jumping towards Nowzad from a good foot or so away, using his teeth to grab the almost healed stumps that had been Nowzad's ears. Nowzad, though, reacted completely differently to how I assumed he would in a fight situation. Instead of defending himself and ripping RPG to pieces, the big dog allowed himself to be forced to the ground, rolling on to his back while RPG straddled him as he continued to mouth Nowzad's stumpy ears.

This was the way they played all the time now. They would stay in that position tussling away for a good ten to fifteen minutes, before RPG would back off and allow Nowzad to stand up, usually before resuming the act all over again.

Nowzad never seemed to tire of RPG's constant attention.

I enjoyed my brief moments when I looked after them; it took me away from the realities of life in the compound. It reminded me of home.

Today, as I walked across the compound in the early-morning sun to feed the two of them I noticed two silver-coloured dishes similar to the one that had been Nowzad's first water basin. They were lying half hidden under an old canvas amid a load of other rubbish stuck in a small unused corner of the ANP mini-compound.

'Just what I need,' I thought to myself.

The dishes would make ideal dog food bowls. Although RPG had been with us for two days I had only the one bowl from which to feed them both, Nowzad's original water bowl. It had made feeding time a long drawn-out affair.

Both dishes, just like the drinking bowl, were charred black from being used for cooking, but after applying a little elbow grease they looked decent enough to use.

Today's feast was going to be the same as yesterday's and the previous day's, but I didn't think they would complain. For two dogs that had, until recently, eaten only what they could scavenge, a packet of pork stew and dumplings with a few cardboard biscuits thrown in was a top treat.

As I mixed up the sickly yellow blob of so-called pork chunks and round plump suet dumplings I had no reservations about giving the food to the dogs. The lads had long ago given up eating this particular dish unless they really had to. It would only end up in the burns pit anyway.

Both dogs sat bolt upright, waiting excitedly as I mixed the goo together outside the run. As I finished preparing their meal I balanced the bowls in one hand like a posh waiter and let myself in. I knew that Nowzad wouldn't try to escape when I brought food. He definitely loved his food more than going walkabout in the compound.

'You wouldn't run away from food, would you, lofty?' I said to him as I placed both bowls down slightly apart.

Both were gobbling at the food before my hands had left the rim of the bowls.

I was slightly rushed and needed to be in a briefing with the OC in a few minutes so I decided to leave them to enjoy their pork stew. I would collect the empty bowls later.

'If you slow down guys you might actually taste that crap,' I said as I let myself out of the run and headed off towards the ops room.

I had covered no more than ten feet when I heard the frenzied barking from behind me. I turned around expecting the worse.

'Nowzad!' I screamed as I charged back towards the run.

I should have known that feeding them both together was a bad idea; I should've remembered back to when Beamer had arrived with us out of the rescue centre. At meal times he would automatically guard his food and then hunt for more from Fizz's bowl when he'd finished. He'd soon realised that Fizz was not going to give it up without a fight. Beamer had learnt the hard way.

Nowzad, however, didn't have that problem. He was the bigger dog and he was still hungry. Unfortunately RPG had been eating a lot slower than him.

As I ran the short distance back I could only watch as Nowzad lunged at RPG. The loud growl he made sounded evil. It made the hairs stand up on the back of my neck.

RPG was trying to mount a pathetic defence of his half-eaten bowl of stew–biscuit mix. But obviously he was no match for the more powerfully built frame of Nowzad.

I yanked the gate open. Nowzad was jumping up; his head was a frothing blur of gnashing teeth as he attempted again to grab RPG around the neck. As he did so, the smaller dog was forced into the corner of the run with no way out.

Without a second's thought my boot connected with Nowzad's midriff. With a yelp he spun in the air and landed on all fours facing me.

'Don't you fucking dare do that again,' I yelled at him.

Nowzad stood defiantly staring me down.

I turned and looked at RPG, who was curled in the corner, clearly shaking. I was breathing in large gulps of air. My heart seemed to be trying to burst out of my chest.

I picked up RPG's bowl with what remained of the food and placed it down in front of him. 'Go on buddy. I am watching this time.'

I turned back to Nowzad and walked towards him, trying to remain as dominant as I could. I knew that I had to show Nowzad that I was boss. He had to learn to obey me otherwise his future wasn't going to be a safe one.

As soon as RPG started to eat the food Nowzad made to move towards him. I held my hand up in what I hoped was a menacing signal; I didn't have time to mess around.

'Don't even think it,' I said to him. 'I am about to be late for my meeting and don't have time for this crap.'

Nowzad stopped and cowered back as I made a pretend move to hit him. I didn't like doing it but I had no choice. Back home I could spend hours training him slowly, one step at a time, but time was not on my side out in Afghanistan.

As RPG finished licking the bowl clean I collected up both empty dishes. Nowzad immediately moved over to sniff the floor where the bowl had sat seconds earlier, looking for leftovers. RPG shuffled to the other side of the run, his long tail between his legs as soon as Nowzad approached.

The situation was depressing. I had really thought the two of them were going to get on fine. Had I been too optimistic? Was I hoping against hope about getting these two rescued? I looked at the two of them, wanting to knock some sense into Nowzad but knowing it would do no good.

'Great, now I have to watch you two eat as well. Thanks fellas,' I said as I kicked the solid mud wall hard with my boot. As if it was going to change anything. All it did was hurt my toes.

I arrived at the briefing out of breath and with two empty silver bowls. As I entered the small operations room the boss looked up at me.

'Just doing some training with the Afghans, sorry Boss,' I answered his questioning glance.

It was only a little lie; the dogs were Afghans after all.

Everybody else was seated. I squeezed to my chair at the front as sarcastic comments floated over from the other side of the room. I ignored them all as I struggled to get my notebook and pen from my pocket. The boss stood to start the brief.

'This isn't the galley, you need to leave your washing-up outside,' one of the signallers whispered from behind me.

I turned and gave him the finger, timing it perfectly to coincide with the Boss turning to point to the map of Now Zad.

The joking stopped as we received a warning order for a patrol to the north of Now Zad in two days' time. Our aim was going to be to make our presence felt and to reassure the locals that we were on their side.

After the meeting I walked around each of the sangars to inform my corporals that we were getting some exercise. The lads were well chuffed as I gave them timings for receiving orders for a brief later that day. It would be a welcome relief from the monotonous routine in the sangars.

I was sitting in the passenger seat of the roofless WMIC Land Rover, refreshed by the blasts of cool, desert air that washed over me. As we drove to our stand-off position in the desert west of Now Zad in a formation of three vehicles, I could also feel every bump and dip in the hard ground travel up my spine.

Steve, the young lad who was driving today, was following the countless old tyre tracks that meandered in every direction across the desert as best he could. Every now and again he would swerve to avoid the white painted rock circles that marked the spot where the locals had detected old Soviet landmines. As we bumped and bounced our way along, I tried to not to think about whether they had missed any.

When we stopped at the appointed spot on the map, a patch of dried desert that looked no different from any other patch of Afghan desert around us, I felt a hand tap me on the shoulder.

I turned to look at Dan, or Dan the Man as we called him, a six-foot monster of a marine who was holding two small yellow pieces of foam out towards me.

'You might need these, Sergeant,' he said, dropping the two small foam earplugs into my outstretched hand.

Dan had a valid point.

I looked up at the muzzle of the .5 HMG, or heavy machine gun, that was about 12 inches from my right ear. The noise they made was deafening even when we were in the sangars, more than a kilometre from their normal position on the hill. I dreaded to imagine what the noise would be like if I had to give Dan the order to engage the enemy. I stuck one of the soft plugs in my right ear and hoped the Taliban would decide to have a day off.

There was no breeze and the heat was stifling. Within minutes of us coming to a halt I could feel the sweat as it began to trickle down my back. I held my hand up over my eyes to block out the blinding sun as the three of us scanned the outer edges of the town to our east. We munched on a packet of Jelly Tots while we waited and watched.

Along with the other two vehicles accompanying us, our focus was on the remainder of Kilo Company as they patrolled on foot up the slowly rising western edge of the town of Now Zad. If it kicked off today then we were their cavalry.

The lads were making slow progress. I squinted into the sun as they worked their way up the northern side of a faint depression in the ground. As the depression widened and headed westwards into the heart of the desert it formed into a deep-sided *wadi* that seemed to be impassable for most of the local vehicles.

The patrol's desert camouflage from this distance was working well, blending the lads in against the yellow cracked and dried mud walls of the compounds. The walls were at least 20 feet high and two to three feet thick and looked as if they had been standing for years. We'd been told they were so compact they could resist all types of small-arms fire, which meant they were ideal for us – or the Taliban – to hide behind. In fact, given the size of these walls the whole of the Helmand Taliban could have been on the other side and we wouldn't have known about it.

There was no hiding, however, from the hordes of Now Zad children who had come out to greet the patrol. It made the lads' progress painfully slow.

As marines across the Helmand province were finding out

as they patrolled their local towns or villages, poorly dressed kids would continually move from one marine to the next, attempting to scavenge what they could.

Through the telescopic sights on my rifle I could make out bearded men in long flowing *shalwars* watching quietly from the roof tops a good kilometre further north. Some wore black turbans, some white. Far to the north we could see a white flag flying high by a cluster of three bare trees, the tribal symbol of the Helmand Taliban. I couldn't see any of the distant figures brandishing weapons and, anyway, I would have had to be the world's best shot to hit anybody from where I sat.

The dwellings towards the north were still the same simple, dried yellow mud compounds that we had seen everywhere. The large rusting metal gates that stood nearly ten foot high were the only entrance to whatever lay within.

I was surprised to see that several women, dressed from head to toe in black burkhas, had appeared at the gates of a few of the compounds.

I guessed curiosity had drawn them out to witness the strange foreigners patrolling their town. It struck me that they were the first women I had seen in nearly four weeks. Watching them emerge from their sheltered existence on the other side of the closed compound walls I couldn't help but think it wasn't much of a life for them, but I guessed they didn't know any other way. The complexities of religion and culture were far too convoluted for me to grasp or to really want to try and understand anyway.

I suddenly caught movement to the left of the women. A small scruffy black-haired child with an enormous smile was playing with an old bicycle tyre and a stick, beating the tyre as it rolled over the bumpy desert floor to keep it moving. The only other time I had seen anybody do that was in a Hovis ad on TV when I was a child. I watched the young child in his light brown long trousers and loose faded shirt play for a few more seconds, totally captivated by the joy he was getting from keeping the tyre upright. I wondered what he would make of an X-box or an iPod, the 'can't do without' gadgets of our generation of Western youngsters.

Every now and again my headset would burst to life with a progress report. I followed the chatter on the map strapped to my leg by mentally ticking off the various report points that we had pre-planned.

'20C A5 out.'

'21A B6 out.'

'0A this is 0, Hill confirms clear, over.'

'0A, roger, out.'

'20C pax on roof in vicinity of K7, over,' I informed all the call signs listening on the radio net.

'Roger 20C keep eyes on, out.'

'22B approaching Exeter now, over.'

'That's us,' I shouted to Steve as I heard our release point being signalled, repeating the order to move to the other two vehicles on the radio.

Steve gunned the engine and we shot forward. The other two vehicles fell into line behind us as we sped across the desert to our next point. As the vehicle juddered across the uneven desert floor, Dan had to ride the bumps like he was a chariot driver at a Roman gladiator fight at the Coliseum. He was straddled across the gun platform in the back of the wagon, constantly turning the big machine gun on its swivel mount so that he could cover the direction of the most likely threat, in this case the part of town that we hadn't explored.

In reality the Taliban could fire at us from any of a dozen nooks and crannies that formed the line of outer walls that jutted out from the main compounds of the northern outskirts of the town.

I looked across to the lads plodding it out as they moved along the patrol line. I was secretly glad that I was the cavalry today; it looked hard work in the morning heat with all the gear they carried.

The plan was for the patrol to cover a large square chunk

of the northern town before heading back to the relative safety of the compound. To get to the eastern side of the town we had to enter the steep claustrophobic walls of the town proper as we cut through the narrowest part of the inhabited areas.

'Keep focused,' I yelled above the noise of the engine, although I didn't have to remind the lads; they knew what they were doing.

Steve gave the thumbs-up signal, never for one second taking his eyes from the road.

This was the danger time. Ambushes in the escape-proof alleys were a real possibility. An AK-47 magazine unloaded on automatic through a crack in a compound wall would seriously ruin our day.

We drove at speed, passing deserted open-plan shops and wooden stalls with their canvas roofs tattered and torn, flapping in the morning breeze.

At one time this looked like it had been a small bazaar, but now it was just a deserted street of broken wood and empty promises. Oil stained the desert floor outside a simple three-sided building that stood on its own. Motorbike parts lay rusting on the ground. As we passed a collapsed table underneath a dried reed roof I wondered what had been sold there. Some large clay pots lay overturned and empty around the broken table.

A few years back I had travelled to Morocco to climb Jebel Toubkal, the highest mountain in North Africa. We had travelled through the old market in downtown Marrakech in the Medina Square. Its hundreds if not thousands of narrow alleys and covered stalls housed traders selling everything from fragrant herbs and multicoloured fruit to caged lizards and tortoises. Row after row of rich-smelling leather goods and finely hand-painted crockery adorned the walls and tables of each stall.

The contrast with this scene was total. Nobody sold anything along here and probably wouldn't for a long time after I had gone home. The only smell in the air here was the stench of rotting waste that was carried by the odd gusts of faint breeze. I felt sorry for the people of Now Zad; it was always the innocent who suffered.

As we headed south I marvelled at the intricate alleys that peeled off from the main thoroughfare. Every now and again a huddle of small children, mostly poorly clothed and with bare feet, would be gathered at a compound entrance. Word travelled fast that we were in town. Dan was waving at the assembled kids like a victorious footballer, returning to his home town with the FA Cup. Many of the kids waved back shyly before darting inside their homes, giggling.

We reached our next position and pulled into a defensive formation while I informed the lead elements of the patrol of our new location.

As we sat waiting for the lads on foot to clear their patrol route, I looked over to the open ground that lay behind us. In among a few pieces of broken junk, I spotted a pack of dogs just lying there.

There must have been 40 or so of them. Most looked like the thick-haired St Bernard that had patrolled the outer walls of the compound. I had no idea if it was the same pack or not. Whatever they were, we seemed to be of no interest to them. Instead they lay there occasionally flicking a heavily dust-covered tail at a buzzing fly. Mostly though, they were just unmoving hairy lumps lying on the desert floor.

I wondered why they had chosen to gather here and then it suddenly dawned on me – the bazaar. In another time, long gone now, the bazaar would have been the place to forage for food when the traders packed up and went home. Old habits die hard, and the dogs obviously had nowhere else to go. They didn't understand that it would be a long time before the tempting sights and smells of the bazaar returned to Now Zad.

I turned away. I couldn't bear to look at the pitiful sight of so many strays with no hope. The relief at finally escaping from the suffocating confines of the compound had disappeared. I tried to focus on the map. Stupid thoughts of trying to feed the strays flashed through my mind. Luckily common sense took over.

'Switch on, Farthing, there is nothing you can do,' I reminded myself. 'Get on with what you're meant to be doing.'

I turned back to my map and followed the remainder of the patrol's advance. The next uneventful two hours passed at a snail's pace, the lads eventually trudging wearily into the relative safety of the DC, the Taliban clearly deciding to have the day off.

But no matter how hard I tried I couldn't shake off the heartbreaking image of those dogs.

It was approaching scran time but I suddenly didn't feel that hungry.

As I held the bag open again and looked in from arm's length I could see a white blob the size of my little fingernail attached to the dog crap that I had scooped up in the run. It looked and smelled disgusting. Not only that, it was moving.

I double checked that it definitely was what I thought it was. It was; the blob was clearly an intestinal worm that had just exited Nowzad.

'That's gross, Nowzad,' I said, shooting a look across at him as he lay curled up on his red satin cushion. I shuddered to think how many of those things were crawling around inside him. 'Don't worry bud; I'll get you something for these,' I said as I patted him on the head.

I looked over at RPG. Chances were that he had them too. 'I'll get Lisa to put some wormers in the post for you too,' I said.

Most pet owners take it for granted that when their pet needs medication all that's required is a simple trip to the vet and, hey presto, it's sorted. No such luck out here in

Afghanistan. We had to rely on friends and relatives sending us stuff but even then the situation was pretty hopeless. Anything that needed to be handled with care or had to be kept refrigerated wouldn't make it to us in a decent condition. Many of the lads had been sent chocolate by their loved ones and opened their mail to reveal letters and other little goodies stuck together with the melted brown goo that the chocolate had become while waiting on a baking hot landing strip. So I knew that to treat the dogs I would either have to rely on simple remedies like worming tablets or improvise treatments myself.

It was the latter approach that I was going to take today as I tackled the other problem the dogs had been displaying: sand flies.

The sand flies crawling over Nowzad in particular had been a nightmare. They were so quick and would burrow into his coat, no matter how much I rubbed and tried to squash the horrible little bugs. Nowzad would try to scratch them off too only for them to reappear as if gloating at him a few seconds later.

In desperation I had rooted through the old pile of stores that had been left for us by the army. I had found light-sticks, cans of paint, old clothing, rations and batteries, everything but what I was looking for. I was about to give up when I came across an aerosol can of fly spray, and not just any fly spray: military-grade fly spray.

'Stand by now you little sand-fly buggers,' I muttered to myself as I gave the half-full can a shake. Nothing survived a can of military fly spray. At first I thought the large 'DO NOT SPRAY ON SKIN' warning on the side of the can was pretty pointless. As if some idiot would attempt to use it as a mosquito repellant. But then I thought of some of the lads I knew and realised that the warning was indeed necessary. Any marine that got hold of a can of this stuff would almost certainly act like a small child, spraying anything that moved to see how effective it was.

I sprayed the aerosol to test it. Breathing in the spray was also not recommended according to the warning on the side of the can. But I couldn't help noticing the smell it left, like sweet candyfloss.

I had decided to treat Nowzad as soon as possible; I knew I would have to act fast. So I tempted him out into the middle of the run with a handful of biscuits and sprayed his coat as fast as I could before he reacted. To my surprise he just stood there, not bothered in the slightest.

As he was acting so placidly, I decided to go for broke and gave his coat another good covering of the spray. By the time I finished the second coat, the candyfloss smell was heavy in the dry, dusty air, like catching the fragrance of a good-looking young lady as she passes you by on the street.

The fly spray had an immediate effect. I watched with delight as one by one, five of the ghastly sand flies fell off Nowzad and on to the ground, writhing around in agony.

'Die, creatures of the Devil,' I shouted perhaps a little too manically as I jumped up and down. Nowzad just looked at me questioningly, his head cocked to one side as I danced the stomping dance of the dead sand fly.

I just smiled at his confused face: 'That'll teach them, eh Nowzad?'

I rubbed his ears and placed the can of fly spray in the shade, hidden away towards the back of the run, just in case it was needed again.

I closed the gate quickly and finished tying up the holding rope that acted as a latch just in time to witness the junior ANP commander approaching us. It was the guy who had pushed me in the chest when I had broken up the dogfight in the alley.

The Afghan army and police who lived in the compound didn't really interact too much with any of us, mainly, I assumed, because of the language barrier. The Afghan army had a Royal Marine as a liaison officer but kept to themselves in a larger building on the other side of the compound.

The ANP, though, were partly my responsibility as they didn't have a liaison officer of their own.

After the dogfight incident, I had offered an olive branch to the police. We had thought a period of some unarmed combat and stop-and-search training would be well received but they hadn't accepted it. We weren't surprised. It would have meant some physical exertion on their part and I didn't really see that happening.

Instead the ANP occupied themselves with eating, sleeping and, when we would let them, operating a so-called police patrol. They would leave the compound, heading south-wards before forming a road block along a small section of desert track that served as the main road along the western perimeter of the town. They chose that spot because it lay in the shadow of the hill, which of course meant they were within the hill's defensive fire perimeter.

The police commander would sit on a rug away from the track while his staff 'worked' the road. The drivers of the few and far between vehicles brave enough to drive along the track would normally be sent to sit with the commander for a while before being allowed to continue their journey.

As he walked up to me today, I noticed that this time the young ANP man was clean shaven, though his hair still fell in straight greasy strands to the collar of his faded brown shirt and his blue long-tailed dress uniform was stained badly and in need of a wash. I guessed he was probably in his mid-twenties but guessing an Afghan's age was not straight-forward. Most rural Afghans probably wouldn't know their birthdays and why should they? It didn't mean that much out here. Just surviving every day was celebration enough.

The deputy commander looked directly at me. There was no morning greeting from either of us. He spoke in Pashtu while pointing at Nowzad, who was hiding towards the back of the run.

'I have no idea what you are saying,' I told him, although really it was pretty clear that he was saying Nowzad was his fighting dog. 'I'll get the translator,' I said, knowing he didn't understand me either. I pointed to the ground and then to him. 'Wait here.' As I moved away he ignored my order and took a step towards the gate, reaching his arm out to the rope that secured it.

'No.' I tried to sound firm as I pushed his long-sleeved arm away and pointed to the ground again. I pointed at my chest to indicate me and then motioned in the direction of the building that housed our Afghan interpreters.

I noticed that Nowzad was still huddled under the cam net but, now fully alert to the two figures arguing just outside the fence of his run, RPG was eagerly sitting by the gate, fully expecting to be able to run out and play at any moment, I imagined.

I couldn't be certain that the ANP wouldn't untie the gate while I was gone but I didn't have much choice. I had known this moment was coming, I hadn't for one moment thought that the policeman would give up his dog that easily. Life isn't that simple. I needed our terp so I could settle this once and for all, but this time, amicably if I could.

I sprinted the 100 yards to the terps' room as fast as I could, thankfully almost bumping into 'Harry the terp' on his way out. Harry was part of the three-man team of inter-preters that lived with us. Without them we would not have been able to interact with the local people. Harry wasn't his real name of course, but we couldn't pronounce his Pashtu name properly. It sounded like Harry and hence, as with most in the military, Harry had been given a nickname. He didn't seem to mind.

Harry had been born and raised as part of a small family in Kabul. He had relished the opportunity to study, where he had excelled at English when the schools had finally been allowed to operate when the Taliban had been driven from power. We all admired Harry as all he wanted to do was assist the coalition forces to rid Afghanistan of the curse of the Taliban. Harry lived with us in the compound in Now

Zad, as prone to being hit on patrol as the rest of us; bullets didn't care whose side you were on. There was no doubt that he was putting his life on the line to bring change to his country.

His only possessions were a small silver engraved teapot and a thick piece of old wood that he had hand-fashioned into a sort of a cricket bat. Whenever we had downtime Harry would pester anybody who couldn't get out of the way quick enough to take part in a miniature game of cricket outside the ops room.

Even though the 'ball' was made from rolled-up masking tape, the marines would reluctantly hit the ball lightly. No one wanted to be the one who snapped the thinly carved handle of the lovingly crafted cricket bat.

Harry and I jogged back over to the run. The Afghan policeman was still standing outside, studying Nowzad and RPG intently.

The two Afghans spoke briefly, totally ignoring me.

Harry turned to me and translated the conversation in his almost fluent English.

'The junior commander says that this is his dog, Penny Dai, and that you must give him back.'

I think Harry knew that wasn't going to happen.

'Harry – please tell him he does not own the dog any more,' I said, looking at Harry to prevent provoking the policeman any more than I already had.

A brief dialogue ensued and Harry turned back to me.

'He wants paying.'

I sighed and looked up at the sky. I could argue all day I supposed, but it was best to settle this once and for all, but with what? I didn't have any money.

'Please tell him, Harry, that the dog is not for sale, but I am willing to give him something as a gesture of goodwill.' I didn't add that I didn't feel any goodwill.

I pretended to listen intently as the two of them bartered between themselves. The ANP never looked at me once but waved his arms and pointed at Nowzad. I couldn't tell if it was a friendly discussion or a heated debate. There was no emotion on either of their faces that I could recognise. Suddenly the bartering stopped.

Harry informed me that he had just sold Nowzad to me for batteries for the police torch. I probably grinned too much with the absurdity of the situation as I shook hands with the ANP junior commander. I promised to deliver the batteries later in the day, leaving them by the faded metal green door of the police living quarters, a small building that looked as if it housed maybe one or two rooms at the most. Outside stood three metal bed frames, where the ANP would bring out their worn mattresses and sit in the after-noon sunshine when it was warm enough to do so.

'Cheers, Harry, I owe you for that,' I said, holding out my hand as the junior commander walked away. I didn't have to tell him how much it meant to have Nowzad and RPG somewhere safe.

Harry slapped my hand in a friendly gesture.

'It's okay,' Harry smiled. 'But you owe me a game of cricket, Penny Dai!'

CHAPTER SIX

Harriott and Oliver

The Chinook powered up with a deafening scream, the down draught from the twin rotor blades churning tons of dust into the air as it lifted gracefully into the sky.

'Something that big shouldn't be able to fly,' I said to myself as I turned away. I had managed to sneak a shower first thing and wasn't about to get covered in dust for no reason.

As I waited for the dust to settle I looked longingly to the mountains that formed a barricade to the west.

The southern Helmand mountains weren't in the same league as the Hindu Kush range further north, but at over 2,000 metres they were far grander than the hills back home in the UK. I would bet that nobody had climbed those silent peaks. With a jihad against the Russians and then the oppressive rule of the Taliban to deal with, I very much doubted that recreational climbing had been on the average Afghan's agenda.

Lisa and I had often talked of setting up a climbing business, and the unexplored mountain regions of Afghanistan would be a gold mine. I stood for a few seconds more, looking up towards the mountains, as I imagined leading clients across the unexplored wilderness, entertaining them with traditional Afghan evenings around desert camps, taking them on camel treks with visits to local villages to witness a way of life hardly touched by modern technology.

I was trying to work out which airport to use when I realised the dust was finally settling. Turning round I could see the Chinook had become just a small dot in the southern sky. I stood up and walked back towards the group of new arrivals. Standing next to the pile of assorted equipment that had been dumped haphazardly on the ground from the rear of the Chinook, they were still huddled in a tight knot of bodies and were covered in a thick layer of dust.

It was the shouted warnings over my headset that brought me back to reality quick time. 'Incoming,' was all I needed to hear.

Our LS wasn't the best place to stand during a mortar stomp, it was more or less football-pitch flat. I looked across to the newly arrived young marines who were still standing there, brushing themselves off and reluctantly lifting rucksacks that were far too heavy on to their backs. They weren't yet wired into our radio network.

'Drop your kit everybody, get into cover *now*,' I screamed across at them.

I was met with uncomprehending looks.

'The Taliban are sending you a welcome, now fucking spread out,' I yelled. The lads immediately dropped everything as they started to run to the four winds trying to find any form of cover.

John was just pulling up with the 4x4 to help shift the kit back to the DC along with the eagerly anticipated mail sacks that had arrived. He immediately slammed the truck into reverse and drove a good 200 metres away from the startled group of marines as they dived for cover. I winced as I saw the truck's rear tailgate smash into a small but solid-looking mound of dried mud. John just pressed the accelerator further into the foot well and drove like a bat out of hell away from us.

The radio was going bananas with different people shouting reports and detailing various groups to engage the Taliban.

I threw myself into a small depression that turned out to be nothing of the sort. It didn't provide any level of cover whatsoever. I stuck out on top of the ground like a sore thumb. I turned back to check that the newbies had got into the limited cover available. Some were completely out of sight, probably burrowing away like little rabbits.

Scanning our surrounding area I was relieved to notice that my force protection had also dismounted and were spread out from their vehicles. They had the advantage of their radios and had heard the warning as I did.

I yelled at the figures lying behind me. 'The Taliban are engaging the hill,' I said. 'Three mortar rounds are in the air and on their way over here.'

There was nothing else we could do but wait.

The hill was a strange place. It was just a bare mound of Afghan mud that rose some 200 feet from the desert floor. It was open to the elements and was devoid of any buildings or compounds. It provided a perfect 360-degree panorama. The 'heads' (naval speak for a toilet) was an open-air seated affair which probably had the best view of any toilet in the world, an uninterrupted view across miles of the southern Helmand desert. To the south and west all you could see was open desert. To the north there was a ramshackle cemetery, which the terps told us was the final resting place of both Afghan and Russian dead.

The lads enjoyed being stationed on the hill. It wasn't as claustrophobic as the DC and they didn't have to man as many sangars as we did. I didn't envy the ones who were up there now though. With its raised elevation, the hill was a prime target for the Taliban.

I strained my neck to look upwards and saw the first mortar round explode on the north side of the hill, close enough to scare the crap out of the guys on the guns, but too far away to make any difference for those of us lying in the dirt on the LS. The hill was definitely the target, not us.

Two more hastily fired mortars landed way off to the east of the hill. The lads were clearly not impressed and the thump thump of the .5s returning fire to the Taliban was deafening, even from where I lay.

The radio chatter was indicating that a full-on battle was getting under way. I had had enough of sitting in the open desert; any small-arms fire hurled at the hill had a good chance of coming over the top and hitting us. It was time to move.

'Up and at 'em, we're moving now,' I yelled to make sure all could hear me.

The look of shock on the lads' faces was clear. With a newfound sense of urgency they gathered their kit together and threw it on top of the pile in the back of the 4x4 that had reappeared and screeched to a halt as soon as I had stood up.

John was grinning like a Cheshire cat at the obvious disbelief on the faces of our new arrivals. I knew what he was thinking. For us it had become routine to be shot at or mortared. We knew there was no point getting too worried about it otherwise you wouldn't achieve anything. It would be like not leaving your house back home in case you got run over. Most of the lads thought that when your number is up then it's up, nought you can do about that. These kids hadn't reached that point yet, but I had a feeling it wouldn't be too long before our new arrivals began thinking that way, too.

As we drove back to the DC, the horrible thought that we might drive right into an incoming mortar kept flashing up in my mind so I urged my driver to go faster. Not that he needed telling. He was thinking the same as me.

By the time we pulled up in the DC the fast jets were on their way to finish the job. I handed the lads over to the company sergeant major, or CSM, who made them wait in the briefing room until the battle had finished before delivering the welcome brief on the dos and don'ts of living in the DC.

I jogged over to the sangars to make sure my lads were okay before I went to check on Nowzad and RPG.

Both dogs were hiding in the mortar run and were extremely happy to see me when I squeezed through the gate of the run. I was relieved that this time Nowzad had found some reassurance in having RPG with him and hadn't tried to jump the gate again. Both of them devoured the handful of biscuits I pulled out of my pocket. I left them munching away on the last few crumbs as I left to find out which of the new lads were joining my troop and what equipment they had brought along with them.

'You're bloody joking,' Dutchy said, kicking the floor.

'Nope, no chef,' the CSM replied smiling to himself.

'What is Bastion playing at?' I said. 'How difficult is it to put a chef on the helo?'

Marines moan about everything and anything and assume it is their right to do so. Food is a constant source of that moaning. We whinge about a lack of food, uncooked food, cold food or too expensive food. (Funnily enough we never moan about too much food.)

We had secretly celebrated the fact that the young chef who could only cook curry was going on R & R before being sent off to deaden the tastebuds at some other location.

But the fact that he had not been replaced was going to cause a riot.

The CSM was slightly older than me and Dutchy and was part of the Mountain and Arctic Warfare Cadre of the Royal Marines. He loved to take the mickey out of anybody who wasn't part of the cadre, which Dutchy and I weren't.

He just looked at us with an impassive grin.

'Troop sergeants, I'm sure you two are both experienced enough to cope,' he said.

'Ahhh no, no way,' we both protested in unison. We knew what that meant. In my case I had been promoted from shit burner to chef. We both just stood for a few seconds in case he was winding us up. But the punchline didn't come.

'Come on then, Jamie Oliver, let's go and see what delights we have to mix up in the next two hours before dinner,' Dutchy said, signalling that we might as well leave the ops room and head for the galley.

'All right then, Ainsley Harriott,' I replied.

'Don't know if you noticed but I am not black.'

'Yeah, and I don't have curly hair and run around like a hyper child all day,' I replied quickly.

The kitchen was part of a small row of buildings. It had a small door and one tiny window. Inside there was just enough room for one folding table for preparing food. Under the one window sat the blackened old military gas hob. It was attached to a long rubber hose that snaked its way through a hole in the wall that the Gurkhas had drilled to the gas bottle hidden outside around the corner.

Piled high on the floor were four big cooking pots. Several large stirring bowls were hung on nails struck into the grey-painted mud wall at the back of the hut. There were no lights.

The food store was in the building next door. We were both slightly surprised when we discovered that the floor was covered in tins of food.

'And all he could cook was bloody curry?' I said, picking up a tin of chicken in white wine sauce and a packet of dried pasta.

'Fruit cocktail over here,' Dutchy yelled as he suddenly lunged for a white packet on the floor as if it was tied to a piece of string and would be pulled from his reach at any minute, never to be seen again. 'And custard powder, he had bloody custard powder,' he added, holding up the packet for me to see.

We had just under two hours to cook something for around 60 hungry lads. The 'one choice café' was about to go into business.

It didn't take long for the rumour mill to starting working flat out. One of the young lads, Simon, coming off sentry stopped by the open door. The surprised expression on his face told us he was slightly confused by what he saw.

Dutchy was stirring the 15 tins of chicken in white wine sauce that he had emptied into two big pots that were now bubbling away on the hob.

I stood at the chopping board with a badly stained apron around my waist covering my desert combats.

'Is it right, Sergeant, that you are cooking scran for us tonight?' the young marine asked. I looked at him with a raw onion in one hand and a large knife in the other. Tears were running down my cheeks from the smelly onions.

'Your observations skills are hoofing,' I said. 'And you reckon you'll notice the Taliban sneaking up on you then, Si?'

He looked at me for a moment longer before realising the absurdity of his question. 'Sorry, Sergeant.'

I couldn't let the opportunity pass. 'Tell the lads that scran may be a little later tonight while we wait for the Yorkshires to cook; we didn't put them in on time.'

'Wow, we've got Yorkshires? That's great, Sergeant,' he said as he walked off looking happy.

It was a well-known fact that our makeshift kitchen was lacking an oven, let alone the eggs, flour and milk needed to actually make Yorkshire puddings. But I was pretty sure that wasn't going to stop the rumour mill.

'How long before that goes round the compound?' Dutchy asked.

'I bet you it will be back here by the time the next nugget walks by.'

I continued chopping away and threw a handful of onion segments into the bubbling pot of chicken and white wine sauce.

'Hey, Sergeant, is it true we've got Yorkshires tonight?' a voice enquired through the open doorway.

Dutchy and I burst into laughter.

*

'Nice work, fellas,' the OC mumbled, between mouthfuls of peach slices as he stood outside the galley.

'No problem, sir. There isn't much an SNCO can't turn his hand to,' Dutchy replied, smiling from inside the doorway.

Armies march on their stomachs. That is a fact. Food is a vital part of the day, not just for survival but to beat the boredom as well. Even though we had individual ration packs for the lads to use for daily rations, the idea of having a chef was to allow the lads at least one decent meal per day that they didn't have to try and cook in between sangar duties and patrols. So Dutchy and myself felt quite chuffed that the 'one choice café' had received rave reviews.

In our two available hours we had managed to cook just enough for the horde of starving marines. We had even surprised them with the chef's special, a dessert, something they rarely saw out here.

It had taken us a few minutes to convince anybody to come and get some of it. No one trusted us. 'Yeah. I come back for dessert and get pinged for the washing-up, eh Sergeant?' was the common response. But when the tinned fruit and custard was laid out on the serving table, word soon got around.

It wasn't long before Dutchy and myself were supervising the queue to make sure everybody got a share.

The OC had been one of the first to tuck in. He was standing in the doorway of the galley, clearing out the last of his peaches as the queue came to an end.

'Good. Looking forward to something even better tomorrow then, gents. I would hate for the lads to be disappointed,' he said, as he put his bowl on the serving table and headed off.

We both looked at each other. We hadn't even discussed the prospect of cooking tomorrow. Tonight had been pressure enough.

We washed up the big cooking pots and cleaned away the utensils in silence as it slowly dawned on us what we had let ourselves in for. Running a kitchen was fun once, but every night would just be a nightmare.

'What are we going to cook tomorrow?' I asked as I dried the last pot.

'God knows,' Dutchy replied.

CHAPTER SEVEN

Jena

It was the barking that roused me from my sleep. It was 1 a.m. and I wasn't on duty for another three hours. The noise was coming from the direction of Nowzad and RPG's run. I dressed quickly and grabbed my gear. I bumped into Dave as I stumbled out of my cell.

'What's all the noise?'

'Don't know,' he replied.

We rounded the corner towards the run at a jog as I had a horrible feeling it was another dogfight.

'Oh shit,' I said as I saw the rear gate was wide open and the area directly surrounding it was swarming with dogs of all sizes and shapes, running around and snapping at each other among the small clouds of dust they were kicking up as they leapt all over the place.

Nowzad and RPG were going berserk locked in their run. I breathed a sigh of relief that it wasn't a dogfight and that they were safe.

Dave grabbed my arm and pointed to the middle of the mass of dogs.

'Oh no, what the hell are they trying to do?' The sight in front of me was just a picture of despair.

There, tied to a lone post by a wire around her neck, was a small terrified dog. She was obviously a bitch as behind her the large male dogs were snapping and baring their teeth at each other for the opportunity to mate with her. It was a scene from doggie hell.

'For fuck's sake,' was all Dave could say.

The moment I had stepped down from the plane on to Afghan soil I knew I had entered a different world, but this was lunacy. Now that I had bought Nowzad's safety, for the time being at least, the Afghans had obviously decided to have a go at breeding their own supply of fighting dogs. This poor dog was going to produce them.

'As if there aren't enough strays already,' Dave shouted above the barking and growling as we both waded into the fray, waving our arms and generally shouting at the dogs. We hadn't thought about being bitten, we were both too consumed by anger and total disbelief to worry about that.

We chased away the male dogs, trying to push them through the open gate and back out of our compound. When the biggest dogs decided they weren't going to leave that easily, Dave picked up a large piece of discarded wood and started to wave it at them. Even that wasn't enough. He had to smash the wood into the ground to scare them in the general direction of the open entrance.

With all the commotion I was surprised that nobody else had come out to see what was happening. I later found out that the lads in the nearest sangar were about to radio the ops room but had heard my voice shouting in the still night air and assumed I had things under control!

Between us, Dave and I managed to close the rear gate and lock the dead bolt bar into place. As silence returned to the compound we just looked at each other.

'Unbelievable,' was all I could say as I tried to catch my breath.

I walked back over to the small dog tied to the stake. She was shivering in the cool night air.

'Are you all right, little one?' I asked her as I reached out towards her small round head.

She sniffed my hand and then immediately started to lick

it as I played with her long oval-shaped ears. She looked much darker in colour than Nowzad and at least half his size. I had no idea what breed she resembled.

'What do we do with you, eh?' I asked, knowing the answer was clearly reflected in her sad eyes.

I reached down to untie her from the wooden stake, holding on to the section of the wire that was bound tightly around her neck. I didn't want her running off around the compound.

I needn't have worried. She happily trotted alongside me as I walked her over to where Nowzad and RPG were waiting desperately to get out. Both of them were jumping up at the gate in anticipation.

I held the young female in one hand while I untied the latch. Both Nowzad and RPG raced out of the run, only briefly stopping to sniff the new arrival before wandering off to continue sniffing and smelling the spots where minutes earlier the pack had been running wild. I guessed they were looking for old friends.

The little female dog's long tail was wagging around, making small whooshing noises. I let her enter the run and slipped off the wire noose from around her neck.

'Guess that's another one then?' Dave said a few minutes later, as he dragged an excited RPG back towards the run by his front legs, the dog's long-haired tail beating madly against the ground as he went.

'What else do we do?' I said. 'We can't just throw her outside; what happens to any puppies?'

I looked back at the main gate. The dusty floor immediately in front of it was a mass of dog paw prints, fanning out in all directions. The wooden stake stood alone in the now empty area, except for Nowzad who cocked his rear left leg against it – admittedly there was a distinct lack of trees in our neighbourhood for him to use.

'What the hell are these people on?' I said out loud as we tried to comprehend what we had just witnessed. 'Apart from anything else, who in their right mind would leave our rear gate open at night with the Taliban on the prowl?'

The fact that the ANP would tie a dog up like that shouldn't have come as a surprise after what we had seen so far.

'I'm going to make the ANP wish they were living with the Taliban tomorrow,' I said, but I knew it would be useless confronting them. What could I do to them anyway?

I chased Nowzad around for a few minutes and then led him back into the run. He didn't seem to mind the young female that was now being stroked by Dave.

'We can't just throw her out the gate, can we?' I said, although I already knew what Dave would say. We could hear the pack still chasing each other around just on the other side of the firmly closed gate.

I had planned to get up early anyway to ring Lisa back home; there didn't seem much point in going to sleep now. So I made use of the fact that the sat phone was sitting in its cradle with nobody booked to use it. I needed to phone her and somehow describe what I had just witnessed.

Before I could say anything Lisa's excited voice bounced across the satellite connection.

'You took your time ringing; I've been waiting ages!' she said.

'I was …'

She cut me off before I could finish. 'I've found a rescue centre.'

I held the handset to my ear, as if I'd misheard her.

'Pen, did you get what I said? I've found a rescue!'

I closed my eyes and breathed a huge sigh of relief.

Lisa was on a roll, however, and carried on talking. 'This animal rescue in London, the Mayhew, helps to run an animal welfare organisation in Northern Afghanistan. They gave me a contact who will take the dogs in.'

'Wow, happy days honey!' was the only thing I could say. A huge weight was lifting off my shoulders.

'How many dogs did they say they would take?' I asked. I still hadn't told Lisa about tonight's shenanigans.

'I told them that you had two dogs that needed rescuing,' she said before pausing. 'Oh no, you haven't?'

Lisa had that pain in the arse knack of being able to read my mind.

'I thought I'd seen it all, Lisa,' I said as I started to explain as quickly as I could what we had seen out in the yard only a few minutes earlier. I doubted that we had got to the young female dog in time; I suspected that she would turn out to be pregnant. So if she was going to give birth then she wasn't going to be on the streets of Now Zad. By the time I'd finished I could tell from Lisa's shocked silence that I didn't need to tell her this dog was going to the rescue as well.

'Okay, how is the rescue going to collect the dogs then?'

'You didn't hear me properly,' Lisa replied.

I didn't guess what was coming.

'I said the rescue would take the dogs, but you have to get them there.'

I took a second to reply, my mind working overtime to process the information.

The large weight was suddenly loading itself back on my shoulders again. 'Where is "there", exactly, honey?' I asked.

'Northern Afghanistan, on the map I found it looks a bit further than Kabul,' she replied. I didn't need a map of Afghanistan in front of me to know that Kabul, let alone anywhere further north, might as well be on the moon.

'I have put it all in an e-bluey,' she said.

The e-bluey was a typed letter that could be sent through cyberspace via the Internet and was printed out in Camp Bastion and then delivered with our normal mail. It meant I would wait probably around a week for it to arrive.

I managed to keep my promise and ask her about life back in the real world, although my mind was already trying to figure out how we could get the carrot that had just been dangled so tantalisingly close in front of us.

I returned the phone to its cradle outside the ops room and walked back outside into the moonlit early morning. My sleeping bag was calling to me. I suddenly felt really tired.

I stooped down to stroke our newest arrival. She had been with us for a few days now and seemed to be settling in well to the routine of compound life. All the attention she was getting helped.

She was sitting upright on her rear legs, her long thin tail swishing madly, on top of what had become her favourite spot on the sandbags that made up the mortar shelter. She almost shivered with excitement when she saw somebody approaching the run to make a fuss of her.

Most of her extremely smooth short-haired coat was a darker brown than Nowzad's, almost coffee-coloured. Yet along the underside of her belly and the front of her legs she was a light tan colour. She eagerly tried to lick me as I bent close to rub her belly. You couldn't help but look into her big eyes that were an unusual brownish yellow; from a distance they looked so sad. But they sparked into life as she watched you approach. I shook my head as I watched her excited little face.

The lads had already named her but I wasn't quite sure I was totally happy with their choice and reasoning. It was after their favourite American porn star, a young lady named Jena. When we had found her the situation had not been the least bit amusing, but I had to admit the lads' sense of humour was.

'So, what do you think to being called Jena, then?' I asked her. 'At least you are not getting named after a Russian weapon I suppose?'

RPG and Nowzad were getting on really well with Jena. Both dogs let her have her own space. Because of this I had the sneaking suspicion that they might have been puppies of Jena's. I don't know what it was but they just seemed to know that she was in charge.

'Enjoy,' I said, laying the food down with Nowzad's bowl a good distance from RPG and Jena's and adopting my own guard position as all three dogs devoured their breakfast with a passion.

Food was the only source of friction between Jena and Nowzad.

I had made a small sign out of the side of a ration box that asked the lads not to throw food into the run. With nobody to stand in between the dogs, Nowzad would gobble down what he could find and then attack RPG or Jena to get whatever they were munching on. Jena would fight back for a split second but then Nowzad would bite her hard and she would dart for the safety of any corner of the run while Nowzad was distracted by the food dropped on the floor. Whenever this happened Jena would squeal like a hurt child until I got into the run and calmed her down.

I needed to spend time with Nowzad getting him adjusted to his new surroundings and life but I didn't have it.

The problem was that Jena enjoyed eating her food slowly. It was a wonder she had survived this long with dogs like Nowzad around. I was determined to keep him at bay today.

'No, Nowzad,' I said, specifically raising my voice and hoping that he would get the message as he finished his bowl and began looking around for more.

An added gentle nudge with my boot helped to steer him away from making a beeline to Jena's half-eaten bowl of bacon and beans.

'You don't learn, do you, nightmare dog?' I said, as yet again I pushed him back towards his empty bowl with my boot.

Nowzad was gradually getting the message; he just growled at me.

'Grrrrrrrr,' I growled back as I threw a handful of dust at him.

I quickly cleaned the run out and left them all lying against the whitewashed back wall, enjoying the first rays of the sun as it warmed their living area. I had the daily brief to attend.

'I'll pop back later and see you then, all right?' I told them as I tied the gate. It would probably be after the promised resupply later in the afternoon.

The meeting revealed nothing new and the rest of the day dragged as it always did when we attended to the general housekeeping jobs that needed doing around the DC. The mid-November sun was still hot enough for beads of sweat to form along our foreheads as we toiled away, filling sandbags to renew the outer wall defences.

The promised resupply helo was half an hour late but within minutes of myself and John returning to the compound the lads were buzzing. A small group of lads eagerly sorted the 14 sacks of mail that we had only just dumped outside the HQ building.

I was still dusting myself down after the dust storm the helo had caused lifting off when the boss called me to one side; he had just finished talking to the HQ back at Camp Bastion. They had updated him on Tom and Matt's condition. As he made small talk about the resupply I waited patiently, trying not to second guess what he had to say. The OC looked tired, but then I guess we all did.

'They apparently drove off the top of a 70-foot-high cliff; we don't why or how,' he said, pausing before continuing, rubbing his hand over his face. 'Matt has fractures of his legs and arms and a spinal injury but he should make a good recovery.' A slight wave of relief washed over me but I knew that was the good news.

'But although Tom is out of immediate danger the docs are still investigating the injuries to his skull and spinal cord; it doesn't look that good.'

He looked me right in the eye as he said it. I imagined he was trying to put a brave face on the situation, as I'd expect of a senior officer. In return I did my best to remain the solid troop sergeant. I didn't quite pull it off.

'Fuck,' I said as I looked away, wearily rubbing my hands across my face.

'He is going to live, so at least that is good news,' the OC added with feigned enthusiasm.

I know he felt as depressed about Tom's condition as I did. I couldn't think of anything remotely appropriate to say. I wasn't sure if I was meant to be reassuring the OC or me.

'I'll go and tell the lads, Boss. They'll want to know straight away before the rumour mill kicks in,' I said, trying to regain my tough exterior.

I walked slowly in the early-evening sunlight along the potted dirt track between the ANP garden and our toilet block towards our living area, trying to figure out what to say.

I pictured Tom's face in my mind as clear as day and recalled the schoolboy grin he'd given me as I told him for the umpteenth time to shave while we had been back at Bastion. With his stubble and suntanned features he looked like an extra in a cowboy film.

Tom was only 18 years old. I had served longer than he had been alive.

I knew some people would ask why lads like Tom and Matt were risking their lives for a place like Afghanistan where no one seemed to care whether the Taliban ruled or not. If the local elders turned up tomorrow and asked for a ceasefire again then I figured we might as well go home. I couldn't see for the life of me what we would achieve by sitting in the DC while the Taliban resupplied and planned a new campaign against us, unopposed. Especially if we were going to start taking casualties like this. But that wasn't what the lads needed to hear.

I thought back to our first patrol in Gereshk. Just before we had been hit by the Taliban I had caught a glimpse of two young girls as I took up a fire position next to an old crumbling courtyard. They were clearly not old enough to wear a burkha; instead the young girls were wearing flowing bright pink dresses that covered their entire bodies, their jet-black hair combed in straight waves over their ears. I had given them my best friendly wave but they both stopped dead and ran to hide behind a rotten wooden gate hanging from its post by a single hinge.

While we held our position I watched the gate with the corner of my eye. I soon caught movement. Curiosity had got the better of them as one of the girls summoned enough courage to pop a wide-eyed head around the corner of the gate. I smiled at her again and waved. This time her face broke into a perfect white smile.

We'd been told winning the hearts and minds of the locals was a huge part of our mission here. At that moment I had wished I had brought some sweets but as it had been our first 'real' patrol my head had been buzzing.

It had been more than enough trying to remember everything that I would need while also checking on the lads as they had prepared. Sweets had not been on the list of 'must have' for this time out. As the patrol had moved off I had waved one last time towards the little girls, their bright clothing a total contrast to the all-consuming, dull, cracked yellow of our surroundings. They had waved back.

Minutes later we had been consumed in an all-out fire-fight with the Taliban. They didn't seem bothered by the fact that innocent children lived in the vicinity of where the conflict was taking place.

Those of us on the ground knew we had a chance at giving those young girls and thousands of others like them the opportunities for a future. As long as we were given the time and resources to do the job then I hoped we would make a positive difference in this screwed-up place.

I knew that was the reason that Tom and Matt came to Afghanistan. Just by being here they had made a small difference. Their accident had just been one of those things. It could have happened here or back home. I had no idea whether it could have been prevented or not, but nothing was going to change that now. It didn't feel much of a comfort though.

I stopped and took a deep breath. I needed to be a troop sergeant. I had to think how I could explain what had happened to the two lads. It wasn't going to be easy.

From my limited perspective I didn't care what politicians thought they had sent us here for or even about the voices of those people back home who called for our withdrawal. I would bet a lot of money that none of them had ever set foot in Afghanistan.

I turned the corner into our small living area and took another deep breath. I saw that most of the lads were still sat outside in groups, happily reading the recently arrived mail. As they compared the goodies they had received from home, discarded parcels and sweet wrappers were scattered on the ground around their feet.

As I approached them a few stopped smiling. They could tell from my expression I wasn't here to give good news. Their suspicions were justified as I shattered the mail morale in an instant and explained the situation. The lads just looked at me expressionless as I told them what I knew. There was no point holding any information back. They had a right to know. As I finished explaining I reminded them all to stay focused.

'I don't want any more of our lads lost to accidents – that's an order, all right?' I looked around the collected sullen faces. 'We came here to do a job, so let's do it properly.'

A few nodded in agreement.

Paul, one of the lads who had only recently joined our troop, piped up after a few seconds of quiet. 'Are we sending them flowers, Sergeant?'

I looked at him slowly. A few sniggers came from the assembled group. I knew that the lad meant well.

'No, we are not sending flowers; would you want flowers if you were lying injured in hospital?' I snapped back a little too quickly. 'Think of something useful and I will see if I can get Lisa to sort it out for us.'

We had no money or credit cards and so no way of ordering anything from the town of Now Zad even if we could find a post office.

'We could book a stripper in a nurse's uniform for them,' Mase volunteered as I went to leave.

I shook my head.

'I'm sure Matt's girlfriend will be well chuffed with that. Think of something sensible, you bunch of jokers.'

The quick exchange had lifted the mood. I walked away as they discussed more sensible options, or as near to sensible as I could expect from them, I supposed.

I knew my R & R would now involve a visit to the hospital. I hated hospitals and already I was dreading it. I had no idea what I would say and how I would react when I saw the extent of their injuries for real.

I still hadn't got around to reading my mail and I didn't have time now either. The boss had planned a short patrol for last light and I now had just less than 90 minutes to get the prep done. Again I was to be OC of the cavalry and that meant checking that all the vehicles we would use had been refuelled and the right kit was on board. The dogs would also have to wait until the patrol had finished before they were fed again.

I rounded up the lads who would man the three vehicles with me and briefed them on our role for the evening and what preparation I needed them to complete prior to the patrol departing.

Just in time we took up our seats in the fully equipped vehicle as the patrol stepped out on the ground. The cool evening air felt quite pleasant as I watched the sun disappear behind the mountains to the west. A few puffy cumulus clouds were just beginning to form to the north, but the air was beautifully still. With the weight of the body armour and our chest webbing pouches stuffed full of ammunition and supplies I couldn't find a comfortable position in the upright uncushioned passenger seat. None of us spoke as we sat in the fading light listening to the constant chatter over the radio as the patrol reported its progress.

The patrol was not going that far out from the compound so I guessed I would hear any sounds of battle long before I got the radio message to assist.

I let my head fall back on to the passenger seat headrest and stared towards the tiny sparkling pinpricks of light that were just making an appearance against the slowly darkening skies.

I looked for the collection of stars that formed the Plough, the starting point for identifying the North Star. I marvelled at how bright the stars seemed here compared to back home, and my mind kept wandering to my R & R time, just under a month away.

I so wanted to get home and see Lisa. I wondered what she was doing right now. I guessed she was probably just finishing off at work before heading out with Fizz and Beamer for a walk along the quiet footpaths and lanes of home.

My headset kept bringing me back to reality as the patrol updated all of us on the net with its progress and location. I mentally followed their route in my head so I could cross-reference it with the map if we were needed to roll out in a hurry.

I listened to the radio chatter for the duration of the patrol right until they trudged wearily back into the compound. Yet again – thankfully I suppose – we were not needed.

As soon as confirmation came from 10A that everyone was back safely in the compound, I lifted myself out of the wagon. For a minute or so I had to stretch to get my back working again; it was locked solid from sitting in the wagon without moving for nearly two hours.

'Dan, take charge of closing down the wagons for me, can you mate?'

'Yeah, no problems,' he replied as he lifted the heavy .5 from its mount.

'Cheers, I've still got to read my mail.' I quickly walked over to my bed space to dump my gear in the pitch-black room.

It was immediately colder as I pushed open the wooden door that stood in the ill-fitting door frame as a feeble attempt to keep out the elements. During the day the room was partially illuminated by the natural light through the low glassless wooden window. I shivered slightly in the chill. I needed to do something about the gaps in the window frame where the glass should have been. I had an old sleeping bag stuffed in between the wood to keep the cold night air out but it still found a way to seep in. I figured a few cardboard sides of an old ration box cut to fit squarely in the window, held in place with masking tape, would cure the problem, when I finally got around to it.

Blindly I fumbled for the small bundle of assorted envelopes that I had placed on the edge of my camp bed.

No matter where in the world we served, the highlight was always without doubt that first moment as you held the newly arrived mail from back home. With the arrival of the Internet, it was a feeling that not many people in the world appreciated any more.

I quickly scanned the front of the assorted e-blueys and letters, recognising the handwriting of my mum and brother and the printed e-bluey from Lisa.

I carried the six or seven letters outside; one of them felt like it contained a small cardboard packet. Both myself and Nowzad were hoping these were the wormers he desperately needed. I sat on the low step to the small dried-mud building.

I put the letters down and tore open the three sides of Lisa's e-bluey along the perforated tabs; it looked exactly like a large pay statement.

I tilted it towards the beautifully bright moon and used the glow to read by. My torch was redundant in my pocket.

Lisa had copied the email she had received into the e-bluey.

From: Joy
To: Lisa and Pen
Subject: Afghan Dogs

Dear Lisa,

We have received your email and have forwarded it on to our contact that helps in Afghanistan.

We assist in running a small animal shelter that was started by an aid worker from overseas. The shelter helps with the welfare of a vast number of animals. If you don't hear back from them within the next week, please contact me again and I will follow up. Sometimes emergencies occur (rather often in this line of work, unfortunately) and emails do get lost.

If you have any more questions, please don't hesitate to contact me.

Kind regards,
Joy
Mayhew International Projects Officer

I was surprised at how short the email had been but as I carried on reading the single-page letter that Lisa had typed I saw that things had moved on from this first contact.

A few days after receiving the email from the Mayhew Animal Home their contact had got in touch with Lisa by phone. The lady who rang was American and it had taken Lisa a few seconds to realise what the call was about. It was only when the woman had started to talk about looking after dogs from Afghanistan that the penny dropped.

According to Lisa's letter, the woman, Pam, sounded incredibly passionate about taking in the dogs for us. She explained how, when working as an aid worker after the defeat of the Taliban, she had witnessed the poor or non-existent welfare facilities for animals. With a grant from the

Mayhew she had founded an animal welfare sanctuary in the far north of the country that was staffed by local Afghanis.

The only problem was that Pam assumed I had permission to use a military helicopter to fly the dogs into a nearby military base so that someone from the welfare centre could collect them by road.

Lisa instinctively knew the situation and had written under that particular paragraph: 'I didn't say anything to her at the time but I don't remember you even considering using the marines? That's not going to happen is it? I told her you want the dogs there by the time you go on R & R and you were working on a plan – was that okay?'

I nodded a silent agreement. Lisa made no mention of what my plan was going to be in getting the dogs to the rescue. Again, a mindreader, she knew very well that I had no plan.

The truth was I had hoped that the rescue would have a means of collecting the dogs from Now Zad. After all, the staff of the rescue were Afghanis and I had naively assumed they would be able to travel freely around their own country. The fact that Pam had not mentioned that rescue option probably meant it wasn't that easy to arrange.

Lisa used the last few lines she had left on the single page to type hastily about life back home. My eyes lit up at the last line as I read that she was still missing me.

'Good, because I am still missing you, honey,' I said to the letter in return, as if it would magically be heard by her back home.

I folded the e-bluey closed again and stared down at my worn combat boots and the dark desert floor. The feel-good factor that had come with receiving mail had been short-lived. Reality was sinking in fast. My shoulders ached.

To get to this animal rescue shelter I was looking at a journey of at least 700 miles. I would have to get the dogs from Now Zad, a town in the middle of nowhere surrounded by nothing but inhospitable desert that was crawling with fanatical nutcases and dotted with millions of landmines for good measure.

'How the hell am I going to do that?' I thought out loud.

Without support from the military I felt it would be a non-starter.

Timing was now becoming a big issue. It was going to be a close-run thing. My R & R slot was 6 December. I had to get Nowzad, RPG and Jena out of here by then. I doubted anybody else would want to take the responsibility of looking after them or fending off any flak that might come their way while I was gone for ten days.

I sighed and looked up towards the night sky and the waning moon. I really needed some divine inspiration.

After a minute or two of silent contemplation I realised that the moon was not going to provide any answers. 'No wishing upon a shooting star tonight, then,' I whispered.

The reality of it all hit me again. Had I really thought I could get them to safety? This was going to be mission impossible. Even Nathan Hunt would have given up after listening to the message on the self-destructing tape recorder. I just didn't have long enough, did I?

It dawned on me that maybe deep down I was just missing life back home and looking after these dogs was my way of pretending I was somewhere else. Maybe, even though I was nearly 40 years old, I had been using the dogs as some type of comfort blanket, although I hoped I didn't need one at my stage of life.

Did the dogs ever really have a chance at getting to safety? I had given them false hope, not that they knew it, but that fact wasn't much consolation. Kicking them out of the compound to go back to a world of scavenging for survival would be heart-wrenching for me and them. I felt the niggling pangs of despair. I had no cunning plan. Kicking them out was probably going to be my only option. That thought hurt.

The problem was that I was always playing catch-up, either waiting for letters or a slot on the phone. The real world was moving quicker than my little world right now.

Maybe, just maybe, Lisa has worked out a plan already? I thought to myself.

Maybe sleep would help and then maybe I could figure something out.

I headed towards the dogs; they needed feeding even if it was late and I still had to crack on with my night-time duties. Sleep would be a long time coming.

CHAPTER EIGHT

Crazy Afghan

'That is some view mate,' I said as I took in a deep breath of fresh air and let the cool breeze penetrate my open shirt.

'Yeah, not bad,' smiled Jim, one of the Fire Support Group marines who occupied the hill. 'Looks even better with tracer winging over your head!'

The cloudless sky was a deep blue that contrasted starkly with the baked yellow earth of the desert plain to the south and the dull mustardy mountain ridges that rose sharply to the east, west and north.

In the far distance to the south through the dancing heat haze I could make out tiny figures working vast fields of farmland. Back home I knew it would take all day in a tractor to turn fields that size. I couldn't begin to imagine how long it would take toiling away with the wooden ploughs they still used out here.

I spent a moment absorbing the view; it reminded me of standing on a Swiss Alpine peak after a gruelling climb to the summit and being rewarded with an awe-inspiring panorama of 360 degrees.

I turned and looked back at the two cages that were sitting nearby on the barren hilltop. Inside them RPG, Jena and Nowzad were waiting patiently, seemingly enjoying the refreshing breeze and the glorious view as much as me.

While RPG and Jena were sitting upright on their rear legs in the bigger of the two crates, Nowzad was resting contentedly in his own space in the smaller container. All three were waiting for the next part of their adventure, but even I didn't know how it would pan out.

Things had been moving fast during the past few days. A plan, of sorts, had finally taken shape.

I was due to go on R & R back to England on 6 December. As we drew towards the last few days of November I had actually begun dreading it.

Slowly panic had been bubbling to the surface. I kept running through the 'what if' scenarios. What if I couldn't get the dogs to safety? What if nobody was able to look after them while I was gone?

It wasn't as if I could order one of the lads to keep an eye on them for me. Apart from anything else, looking after all three was now becoming hard work.

Jena had become a right little madam, bossing both Nowzad and RPG around the run. She would yap away incessantly, seeking attention from anybody that walked by. It was becoming noticeable that she was beginning to fill out. Dave and I agreed that she had probably already been pregnant when we rescued her from the wooden stake.

At least Jena would let strangers approach her. If one of the lads came up to the run she would sit patiently at the front with RPG, waiting for the odd stroke to come her way. Nowzad, on the other hand, would still bark at everyone he didn't know, always from the safety of the rear of the run. I was still the only one he really trusted.

Time was at a premium at the moment but I tried to give each dog at least a few minutes of fuss when I was in with them. The bond was getting stronger and I had no idea how I was going to break it.

I'd spoken to Lisa a couple of time since reading her e-bluey. Over the satellite airwaves, we'd agonised over how to get the dogs to the rendezvous with the rescue truck. I was sure a local 'jingly' truck driver from Now Zad would have welcomed the business. Now and again I'd seem them in the distance, heading south to Lashkar Gar. But as we hadn't patrolled that far into the inhabited areas of the town I hadn't had the opportunity to talk to a driver and broker a deal.

With a local driver ruled out, the only alternative was for Pam or someone at the rescue shelter to send an empty truck southwards to collect the dogs. It would cost a fortune, hundreds of dollars, but right now if we were to get the dogs to safety then it was worth it. Talking on the phone, Lisa and I agreed the alternative was not an option. Lisa would have to wire the money to Afghanistan once the pick-up had been made.

I felt bad. I'd had to leave it to Lisa to try to make the arrangements long distance from England. I knew it must have been a nightmare for her, with the time difference and lack of decent phonelines in Afghanistan. So during the days that followed the arrival of her letter, I had tried to call her as often as possible on the sat phone. When I managed to get through, it was invariably to find out that she had no news. In a vain attempt to save my allocated welfare minutes I would quickly tell her I loved her and then end the call. But they still always expired all too soon.

Luckily I had a collaborator in Dave who stepped in and offered me the use of his phone card. From the way he chain-smoked as we stood waiting for the phone to connect I figured he was as anxious as I was. We both had every reason to be. The more I phoned Lisa, the more I thought our vague rescue plan really wasn't up to much. I would shake my head towards Dave as Lisa told me that she had nothing to report.

As if the situation wasn't tense enough, my improvised dog rescue centre had attracted the attention of the Powers That Be at Camp Bastion.

With people heading in and out of Bastion on their R & R, the rumour mill had gone into overdrive with talk about how the so-called dog warden of Nowzad was planning to move his strays to an animal rescue shelter. Of course everyone immediately assumed that it was going to be via a military helicopter and it hadn't taken long for the top brass to catch on.

The boss had soon been on the receiving end of what must have been a rather one-way radio conversation with Bastion reminding him of the strict policy on animals. He had no choice but to pass the message down to me. He'd pulled me over to one side at the end of an intelligence brief one evening.

'Sergeant Farthing, I have been asked to remind you of the brigade's policy on the adoption of feral animals as unit mascots,' he said. 'There will be no dogs adopted by anybody in this unit. End of subject. And I shouldn't have to tell you that there will not be any use of military assets to transport the animals back to the UK or anywhere else for that matter, due to the health risk they impose.'

He'd said it so matter-of-factly, without any hint of emotion on his tanned face, I couldn't tell whether he was serious or not.

'Fine, sir,' I said after taking a deep breath. I really wasn't sure if he was about to tell me to get rid of the dogs. But I figured I should say something. 'Just to set the record straight, I had never intended to adopt them as unit mascots and they are not being sent to the UK anyway,' I explained.

This was the truth. I hadn't even thought about putting them up as the unit's mascots, let alone arranging for them to travel to the UK. Hell, getting them to the Afghan rescue was hard enough in itself. I already had two dogs at home. Why would I want four?

The boss remained impassive so I pressed on.

'I am just trying to do a little bit of animal welfare work to pass away the quiet hours, Boss.'

The smile that broke out on his face gave away a lot. He wasn't going to say what he was thinking out loud, though. 'That's what I thought you would say,' he said, relaxing now that the official bit was out of the way. 'So how's it going? I hear there are three dogs now.'

'Really well, Boss. Yup, we now have three. The new one is probably pregnant, just to complicate matters a little. So I need to get them out of here ASAP really,' I said, a big grin spreading across my face.

The OC just shook his head in mock amusement.

'All right,' he said. 'Just don't drop me in it.'

'Boss, would I do that to you?' I said, feigning mock hurt then turning to leave.

As I'd headed out into the compound I'd known that everything now came down to Lisa finding a way to get the dogs to the rescue in the north. Deep down I had thought about using the helicopter option on the quiet as a last resort. Now if I did so, it would be in the face of a direct order. It was so frustrating to know that I could put the dogs on a resupply helicopter and fly them to Kandahar in about 45 minutes and the problem would be solved. 'But that is never going to happen now, is it?' I told myself.

To be fair there wasn't anything malicious about the orders. I knew that. Of course we hadn't come to Afghanistan to rescue dogs. Our top brass couldn't condone something that would set a precedent for dogs being rescued during military operations.

But it didn't make it any easier. At least I could cheer myself with the knowledge that the boss had – unofficially – let me carry on for now. I didn't want to think about what I'd be doing if he had told me to set the dogs free here in Now Zad immediately.

It was 27 November, just four days before I was on notice to move for my R & R, when Lisa's hard work finally paid off. She had spent countless minutes on the phone to Afghanistan talking with Koshan, the supervisor at the animal shelter, who also thankfully spoke English. Lisa had been pestering him to arrange a truck that would make the long three-day journey south to Now Zad.

At first he had said no driver would risk the trip; it was too dangerous. But once Lisa gets her teeth into something she doesn't give up easily. After endless encouraging phone calls at his end Koshan had apparently found a driver prepared to make the journey.

As soon as I finished the call in which she told me the news I ran over to find Dave, who I knew was cleaning his rifle. We high-fived each other as I filled him in on developments. The truck was coming from Kandahar and would drive into our valley on 30 November, three days' time. Because our satellite phone was not secure I had not been able to give Lisa our exact location. The Taliban knew exactly where we were; they didn't need to listen to my phone call to find that out. But so as not to compromise anybody I asked Lisa to let the driver know that once he came over a pass we called Crazy Afghan, he was to head for the only high feature that stuck out like a sore thumb from the flat valley floor. Which was, of course, our fire base on the hill.

My plan would be to watch for a truck coming towards the hill. He shouldn't be too difficult to spot as it would be the first vehicle to drive directly towards our position on the hill since we had taken up residency.

'This has to work,' was all I could keep saying to myself.

It was the following day, while the self-elected dog rescue committee of me, John and Dave were having our morning cup of tea that it had hit us that we would need something in which to transport the dogs. We couldn't expect them to just get in the back of a truck and happily drive all the way to the rescue.

The next day John and I made an even earlier start than normal so we could search among the engineers' scrap pile. We managed to scavenge enough discarded old HESCO panels to make two decent-sized transportation cages. I reckoned that the dogs would probably be confined in the cages for at least three days, maybe more, so they needed to be comfortable. I didn't expect the driver to attempt to let them out at any time during the duration of the trip.

It took three hours to build the first cage. It was roughly a two-foot-square cube of HESCO with a small hinged gate built into one side. It seemed fairly sturdy and would withstand being lifted in and out of a truck.

We both took a step back to admire our handiwork. This DIY thing was getting easier.

'Good effort John; that isn't half bad. Guess we got a career in Civvy Street after all this.' I slapped him on the back.

'You might need these.' We turned to look at Pat, one of the company's older marines who, as an extra duty, had been tasked with maintaining the company's reserve supplies such as batteries and ammunition. He was holding out some plastic cuff ties.

'You need to build something to line the bottom a few inches along the walls of the crate,' he said. 'It will stop the dogs' paws from sliding out and becoming trapped.'

'Good point.' We hadn't thought of that.

'Why don't you use some ration pack cardboard to line the lower sides and floor of the crate?' he suggested.

Pat's idea worked well and we secured the cardboard to the cage bars with the plastic cuff ties. I had no idea whether the back of the truck would be covered or not, so to provide some shelter from the elements we enclosed half of the crate with some torn canvas that had been part of an AID Agency tent.

Not for one moment did I think that the journey was going to be a pleasant experience, but with T-shirts donated from a few of the lads, the dogs now also had a semi-cushioned floor which would hopefully absorb some of the bumps and jolts as the truck made the long journey north. It wasn't RSPCA-approved but it would do the job.

Up on the hill I bent down and let Nowzad lick my fingers through the cage. 'Not long now, buddy,' I reassured him. 'You, my friend, are going on a bit of a journey,' I added, which was probably the understatement of the century.

I fished out three biscuits and fed each of the dogs in turn. Jena seemed more interested in being stroked along the top of her head.

I stood up and looked back east towards the pass in the mountains that I knew the driver would have to come through. We had named it 'Crazy Afghan' because it had been the scene of several encounters with the mobile patrols of Danish troops who roamed this part of Helmand. No matter how hard the Danish seemed to hit the position, the Taliban holed up in the pass would always come back for more.

We'd seen it firsthand. One night we had watched mesmerised as tracer rounds had lit up the night sky. We had even watched as an Apache helicopter had used hellfire missiles to destroy the contents of an immobilised Dutch vehicle so as to deny it to the Taliban. Luckily, the crew had all escaped uninjured.

With the view from my vantage point today I could clearly see the road snaking over the pass and into our valley. It was going to be a quiet day so the boss had cleared it for me to sit on the hill until the driver showed. We had no idea what the truck looked like or even what the driver was called.

I sat down on the barren dirt of the hill and leant back against Nowzad's cage, getting comfortable for the wait. There was still an hour until midday, the agreed pick-up time.

The hour passed slowly and so did the one after that. Throughout I kept scanning the distance, using the high-powered sights that the hill used to spot the Taliban.

'Nothing yet, Nowzad,' I called out over my shoulder. There were only two dusty roads that led through the desert towards Now Zad from the direction that the truck would mostly likely have to come. The rare vehicle that did drive along the heat haze on the edge of the horizon towards Crazy Afghan always caused a cloud of dust to follow it as it crossed the desert.

I scanned again for the thousandth time, but still no sign of any truck anywhere. As the afternoon dragged on I found myself thinking about what might lie ahead for the dogs. I hadn't even asked Lisa what facilities the rescue centre had. Who ran it? How many animals were there? How did they rehome them? I began to feel slightly sad at the thought of letting the dogs go. I knew it would be for the better if they did make it to the rescue but I had enjoyed looking after them. It would be weird not having them around.

We had spent nearly four hours sitting in the crisp fresh air on the open hill when the uneasy feeling that something wasn't right finally broke free of its shackles. Something must have gone wrong.

I knew that Afghans' timekeeping had the potential to be, shall we say, a little slack, but this wasn't right. It confirmed the feeling I'd felt all along today. Deep down it had all felt too easy to actually work. Deep down I hadn't really believed that everything would run as smoothly as it had sounded over the phone.

Using the trenches and sangars that lined the top of the hill I made my way to the spot where the sergeant, who was in charge of the hill position, was enjoying a freshly brewed cup of tea.

'Want one?' he asked.

'No thanks,' I said, sitting down on the top of the sand-bags that lined the entrance to his living quarters in the sangar. 'No sign of the truck. I am going to make a move back down the hill so I can use the phone.'

'All right, mate, I'll keep an eye out for a truck if it does turn up,' he replied. I got the feeling he wasn't totally behind what I was attempting with the dogs. As I stood up to leave he joked: 'And we promise not to shoot him.'

'Yeah, I would appreciate that,' I said, although I didn't feel like laughing. Secretly I didn't hold out much hope that there was a truck coming. Which meant the dogs weren't going anywhere.

As we got ready to move off the hill, I looked one last time in the direction of Crazy Afghan. There was no magical image of a truck on the horizon. Reluctantly I loaded the two cages into the back of the open flat bed that we used for moving the bigger defence stores around.

The dogs seemed extremely chilled about the whole ordeal; it was as if they had been transported around in cages all their lives. They were showing absolutely no signs of stress. I guessed they trusted my judgement. I hoped it wasn't going to be unfounded.

I sat in the back of the open truck with the two crates as we drove back to the compound and for once I didn't have anything to say to the dogs.

We dropped the dogs by the run but I left them in the cages, just in case, as I sprinted over to the HQ building to grab the sat phone. It seemed to take for ever to dial the access codes and then the number for Lisa. I was about to hang up when the phone connected.

'Lisa, it's me,' I said. 'I need you to ring Koshan. The truck hasn't turned up yet; have you heard anything?' I blurted out without waiting for her to say hello back.

'No, I haven't, and you want me to ring him now?' she asked, sounding surprised.

'Of course,' I snapped back, 'I need to know what has happened or where the driver is. I can't just sit around all day.' I could have, really; it was down to be a slow day, but that wasn't the point.

'I am about to go out the door to work,' she replied. I hadn't even thought what time it was back home.

'*Please*, honey,' I begged. 'I need to know if he is on his way or not. I will ring you in an hour, okay?'

'All right,' she said reluctantly. 'I'll be at work so you may have to wait for me to answer it if I am teaching a class. I'll see what I can do.' And with that she hung up the phone.

I knew the next hour was going to be a nightmare while I waited to ring Lisa back. I tried to focus on checking the lads in the sangars but I couldn't stop wondering where the truck was or what had happened to it. It didn't help that as I did my rounds most lads were asking me why the dogs were still in the compound.

With another five minutes to go before I was meant to ring Lisa I found myself dialling the number on the phone. Lisa, luckily, wasn't in a class but she had no news for me. She couldn't get through to Koshan and anyway she would then have to wait for him to get in touch with the driver, no doubt.

'I love you, honey,' I said as I frustratingly clicked the end call button and then went to let the hounds back into their run.

I couldn't leave them in their travel crates any longer; they had been holed up patiently for nearly seven hours. All three dogs trotted happily into the cramped run just as if they had been out for a jolly in the car. For a moment they reminded me again of Fizz and Beamer. Both our dogs loved nothing more than staring out the window of our van as the world went by outside.

I grabbed the dogs' bowls and the stash of the lads' unwanted boil-in-the-bag meals from the pile outside the run. All three adopted their normal stance of sitting immediately upright, tails – or stumps in Nowzad's case – swishing from side to side along the dried dirt floor as they watched me like hawks while I measured out their food.

I stood guard in front of Nowzad while they ate before clearing away the bowls and making a fuss of each dog in turn prior to tying the gate securely. I had no idea how long they were going to be back in the run this time.

I rang Lisa again in the early hours of the next morning, timing it purposely in the hope she was about to go to bed. 'Where the hell has the driver got to?' I asked her.

I felt hopeless as I listened to her again explain she had heard nothing back from Koshan, then promise she would try to ring him again as soon as she woke.

'I wish I was getting into bed with you,' I said as I remembered the feel of snuggling up next to her warm body. 'Boy, do I wish I was,' I repeated as the image filled my head. 'I could close my eyes and fall asleep without a care in the world.'

'Dream on, lofty, you'd have to move the Rottweiler out of the way first,' Lisa said.

I suddenly felt really homesick.

I hung up. I looked at my watch; it was nearly two in the morning. I needed sleep. If I was lucky I could get two hours in before the day started again. It would have to do.

As the morning crawled into another afternoon I stood on the roof of the HQ building looking out towards the mountains in the north. Somewhere out there stood Noshaq, the highest mountain in Afghanistan at 7,492 metres. Attempting to climb it was not going to be a good idea, however. The route to it was blocked by landmines, laid, not by the Russians, but the Northern Alliance to prevent the Taliban from attacking their towns. The mines also meant that valuable farm and grazing land was now a no-go area. It was just so sad that nobody could ever just get on with each other but then I guessed I would have been out of a job if they could.

I glanced down at my watch; it was a few minutes before 3 p.m.

Over the last few days big grey storm clouds had been

forming, enclosing the high peaks around this time in the afternoon. They looked more menacing every day. It was definitely threatening rain and I didn't think we would have long to wait.

Added to the cool wind that was more or less a constant nowadays, I knew the rain would make life even more unpleasant around the compound. It wasn't as if we had anywhere to dry our clothes.

I looked over in the direction of the dogs' run. It was obstructed from my view by the old building that I had first found Nowzad hiding in. But I knew it so well I could visualise it in my head. I would have to do some more DIY on it if the dogs were staying for any longer. The only protection was the mortar shelter, and that wasn't water-proof. Jena spent most nights curled up under the camouflage net. Yet again my mind was drifting towards the plight of the three Afghan strays that I had become inexplicably connected to. Surely there had to be a way I could get them to the rescue centre.

Where was that bloody driver?

News that the boss had ordered a patrol to the southern village of Barakzai spread quickly around the compound. We were leaving at first light. It was a welcome relief for me. It would mean I could occupy myself with the briefings and rehearsals that my lads would need before we went out.

It wasn't until that evening that I was finally put out of my misery about the driver. He'd tried to travel here, but hadn't made it.

I managed to place yet another call to Lisa. She told me she had finally got hold of Koshan. He explained the story. Lisa recounted it again for me as best she had understood it.

The driver had been stopped at two Taliban checkpoints on his way into the Sangin valley that led towards Crazy Afghan and the town of Now Zad. The Taliban had wanted to know why a driver with a northern Afghan dialect was this far south and what business he was undertaking in their area. Obviously he couldn't tell the truth and say that he was collecting dogs for a Royal Marine who was part of ISAF. That could have been a death sentence for him.

I was angry with myself. It was a stupid mistake. If I had thought the plan through we could have got the driver to fill his truck with much-needed supplies to deliver to the local people. He would then have had an excuse to drive through the valley. But his truck had been empty and there was nothing in the Now Zad valley that he would have been collecting. The Taliban had turned him away and scared the living daylights out of him in the process. He wasn't going to try coming back.

There was, it turned out however, a Plan B.

'Koshan said that he can get a driver to go to Kandahar if you can get the dogs there,' Lisa said.

'Lisa, I only have tomorrow to find someone to do that,' I said quietly.

She didn't ask why I only had tomorrow and I couldn't have told her we were going on a patrol anyway.

As I put the phone down I closed my eyes and let out the air in my lungs slowly. This rescue really wasn't going to happen. The feeling of being unable to do anything was slowly balling up in my stomach and I couldn't stop it.

I slumped down on the broken wall I was leaning against and just sat there for a few minutes not moving.

'Get a grip, for fuck's sake,' I said to myself eventually, standing up. 'Have a bloody word with yourself, Farthing.'

I hadn't come this far to give up now. There had to be a way.

'Never give up,' I said aloud to myself in the afternoon air. The saying had been continually drilled into us during Royal Marine training; if you wanted the Green Beret, the sign of a commando, then you never gave up. Yet again it was time to put it to the test.

Maybe, just maybe, I could find a truck in Barakzai. And

maybe, just maybe, I could persuade a driver to get the dogs out of the valley and to meet up with the driver from the rescue? I had to hope. What else was there?

CHAPTER NINE

Barakzai

It was late morning but I was sweating already. Even the cool air was failing to stop the perspiration forming down my back as the heavy kit pressed into my shoulders.

The cold of the Afghan winter wouldn't be so unwelcome after all, I thought to myself. I couldn't imagine carrying all this kit if it got any hotter. I didn't mind admitting I was impressed with the army lads who had fought through the height of the high Afghan summer before us.

We had walked across the open desert for a good few kilometres before we approached the familiar brownish orange mud walls that signalled the start of the village.

Just being out and walking was a refreshing change. I looked around at the rest of my troop and even with the bulky equipment that most of the lads wore, I could tell they were chuffed at being out of the stifling confines of the compound.

During the walk I'd seen a couple of trucks driving around the dusty landscape. But, typically, they'd deliberately avoided coming anywhere near us. They knew we'd stop and search them. I'd already resigned myself to the fact that my only chance of talking to a driver would come if I found a truck parked in the village.

Even this early on in the morning, the sky was overcast with dark clouds that had now started to fill the vast desert plains that sprung southwards from the mountains. Our weather reports from the RAF indicated that we were probably going to get the first of the winter rains later today. I hoped we would make it back before that happened.

Barakzai was much smaller than Now Zad and sat at the head of the farmed land that supplied the Now Zad valley. The village consisted of a collection of the same small gated, walled compounds that were to be found in Now Zad and, I suspected, most of Afghanistan. The compounds were all connected by network after network of narrow alleyways. As we advanced further into the alleys, small children in dirty baggy trousers and shirts appeared and immediately pestered us for pens or crayons.

None of them wore shoes. I made the mistake of handing out a pen to one little dark-haired chap with bright blue eyes who was very good with his hand signals and had been clearly asking for one. Sure enough, within seconds I had a small crowd grabbing at everything I wore.

I didn't want to seem cruel but I had to push them away. The last thing I wanted or needed was one of them running off with a grenade. I gestured at our interpreter who came across and quickly sent the children on their way with a volley of shouted words and much waving of his arms. But the kids made sure they didn't go without relieving me of another pen and some light-sticks.

Winning the hearts and minds of the locals was a huge part of our mission here, yet since getting here I hadn't known what to expect from the people of Afghanistan. We had been told that President Karzai had requested our presence, but that was just the public face of politics. The truth was he needed us, such was the instability of the region. Some of the people would welcome us and others would resent our presence, but that was the same with any society. One thing I knew for sure, however, was that if the coalition forces didn't provide the security and stability that Afghanistan craved then we would definitely lose the support of the ordinary people.

It didn't matter what you felt about the decision to invade Afghanistan in the first place; leaving the Taliban in power to create a safe haven for terrorists would be bad news for everyone.

My headset crackled into life. One of the lads ahead wanted to know how he should respond to someone who'd asked if he was a Russian soldier. Again it was a sign of how isolated and cut off from the world these people were. The Taliban had banned radio and television so all outside broadcasts had stopped when they came to power. As a result there were many in Helmand province who didn't know about the US-led invasion in 2001.

Before I could press my transmit button, the boss replied from towards the head of the patrol. In a sarcastic tone he said it was probably a good idea to say that we were British and here to help.

As the patrol moved southwards, the village seemed alive with faces, all staring round corners, looking at us unemotionally. It was obvious this was a male-dominated society. There were no women to be seen anywhere. Nearly all the men old enough to be able to grow a beard wore one. They were all dressed the same: a grey or blue long-sleeved shirt that came down over baggy trousers and black leather shoes that had seen better days.

As we passed into a street wide enough for a vehicle I watched as a small mini-van drove by. The passengers perched on the roof were all children. I waved up at them. Two of the younger boys waved back.

As we patrolled along the street we walked in front of a makeshift stall. It didn't seem to hold much stock, just a few bits of fruit and some vegetables that had seen better days.

Two teenaged lads lazed outside a small open-fronted building that served as a garage workshop. The odd bits of what I guessed were motorbike parts were laid out on the ground in a haphazard fashion. Oil stained the dried ground.

From a dilapidated building that at one time or another had served as a shop emerged an old guy with sparkling eyes that seemed younger than his wrinkled face.

He was carrying a small wooden birdcage that housed a bright bird that was trying unsuccessfully to flap its wings. I didn't know whether it was just for decoration or for eating. Whatever it was, he wanted me to buy it. I didn't have any money on me and I didn't think patrolling back with a birdcage in one hand would've gone down too well with the boss anyway. So I waved my hand to indicate: 'No, thank you' and tried my basic Afghan, '*Salaamu alaikum.*'

I was greeted by nothing but a blank stare. Maybe I should've stuck to French at school. If Harry had been around to interpret I would have asked the man with the birdcage whether he knew of any truck drivers. But he wasn't around so there was no chance of that.

Trying again to communicate, I held up my right hand across my heart, a universal peace greeting. It meant letting my rifle hang by my side on its sling but Afghan custom dictated that the only thing you did with your left hand was wipe your backside so I had no choice if I didn't want to offend him. I nodded goodbye and left him.

The alleyways all looked the same and none had names or markings. If there was such a thing as a postal service out here, the local postman would have his work cut out.

With the walls of the compounds on either side of us we had no way of knowing which one led where with any certainty. To no one's great surprise a few minutes after turning back into one of the smaller alleyways a radio message came up the line telling us we had missed our first checkpoint.

The boss wanted to check out a small building that was being used as a school and to meet the village elder to discuss any support we might be able to offer in the form of reconstruction or aid.

The lead section regained their bearings and headed off

while the section I was attached to held position for a while before heading back the way we had come and into another series of alleys and cluttered buildings.

I followed slowly, keeping tabs on the marine in front. With no breeze in the alleys it was still relatively warm. The smell of rotten food and human waste stung the inside of my nostrils.

Whenever the patrol stopped each of us had to take a quick look around before crouching down to adopt decent fire positions. The weight of the kit made sure we conserved energy. The getting up and down as we stopped was becoming hard work for my old knees in particular; they really didn't like the stop-start that patrolling entailed and given the amount of revolting stuff on the floor I was also careful about where I put my knees.

The message came up the line that the boss had arrived at the centre of the village and had asked to talk with the elder. A flurry of activity indicated that the local men had gone to seek him out.

I walked up the line of crouched marines, stopping now and again to check on a few of them. The centre of the village was just an open area of barren wasteland no bigger than a normal-sized swimming pool. There were low mud walls and a few empty wooden stalls that jutted out from the ends of several unkempt buildings.

By now a group of local men and kids had formed. Most wore the faded blue grey *shalwar* robes that were traditional in these parts. A group of shoeless children were grouping around the marines who had taken up positions around the open ground.

I approached the boss and Harry the terp. They were both deep in conversation with a tall distinguished old man wearing an immaculately clean white turban. His grey beard was one of the longest I had seen and tumbled down on to the top of his chest.

As I walked past them on my way to tell a marine on the

opposite side from me to look outwards and not inwards as he was currently doing, I caught snippets of the conversation.

'Boss, the elder says he is still waiting for the promised medicines, food and school equipment that he was told would be here by now,' Harry was saying.

The boss responded to Harry, but I was by then out of earshot. I could guess what he had replied though. Without the security that this region desperately needed no aid agencies would attempt to deliver anything. The locals would have to work with us to deny the Taliban freedom of movement. Only then could we provide the resources the villages badly required.

The conversation in the middle of the village lasted a few more minutes and ended with all three shaking hands before the boss signalled it was time to move.

The outskirts of the village ended sharply and I found myself once more about to step into the open expanse of the desert plain.

I felt a tug at my sleeve and looked down to see a small brown-haired girl with piercing green eyes staring up at me. She could not have been much more than ten or eleven. She held out a grubby hand in my direction.

'Hello little one,' I said as I crouched down so I was level with her. 'Let me guess. You want a pen, eh?'

I did a quick check around to make sure I wasn't going to be swamped by hundreds of her friends. The coast was clear so I fished out a pencil from my top pocket and a couple of boiled sweets that I had placed there just for this reason.

She grabbed them from me, an oversized grin spreading across her face. But instead of running away she stood and spoke to me in quick-fire Pashtu. Luckily I looked up to see Harry a short distance away walking alongside one of my corporals.

'Harry, can I borrow you?' I shouted over to him.

He jogged over and said hello to the little girl who surprisingly stood her ground.

'I have no idea what she is saying, mate. Can you translate for me please?'

Harry spoke to the girl and they exchanged words as I listened intently, unable to understand anything.

Harry looked at me. 'She wants you to teach her to write,' he said matter-of-factly.

'Oh,' I replied. The youngster was staring up at me as if I was about to give her a lesson there and then. Harry was still looking at me too, his piercing dark eyes testing me, waiting for the answer he already knew I was going to give.

'I can't, little one, not yet, maybe soon,' I said, talking more to Harry than the child.

He looked at me a moment longer before he translated it into Pashtu. I pulled out my small black notebook and opened it towards the back where the remainder of the blank pages were. I ripped out a handful and held them out to her. 'This is all I can give you for now, okay?'

The little girl didn't need Harry to translate; she reached for the paper and with it securely gripped in her hand promptly turned back down the narrow alley towards the centre of the village.

'Harry, is there a school here?' I asked him as we moved off to rejoin the patrol that was now fanning out into the cool crisp wind blowing from the north.

Harry replied without looking up. 'Yes, but there is only one teacher there. He uses an old building as the school but he has no materials. It is not well attended any more.'

As we patrolled back northwards across the rough desert floor I wondered what we could do to improve the lives of these people.

My attempts at trying to rescue the dogs seemed fairly trivial in the grand scheme of things. But as we headed back to the compound, it was bubbling back towards the forefront of my thoughts again.

I'd failed miserably to find a truck driver in Barakzai or any of our local area patrols and I probably wasn't going to find one in time for the trip to Kandahar.

It was looking like I had only one option left. It was time to break some rules.

CHAPTER TEN

Lift Off

I tried to spend as long with the dogs as I could over the next few days. I even missed out on some opportunities to sleep so that I could sit down and enjoy the quiet moments with them in the run instead. I was going home so I knew I would have nearly a day on a plane to catch up with sleep and with no major patrols planned we had lots of time on our hands.

Nowzad would recognise my voice immediately as I rounded the corner to the run. He would push himself up on to all fours from his curled position on the red cushion and push his nose through the bars of the run, his little stumpy tail wagging from side to side. RPG would just dance around behind him while Jena made her normal high-pitched squealing until I opened the gate and forced my way inside.

A few broken biscuits would do the trick and quieten them down. It often made me wonder if it was me they were happy to see or the food I offered.

'Probably the food isn't it?' I would tease them.

Perhaps it was hard for some to understand but the dogs were a source of companionship. They didn't ask questions of me, they never got a 'sad' on with me because I hadn't been around to see them. But they were always happy when I did turn up. It was kind of relaxing to just sit there and make a fuss of them. Jena, in particular, was the ultimate soft dog and loved nothing more than rolling on to her back so you had no choice other than to rub her belly.

In my desperation to see the dogs make it to the rescue, I had now formed the only plan that had a remote chance of working. And it was a very remote chance at that.

Although simple it was fraught with massive pitfalls and ran the risk of severe reprimands if it went horribly wrong.

Koshan had confirmed to Lisa that the Afghan driver he had lined up, who we now knew was called Fahran, wasn't willing to try coming to Now Zad again. However, instead of coming to Kandahar as had been previously suggested, he was willing to drive to Camp Bastion.

I was sure Fahran would have no trouble finding Bastion. During the brief spell we'd spent there I'd witnessed hundreds of 'jingly' trucks forming outside the camp every day, attempting to sell goods and supplies to the Afghan people. Any local person south of Kandahar would know where it was.

We'd agreed to go for it and I had told Lisa to tell the driver to drive to Camp Bastion for 6 December, the day I was due to fly out for my R & R. I asked her to make sure that he knew to place a sign in the window of his truck with my name clearly written on it.

My job now was to get the dogs to Bastion. And there was only one way to achieve that. The dogs would have to fly with me on a military helo.

This was, of course, a really risky strategy as I didn't have permission.

The plan was fraught with possible pitfalls. What if bad weather barred me from catching my helo flight on the allocated day? How long would the truck driver wait?

If the helo did arrive on time, would my plan work? The idea was that me and one of my lads, Mase, would run up the ramp with the dogs hidden in boxes. We were gambling that the loadmaster would be too preoccupied with looking out for incoming mortars and would simply assume the boxes were carrying equipment. If he noticed I had three dogs on board it would be too late. We would be airborne. I could face the music later. And anyway what was the worst thing they could do: send me to the front line?

Getting to Bastion was only the start of my problems. Even if I got the dogs to the camp there were still too many variables that could go wrong.

I would have to successfully rendezvous with the driver. If we didn't meet up in the small window of time that I would have before my military plane home, I would have nowhere to put the dogs. I would have to just walk out the front gate and release them. Bastion was situated in the middle of a barren wasteland; it would be an instant death sentence.

Leaving them on site at Bastion was not an option either. They would be shot.

Even so, if the timings were right there were other things that could go wrong.

If Camp Bastion was attacked and the camp locked down, for instance, I wouldn't be able to leave to hand over the dogs to the truck driver.

Then there was the stress the dogs would experience being cramped in a small cardboard box for possibly two or three days and facing a helicopter ride, not the quietest experience in the world.

The odds on this working were about as good as the odds of me winning the lottery, but it was the only plan and it had to work.

Dave was the only one who wasn't completely onside with my strategy. 'What about the noise of the helo mate; they'll be scared stupid,' he'd reasoned.

He was right of course. The deafening sound of the helo would be terrifying, but I had no option.

'I know, I know,' I said quietly.

Despite this, however, he helped me to build some new

travel boxes. They really would have to be tiny. The dogs would be able to stand up, but little else. But what choice did I have?

It was less than three hours before the flight that was going to take me and Mase on R & R would land at the Now Zad LS. Suddenly it struck me that Fahran, the driver at Bastion, might have a mobile phone. Perhaps I could get through to him and find out if he made it to Bastion? I ran to the sat phone to call Lisa who, luckily, was at home.

'Lisa, can you see if you can get the driver's phone number from Koshan? I'll call you in 30 minutes; it is now or never, okay?' I said, the anxiety obvious in my voice.

When I got through to Lisa again it was only an hour before the helo was due to land. Koshan had been reluctant to hand it out, but Lisa was persuasive. I scribbled the number she gave me down on my notepad.

Harry was in the ops room and offered to ring Fahran for me. The sat phone seemed to take for ever to connect with the Afghan mobile. Finally, I heard Harry saying the customary Afghan welcome. But the conversation was over a lot quicker than I expected.

Harry turned and looked at me.

'Sorry, my friend, this is not the driver.'

'Are you sure, Harry? Check the number again; what was his name?' I asked frantically, waving my notepad.

'It is not Fahran and he told me not to ring again,' he replied.

I checked the number on my pad again. It corresponded identically with the dialled number on the sat phone screen.

'Bollocks.' I kicked the HESCO block in front of me. I had repeated the number as Lisa said it to make sure it was correct. Had she written it down wrong in the first place? Had Koshan palmed her off with a wrong number?

I tried calling Lisa but it went straight to the answerphone.

She was at work and unable to answer her phone. I didn't bother leaving a message. I had nothing to say.

'Sorry,' Harry repeated again. He knew how much it meant to get the dogs to safety.

I touched his upper arm. 'Don't worry, mate. Marines always have a back-up plan.' I smiled as reassuringly as I could.

'This really isn't one of your better ideas, Pen,' Dave said as we put the finishing touches to the new travel crates.

'Thanks for reminding me Dave, but what else are we going to do?'

'You get caught, you know you're fucked, don't you?' He looked directly at me. 'Is it worth the risk?'

'What do you think?' I replied.

Surprisingly Nowzad hadn't minded being picked up. It was the first time I had ever attempted it. He didn't fight either when I placed him into the extremely confined cardboard box. We had reinforced the inside of the box with metal strips so that it was crush proof and lined the base with the T-shirts from the larger crates for comfort.

'Sorry bud, it's for the best,' I said as he squeezed into the confined space.

Nowzad's sad eyes just reflected the resignation of whatever was happening to him.

We placed all three boxes with their precious cargos into the pickup and set off for the rendezvous with the resupply helicopter. As I stood in the back holding their boxes in place, all three dogs were looking back up at me, confusion in their eyes.

The two expanding dots on the horizon were unmistakable. The faint chopping sound of the inbound Chinooks was building. The corporal who had taken over from me prepared the smoke flares that would signal our presence on the LS. I had only a few minutes. It was time for the last throw of the dice.

I had found a phone number for Arnie, the corporal in charge of the security detail at Bastion during my last night-time duty. I knew he had a vehicle and the necessary passes to be able to drive out to the holding area of assorted jingly trucks that formed outside Camp Bastion.

I had got to know Arnie during our last winter training deployment in Norway. We had trained together in the gym from time to time and then refuelled with Norwegian beer afterwards in the local town. It hadn't taken much to convince him to have a look for the driver.

With the helicopter within minutes of landing I needed to know how he had got on. The signal from the sat phone was weak. For a moment or two I could only hear static. But Arnie's voice was soon coming through. And his message was clear.

'No joy, mate,' he said matter-of-factly.

'Are you sure?' I asked. Deep down I had known this was going to be the answer, but I was still gutted.

'Yes, mate. I have driven round all the vehicles; no signs with your name displayed in any truck windows.'

Reluctantly I accepted the truth. It was over.

'Okay, Arnie. Thanks mate for looking. I owe you,' I said.

'Damn right you do. Beer tokens when we get home mate.'

'Roger. Stay safe,' I said as I hung up.

The corporal who was standing in for me now on the LS was popping smoke to signal the helo. The game was up.

Dave stood next to me; he knew what I was going to say.

'The driver isn't there.' I looked at the three boxes sat waiting on the flat bed.

The noise from the incoming helicopters was growing louder.

'Look after them?' I said to Dave.

'No worries, mate, it is not as if I have a lot else to do, is it?' He held out his hand. 'Enjoy your R & R and come back with a new plan.'

I shook his hand and then touched the dogs each on the nose. Nowzad tried to lick my gloved fingers through the bars as he always did.

'Sorry, guys,' I whispered.

I grabbed my small day sack from the back of the flat bed along with my rifle and signalled Mase that we were going. The helo was making its turn to get in position for the landing on the rough desert floor and was already swirling up a cloud of dust and dirt. As it prepared to land on the deck we both broke into a jog, heading for the back of the helo. I didn't look back as we ran into the maelstrom.

CHAPTER ELEVEN

R & R

My uniform stank. My grubby day pack, body armour and helmet were dumped unceremoniously on the floor next to me.

I caught my reflection in the mirror behind the optics of the bar. My hair was unkempt and would definitely have earned me an extra duty on parade.

'Add a few more days for this as well,' I smiled to myself as I rubbed the two days of stubbly growth around my chin.

I looked down at my desert boots. Yellowish brown dust from the Afghan desert had collected between the laces. They definitely didn't match the red carpet I was standing on.

I lifted the full pint of beer to my lips. I closed my eyes and took two large gulps, my first alcohol in over two months. It tasted damn good.

I didn't think I could look more out of place if I tried, but as I scanned the bar for anyone taking a tell-tale sneaky glance in my direction I realised that not a single person was looking. The pub clientele were far too preoccupied chatting away over their lunch to pay me much attention. I had assumed that everyone would be racing to find out about the real Afghanistan but nobody had even looked since I walked into the bar. I felt slightly disappointed.

It was early December and the pub was already decorated in gold and silver tinsel. A large Christmas tree spilled out from one corner of the bar, brightly wrapped fake presents stacked underneath.

'Book your Christmas party now to avoid disappointment,' the signs warned on every available wall space.

I knew where I would be in seven days' time and there wouldn't be a Christmas dinner on the cards when it came to 25 December in the Now Zad compound, that was for sure.

A few feet away from me a group of businessmen were engrossed in conversation, their table cluttered with empty plates and half-full pint glasses. I assumed they were talking about a world that had no bearing on where I had just come from. I imagined they had no idea about my life in the last ten weeks. But then why should they? I was the one who had decided to join up, not them.

It was the brunette barmaid who broke my train of thought, or more accurately the revealing low-cut top she was wearing. 'Want another one, love?' she asked without really looking at me.

I waited for her to ask me why I was standing in her pub with body armour and a combat helmet. But she didn't seem interested either. If she was wondering where I had just come from she didn't show it.

'Yeah, that'll be good, thanks.'

She poured me another pint and turned to serve another customer as I placed the money on the bar surface. I was glad I had borrowed ten pounds from the unit photographer on the flight on the way home. I hadn't a penny to my name when I left Now Zad.

I hadn't stopped since that fateful moment when, through the open rear cargo door of the helicopter, I watched as the truck with Nowzad, RPG and Jena became just a small blotch in the vast expanse of the Helmand desert.

As soon as we touched down in Camp Bastion, Mase and I had been lucky, as a transport plane was about to lift off for the real world. Those of us who had been allocated spaces just made the flight back to civilisation. We stopped en route a few times for refuelling and a change of aircraft. Time had no meaning, really. I just knew I was going home.

The coach that had been sent to collect us from RAF Brize Norton had stopped several times to drop blokes off along the motorway so loved ones could pick them up. My stop had been on the first roundabout as we had entered Plymouth. I had borrowed a mobile phone from the lad who sat next to me on the coach to call Lisa and let her know where I was going to be.

I had just downed the last mouthful of my second pint when I saw our car through the fake snow sprayed on the bay window of the pub. I grabbed my gear and bounded out of the main doors. I found Lisa looking for a space in the almost full car park.

She had brought Fizz and Beamer along for the ride and they were going berserk as I reached the passenger door of the car. No sooner had I yanked the door open than I was smothered by a pair of overexcited dogs. I tried to make a fuss of both of them at the same time.

'Wow, guys, stop licking me, yes, I missed you too,' I said as I pushed them both away just in time to turn and face a grinning Lisa as she arrived around the side of the van.

Her smile was just as I remembered it. We grabbed each other and embraced for a long while. 'I've missed you loads, honey,' I said as we finally parted.

'So have I.'

I wasted no time in hurling my gear into the boot of the car.

'Have you been on the beer already?' Lisa teased me as I climbed into the passenger seat alongside her.

'The barmaid may have forced me to have had one or two,' I said, smiling guiltily. 'Just warming up for later!'

Home was just as I had left it, well, more or less. Lisa had done the normal woman thing of moving everything in the house around while I'd been away.

A few more cold beers from the fridge went down a treat before we braved the wind and rain to stroll out with the dogs along the deserted beach.

The storm surf was crashing chaotically against the shore as Beamer chased the tennis ball I threw for him across the damp sand and Fizz hunted around every rock for the elusive sand squirrel of her dreams.

As Lisa and I walked hand in hand, the refreshing sea breeze battering us as we went, we chatted about everything and anything of the last two months.

Over another beer from the fridge when we got home I showed Lisa the pictures from my digital camera of Nowzad, RPG and Jena. I felt a lump in my throat as I described their individual characters and recounted in detail how each dog had come to be in the compound.

As she looked at the images of the compound and the town of Now Zad on the computer screen, it began to dawn on Lisa just how remote and cut off we had been there. But seeing it as an image now instead of my real-time view and the associated smell of rotting waste and dust, I felt a million miles away from Afghanistan and my life of the last two months. It all seemed slightly surreal now that I was back in the comfort of familiar surroundings.

As I had access to the Internet I emailed the American lady who had first been in touch with Lisa. I attached a couple of the photos of the dogs.

From: Pen Farthing
To: Pam
Subject: Afghan dogs

Hi Pam,

It's Penny F here – Lisa Farthing's other half. I am home on R & R for a while and have access to the Internet.
Firstly thanks for all your help with trying to rescue the dogs. They are quality dogs and I will rescue them but I am

now open to all suggestions. The British military won't help me.

I am utterly gutted that I had to leave the dogs at Now Zad as the helicopter came in. The driver that had been arranged had not confirmed he was at Bastion so I could not risk flying them as if I had arrived at the camp with the dogs and with no transport for them then the camp CO would have had them shot. (They are really paranoid of rabies etc., there is nowhere I could have left them at Bastion.) The driver that you arranged would not speak to me on the phone through my translator – he told us not to ring him ever again. I am not 100 per cent positive that he actually drove to Bastion. None of my guys at Bastion could find his truck outside the camp, which is why I couldn't risk flying them.

Let me know what we owe you though and I will get it paid as soon as possible. I have until about the end of January to get them out of Now Zad – any ideas, Pam, will be much appreciated.

Look forward to hearing from you.

Penny F

It didn't take long for Pam to send her response. It didn't deliver anything new but I guess I hadn't expected it to.

From: Pam
To: Pen F
Subject: Re: Afghan dogs

Hi Penny,

I recognise both these dogs as very similar to other Afghan dogs we have saved and loved. We must not allow this mission to fail. Is there ANY way you can get them driven to Gereshk or Lashkar Gar? I am sure I can get them picked up there. I will send Lisa info about how to get me the money. I spent $600, which I had been sent to ship another

dog to the US. But still we do not have the dogs safe. There
must be someone you can trust to get them to Gereshk or
Lash. What about one of the drivers that is always waiting
outside Bastion? Could someone at the camp talk to them in
advance and get them to agree to take the dogs to Gereshk or
even to Lash?

'Great, it looks like it is just down to me to sort something out,' I said, closing down the computer and heading for the fridge in search of some liquid inspiration.

I had seven days at home but the more I tried to get time to slow down the quicker it slipped away.

The planned visit to the hospital to see Tom and Matt was a no-go. The doctors had said neither of them were to receive visitors except for immediate family. I felt relieved in a way; I wouldn't have known what to say to either of them.

Lisa had booked a hotel in South Wales for a few days so we could spend the time strolling along the ridges of the bleak mountain slopes. Unfortunately it rained, but both dogs were in their element as they ran ahead along the stony mountain paths, Beamer finding every muddy puddle he could to lie in. He would sit there, his tail splashing around madly in the puddle, before charging off to find the next one. Meanwhile Fizz would run along nose to the ground curiously searching for her mountain squirrel, oblivious to the fact that we were the only creatures daft enough to be up on the mountain in weather like this.

When we reached a summit we were generally rewarded with a view of nothing but thick cloud and mist. Visibility was almost zero at this altitude. We didn't linger there long and were soon starting our descent towards the warmth of the hotel bar and a hearty meal washed down by several pints.

We had a TV in our room but I refrained from watching it. We had enough to fill our days. Every now and again I would find my mind wandering away to that distant place and the three dogs I left behind on the back of the 4x4 truck.

Before I had left Now Zad I had asked Dave to give me a call to let me know that the dogs were back safely in their run.

He was as good as his word. Unfortunately, when he did call he got the time difference wrong and left me a message on my phone in the middle of the night. It was brief but said that the dogs were doing fine, although he revealed that Nowzad had been unwittingly allowed to escape the run one day. Dave had spent a good hour roaming the compound trying to coax him back.

I chuckled as I heard it. I had needed to know the dogs were doing well.

Time continued to fly by and all too soon we had to leave the hotel and start the journey back to Brize Norton. We stopped briefly at Lisa's parents to drop the dogs off before we continued to the air base. We arrived early in the morning and as I walked up the path Lisa's dad was leaving to attend to the cows on the farm. His words stopped me cold. 'Have you seen the news today, Pen? Did you know him?'

'What are you talking about?' I asked, my heart starting to race now.

'The marine that was killed yesterday in Now Zad.'

'Oh shit. What was his name?' I shouted, already sprinting for the living room and the television.

It took me several frustrating minutes to find the item on the rolling news headlines, but eventually it flashed in front of me on the screen.

The BBC reporter was based at Bastion; behind him now and again clips of unknown soldiers would appear departing on various patrols. Then in the background was the square insert photograph of a Royal Marine in desert camouflage uniform. I recognised the face immediately.

It was Marine Richard Watson, part of Dutchy's troop from our company.

'Oh no,' I said.

Lisa stood quietly behind me and grabbed the hand that was hanging limply by my side. She squeezed it gently. I squeezed her hand back.

CHAPTER TWELVE

The Green Green Grass of 'Home'

On the flight back to Afghanistan I slept during the whole journey, more or less. I opened my eyes occasionally and looked around the crowded hold of the transport plane, but it wasn't long before I closed them again and drifted off to the constant hum of the engines as we cruised across a barren night sky. Everybody on the plane was going back; nobody was new to this any more. I knew what to expect when I arrived at my destination; there wasn't the apprehension that is with you when you're first deployed to a new area.

I had held Lisa for a lot longer this time as we said goodbye. Being with her when I found out that it was Richie who had been killed wasn't good. It had brought it home to both of us just how close we were to harm's way in Afghanistan.

When the C130 transport plane landed on the dirt strip runway in the Helmand desert outside of Camp Bastion it felt like I had never left.

I walked down the cargo ramp as the loadmaster and crew were already making preparations to get the big beast airborne again. The air felt colder than I remembered, and dampness hung in the air. Low white clouds clung to the mountains to the north.

The mud under my boots was wet and sticky. But I had brought back my winter leather boots; the canvas ones – useless when the weather wasn't dry – were in my day sack slung over my shoulder. I wouldn't be using them again in a hurry.

Mase and I headed over to get our rifles and gear from storage. I popped my head into the operations tent to sign us in. It hadn't changed in the ten days I'd been away. Radios crackled into life from every desk, reports and demands coming in from across the Helmand desert. Maps and charts were stapled to every available wall space. It even felt damp in here too.

The duty officer for the day was also the unit's training officer. I had reported to him directly on a day-to-day basis when we were back in Plymouth.

'Ahh, Troop Sergeant – what's up?' he smiled as he saw me walking towards his cluttered desk area.

'Just got back from R & R, Boss; two of us need a lift back out to Now Zad. Got any flights heading out that way?'

'Yeah, if you're ready to go in twenty minutes,' he said as he checked a screen in front of him. 'You can get a lift with the Immediate Response helo.'

I took a breath. The IRT helo was launched only when it needed to collect a casualty.

'What happened?'

'One of the lads has broken his pelvis, not sure how.'

'Shit, do you know who it is?' My mind was racing, wondering who it could be.

'Marine Smith,' he replied without looking up from the screen.

Marine Smith had been sent to Afghanistan to work as a clerk but we had requested him to help bolster our company in Now Zad. He had been with us only a few weeks.

My brain had also worked out that it took at least five minutes to get to the helo pad at a jog. I had already started mentally counting down the minutes.

'We will be on that flight; can you let the pilot know, Boss?' I asked.

'Roger, see you in another three months. Hope you enjoyed your R & R,' he smiled as he picked up the internal phone.

I charged out of the busy hum of the ops tent to find Mase casually leaning against a section of the HESCO barricade that surrounded the tented HQ complex.

'No rest for the wicked, mate. We need to grab our gear and get down to the helo pad. We're out of here in fifteen minutes.'

He just looked at me; his brain slowly registered what I had said.

'Oh crap,' he replied.

We just made the flight, running up the cargo ramp and into the hold, struggling with three large blue bags of letters and parcels for the Kilo Company lads.

Mase had noticed them dumped in a pile waiting to be sent to Now Zad as we had signed out our weapons. It had been a nice thought at the time but after running the kilometre to the helo pad with the heavy postal sacks and our personal gear we seriously wished that bright idea hadn't occurred to us.

Sweat was pouring from me as the loadmaster pointed out two empty seats either side of the medical crew. I hadn't even sat down before the Chinook powered up into the overcast sky.

I smiled at the Wren medical assistant, a member of the medical response team, in the next jump seat along. She smiled back as I dumped the mail sacks and plonked myself down.

I noticed that she already had her medical mask tied neatly to hand around her neck and was holding a pair of rubber gloves and bandages in one hand. She had a fully stuffed medical bag lying closed between her feet. Her rifle had been treated almost as an irrelevance and had been stuffed under her seat.

'Keen for postmen, aren't you? Maybe you can come and give me a personal delivery sometime?' she shouted above the roar of the helo engines, a stupid big grin on her face.

I looked back at her. She caught me by surprise. Had I heard her right?

As I stumbled to think of something appropriate to say she burst into a fit of giggles. She was winding me up. Flying out on the IRT helo as the duty medical team must have been fairly stressful. Not knowing what to expect, then arriving at a destination to be presented with a casualty and expected to deal with it as the helo flew back to Bastion was not a job I envied. Humour was often the best way to deal with stressful situations, and she had just succeeded in getting me flustered good and proper.

'Nice one,' I shouted back as I regained my composure. 'Maybe if you're lucky I'll let you bandage me up one day, okay?'

She gave me the thumbs up, the stupid big grin still on her face, and then went back to checking the medical bag on the floor in front of her.

I looked out the back of the cab. We were flying low, really low. But we had no choice as the clouds were almost down to the deck. It was raining too, not too heavy but enough of a drizzle for the pilots to have their work cut out for them.

The 20-minute flight passed quickly as my brain flitted between memories of my R & R, which already seemed so long ago, to wondering how the lads were coping with the loss of Marine Watson. I was also desperate to find out how Nowzad, RPG and Jena were. I hadn't heard from Dave since that one message he left on my phone, so I didn't even know if the dogs were still in the compound. I knew compared to losing one of the lads the fate of three strays was nothing. But they had been my three strays and I still needed to know.

The signal came back from the loadmaster – one minute to touchdown. Mase and I stood up, coping with the bucking movements of the helo by holding on to the webbing straps hanging from the ceiling of the airframe, our legs planted firmly apart, our knees slightly bent as if riding a giant surfboard. The medical crew was still seated, waiting for the casualty to be brought on board.

As the jolt confirmed that we had landed both of us were already running down the ramp dragging the three mail sacks out into the stinging miserable hurricane of wet mud and rain that the downdraught from the rotors was churning up. Even with our goggles on and scarves pulled up around our mouths we fought to see where we were going as we tried to get a safe distance from the back of the cab. Partially obscured by the storm of soggy mud I caught a glimpse of four crouched figures struggling to carry a body in a sleeping bag back up the ramp.

I assumed that was Marine Smith on his way to the hospital.

Within seconds the four figures were back on solid ground, huddled next to me and Mase 30 yards from the helo. It was just the right spot to be hit full blast with the stones and mud as the Chinook launched back into the overcast sky. I winced as I took a stone direct on my upper left arm.

As the noise and hurtling debris subsided I pulled down my mud-coated goggles. They were completely useless now. I couldn't see anything out of them.

A fist punched me on the arm, right on the spot the rock had just hit. I winced again. 'Welcome back, Sarge, how was the R & R?'

I recognised the voice. As he took off the goggles and scarf, his gringo moustache, even bushier than normal, confirmed to me that it was Dave. His dark unwashed hair seemed to have grown even longer than I had expected it would.

'Yeah, hoofing mate, still missed this place though,' I lied as we all stood up and shook hands. 'How have you guys been?'

I didn't need to ask about Richie directly; he knew what I meant.

'Yeah, better, the lads are dealing with it okay,' he replied. 'It was a hard few days at first.'

I looked around the desert; the familiar 4x4 with John driving was just screeching to a halt. The mountains at either side of the town were completely enveloped in low cloud. It was now drizzling steadily.

I turned back to Dave, but he already knew what I was going to ask.

'Don't worry, the dogs are doing good, they are still in the compound. Jena has put on a bit of weight though.'

'I still don't have a plan to get them out,' I replied as we dumped the mail sacks on the back of the flat-bed truck. Dave didn't respond. The chill wind from the north was cooling me down quite rapidly now that the exhilaration of the helicopter ride was over.

'Hey John, are you still driving this thing?' I extended my hand through the open passenger window of the truck so I could shake his. It was good to see familiar faces again.

'Don't trust anybody else with my baby,' he laughed, 'You should know that!'

I jumped into the cab next to him for the short ride back to the compound with the rest of the lads riding shotgun on the back of the flat bed. I looked down at what had, only minutes ago, been my clean washed uniform. It was now wet and covered in mud. I knew that it would stay that way for several weeks to come.

As I stared out of the window I realised what had been puzzling me about the desert floor: it was the wrong colour.

Instead of the dull cracked yellow of the last few months there was now a thin carpet of green vegetation extending as far as the eye could see.

'Wow, when did that happen?' I asked, pointing out the front of the cab windscreen.

'Day after it first rained, overnight and just like that, boom, we got grass,' John replied, not taking his eyes from the potholed track.

The compound, on the other hand, hadn't changed one bit. Everything looked exactly as I'd left it when I'd last driven through the metal gates. Except, that was, for the water that had now been unable to run off through the thickset walls of the compound and was now pooled in vast puddles over every depression in the ground.

'Nice, wish I had bought my wellingtons back with me,' I said as John drove the truck through a particularly deep puddle to arrive outside the ops room.

I reported straight to the nerve centre to inform the boss I was back. The surprised look on his face told me that he hadn't expected me back till the next scheduled resupply flight in another few days.

'Nice haircut, Sergeant,' he smiled as I removed my combat helmet. I had to admit I had had it cut slightly too short during R & R. I now looked like the new boy of the compound as most lads hadn't had a haircut in over two months.

We exchanged pleasantries about my R & R before getting stuck into the situation report so I could get up to speed on the events of the last ten days.

I listened intently as he explained how Marine Watson had died. The company had been ambushed by the Taliban two days on the trot as they mounted patrols towards the north of Now Zad. On the second occasion Richie was in the passenger seat of the WMIC that I sometimes commanded. He had been shot as the cavalry were responding to the request for fire support.

The lad who had just broken his pelvis had been riding top cover in a WMIC as part of a night patrol to resupply an observation post that had been in operation for a few days out in the desert. Even wearing the night vision goggles that intensify the ambient light the driver had still failed to see the edge of a steep-sided *wadi*. Marine Smith had been lucky not to have been more seriously injured as the vehicle tyres lost their grip in the wet mud and the wagon rolled down the bank.

The boss had almost finished getting me back up to speed when the Taliban decided to welcome me back to the compound.

'Hope you haven't forgotten what to do,' were his parting words as I charged out of the ops room. Checking on the dogs would have to wait.

I sprinted to take up my place in the sangar. Only 24 hours ago I had been drinking beer in a posh hotel. I was now wet through in a crammed sangar listening to gunfire reverberate around the mountain walls as the Taliban reminded me that nothing had changed.

Hutch was manning the gun to my right. I hadn't managed to chat to him yet. He just shouted across as he engaged a target in the far distance. 'Welcome back, Sarge.'

I looked out on to the dull rain-soaked town of Now Zad. It wasn't funny but I had to smile. Despite the rain and the new grass it was like I had never left.

I dumped my day sack by my bed and retrieved the special dog chews I had bought back in the UK from a side pouch. I quickly called in to see if any of my lads were off duty in their compound. I found the open windows in the accommodation areas decorated with sparkly tinsel and Christmas banners that were now dripping from the continuing downpour.

There was even a small spruce tree in the corner of the room that looked as if it had seen better days. I had no idea where that had come from.

Most of my lads were around the sangars or asleep in their racks. I spoke briefly to the few who were getting on with personal admin. I deliberately avoided raising the subject of Richie. If the lads wanted to talk to me about it they would. But for now no one did. I tried to wind them all up with tales of my R & R and the amount of alcohol and good food I'd stuffed down my neck while at home.

As I headed back out to see the dogs across the compound it was hard to avoid the puddles of water forming in every dip in the ground. Arriving at the run I stared inside, but no dogs ran out to greet me. There was a new corrugated shelter that I imagined Dave or John must have built. Peering inside I saw two dogs curled up together, Jena and RPG.

I figured that Nowzad must be in the mortar shelter that now had a plastic waterproof covering fixed over it. I quietly untied the gate and slipped through the gap.

I stood in the water that had collected at the lower part of the run by the gate and rustled the chewies out of my soaked pocket. 'Is nobody pleased to see me then?' I shouted into the corrugated shelter.

RPG and Jena both raised their heads immediately to see where the noise had come from. At the same time, a familiar nose pointed out into the rain from the depths of the mortar shelter.

They recognised me instantly and I was soon covered in muddy paw prints as all three dogs jumped up and down around me in the mud. Jena's little yelps of excitement told me she had missed me.

'Yes, yes, I have missed you all too,' I said, as I placed one of the chewies first into Nowzad's mouth then gave one each to RPG and Jena. It always surprised me that even though they were street dogs they were as gentle as anything taking the treats from my hand.

'Calm down, Jena, I don't think you need the excitement by the look of you.'

Jena was now looking quite plump. We were definitely going to be the proud owners of some pups pretty soon.

The dogs calmed down as they took the chewies away to their own little corners around the muddy run. I stared and watched over them while they ate before making a fuss of Nowzad to distract him from the fact that Jena was still taking her time with her chewie.

Every now and again she would stop eating and just stare at me as if I was about to disappear off again.

'Just get eating, Jena. I'm not sure how long I can keep this nightmare dog occupied,' I said.

CHAPTER THIRTEEN

AK

I had to be quick feeding the dogs today.

We had a patrol planned and were then going straight into greeting a resupply flight. It wasn't just any resupply flight either. It was the big one, our Christmas mail delivery.

Bastion had informed us that there were 35 sacks of mail on the flight along with a few surprises. The compound was quietly buzzing with expectation. Even the rumour mill wasn't giving anything away.

I emptied the contents of the ration packets into the three bowls. It suddenly struck me that the dogs were not as enthusiastic as normal. Maybe it was the weather, which as well as being wet had turned extremely bitter with freezing cold northerly winds blowing in.

Every day now we went through the same cycle. We would wake up to a frozen compound. It would slowly defrost until the mid-afternoon downpour began, then turn to ice again overnight. It was miserable. The plunge in the night-time temperature had been sudden and it was only getting colder. The mountains to the north were now a picture-postcard scene of white-capped peaks.

The night-time sentry duties were becoming a severe endurance test. Getting out of the toasty warmth of a down sleeping bag at 0100 in the morning wasn't easy. I had recorded minus ten on the thermometer on my watch only the night before.

With the onset of the real Afghan winter, the unofficial dog rescue committee that was made up of me, Dave and John had come to the conclusion that the dogs needed more shelter from the elements, especially with Jena on the verge of having puppies.

There was one small courtyard building next to the rear wall of the compound that was still disused. We'd given it a quick once over when we had first arrived and concluded that it didn't look that stable as a structure, so it had remained an empty shell.

With some imagination and a bit of effort, however, we decided it would be ideal for a two- or maybe three-run dog pound, especially as it contained three small storerooms that were built into the main back wall. The spaces would be ideal for the dogs to shelter from the freezing downpours. As we set about fixing them up, for added warmth we taped up three large cardboard boxes and cut a flap just big enough for a dog to enter through one of the ends. We placed a box in each of the rooms, lining the insides with the unused T-shirts from the failed rescue travel crates.

The courtyard was over on the west side of the compound and well enough away from most of the lads as not to cause a nuisance if the dogs started barking as they sometimes did when the Now Zad pack wandered close by at night around the outer wall. I guessed that Nowzad missed his days of roaming wild after dark. I never really understood that. I figured having two square meals a day and somebody looking after him was a fair trade.

Another morning of frenzied activity saw the new dog pound up and running. The work had kept John and me warm as the wind was blowing a bitter chill from the north most days now.

Our plan was to eventually separate Jena from Nowzad and RPG. I had no idea how the two male dogs would react to her puppies when she had them. We had cut the fencing ready to split the run up and left it lying against the wall, for now leaving it as one big run.

'What's up with you guys?' I asked as I held up a bowl of what they usually considered a gourmet meal. 'Don't you like your new accommodation or have you just gone off food?'

I didn't believe that last statement for a minute.

Nowzad wasn't looking at me, which had to be a total first during feeding time.

'What the hell are you looking at, Nowzad?' I asked him, turning to follow his gaze behind me. 'Wow, where did you come from?'

Behind me was a small mud alcove that didn't seem to have much of a use. Until now it had been a place to ditch the empty ration packs when we didn't have time to clear them away.

Today, however, a small, funny-looking dog, a similar colour to RPG, was lying panting heavily on its side in among yesterday's rubbish.

I stopped arranging the dogs' breakfasts and took a closer look. I could see she was a bitch. It wasn't hard to see why she was in distress. Her neck was nearly double the thickness it should have been for an animal this little guy's size.

'What's the matter, little buddy?' I said as I reached out a hand. It didn't move but the dog's eyes followed my hand as she decided to give out a soft little growl in my direction. She didn't seem to have much fight in her.

To get a better look at her, I shifted my position until I was looking down on to the dog and the back of its head. 'Okay, buddy,' I said, 'I can see why you aren't moving too much.'

There was a nasty-looking wound at the base of the dog's enlarged neck. The area around the bloodied patch was a matted clump of bloodstained hair and broken skin. As I looked closer I realised that I was actually studying two small puncture wounds about half an inch apart. I was no expert but it looked decidedly like a snake bite to me. Afghanistan has around 270 varieties of snake, of which about 50 are poisonous. I imagined that was why the neck was swollen so badly. I reached out my hand again gently and slowly towards the dog's head. Again she didn't move, just growled steadily back at me.

'Okay, I'll get you something for this but I don't know if it will work.'

I stood up and turned to face Nowzad. 'Sorry buddy, but breakfast will have to wait.'

I quickly ran over to the store. I spied the cardboard box I was looking for immediately and emptied the contents on to the floor. I could pack them away later.

When I returned the little dog was still lying on her side, panting heavily. She hadn't moved. I pulled on my leather combat gloves and gently reached my hands either side of the dog and under her back. I tried my best to support her swollen neck as I lifted her carefully into the box. Because of the cold, I had my thick combat jacket on. As I cradled her I hoped the little dog wouldn't be able to bite through that. Luckily her attempts at growling were fairly pathetic.

The dog was about half the size of RPG, but her legs were nowhere near as gangly as his. I placed the box carefully down under the shelter of the discarded corrugated tin, covering the injured dog over with an old T-shirt before I went to find the doctor.

As I walked across the yard, aware of the time, I couldn't quite figure out why I was suddenly the focal point for all the waifs and strays of Now Zad. Why had the little dog found her way into the compound? How did she know I would try to do something to help her?

There was no way Dave or John would believe that I hadn't brought the dog in from outside, I thought to myself.

I walked into the medical room. The doctor was doing a stocktake.

'Doc, you got a minute?' I asked.

'Yeah, what's up? Are those warts playing up again?' He made sure he shouted so that his medical assistant, who was quietly reading a book, looked up.

'Ha ha, nice one, Doc, cheers for that.' He knew I didn't have warts but it would be good for the rumour mill. It was his way of getting back for those early-morning wake-up calls. 'Doc, hypothetically, suppose a little baby was bitten by a snake. What medicine would you recommend?' I asked.

'A snake bite? Well, it would be some form of anti-venom depending on the snake involved,' he said, looking up at me.

'If you had no idea what type of snake?'

The doc looked up and gave me a knowing look.

'This small baby of yours, it wouldn't be a dog by any chance?'

'Yeah,' I replied with a sheepish grin.

'Okay, antiseptic cream over the bite area and then one of these pills twice daily for three days,' he said, reaching for a packet on one of the higher shelves in the crammed medical centre. 'I can't vouch that it will work though,' he added.

'No worries, if it doesn't I'll try it on the warts,' I yelled as I rushed out the door.

I knew I would have to administer the cream and attempt to get the dog to eat the tablet all in the space of a few minutes. I didn't think I had to worry too much about the little dog putting up a fight. She looked knackered.

The Christmas mail drop was big. As the Chinook flew away we were left with a large under-slung pallet and nearer 40 sacks of Christmas mail lying in the damp air of the desert LS.

John and I, along with our small working party of four lads, stood transfixed as we worked out what the hell we were going to do with all that mail.

Big cardboard boxes, far too heavy for even two men to

lift comfortably, were strapped down tightly to the base of the wooden pallet.

On closer inspection of the pallet boxes, I discovered one marked for the attention of the chef at Now Zad.

'That'll be me or Dutchy then,' I said. We really were hoping that a new chef would have arrived by Christmas, but that was not to be.

John and I peered eagerly into the box to discover four large frozen turkeys along with an assortment of fresh vegetables, strips of bacon and sausages and Christmas crackers.

'Better get your pinny on,' John sniggered as we loaded the bags of potatoes and carrots on to the pickup.

The real surprise was at the bottom of the box: three crates of lager. There was then much back-slapping as we discovered another box containing even more crates on the pallet. A quick calculation and we worked out that, in all, there was enough for one can for each man in the compound on Christmas Day.

We'd been feeling a bit sorry for ourselves since discovering that for once the rumour mill was correct and Gordon Ramsay *was* to cook Christmas dinner in Bastion. It was a nice gesture but not one that was going to benefit any of us fighting in the out stations. This delivery was obviously to make up for it. Bastion really did care about us.

As we made the short drive back to the compound, my main concern was how on earth we were going to cook four enormous turkeys with just a gas-operated hob.

Over the next couple of days I administered the cream to the small dog's neck. She had taken well to the tablets the doc had given me, as I'd cunningly stuffed them in a slice of corned beef.

Towards the end of the second day I found her sitting upright in the box, her head just poking over the top. I noticed her small tail wagging as I got closer.

We had named her after the Russian AK-47 automatic

AK

weapon as she was just a smaller version of RPG. We thought
we might as well stay with the weapons theme.

'I see you are feeling better then, AK?'

The swelling in her neck had gone down too. I could now
stroke her head without fear of any reprisal. I lifted her up
and placed her on the floor at my feet. Nowzad, RPG and
Jena were glued to the fence to see what would happen
next.

Little AK sniffed the ground, slightly wobbly on her feet,
before promptly sitting down again.

The dogs in the run all let out a slight whine.

'Not ready for the big world yet, eh bud?'

I picked her up again and placed her back in the box along
with another slice of corned beef.

CHAPTER FOURTEEN

Santa's Sleigh

Christmas Eve started the same as every other day over the past week or two: wet.

By now the Christmas decorations that hung from most of the doors and windows were really looking the worse for wear. The constant drizzling rain saw to that.

I stepped out into the mud of the compound and wished for the thousandth time that I had brought back my wellingtons with me. I could feel the water seeping through my now constantly sodden leather boots within minutes of putting them on. Clean dry thick wool socks were the commodity of the moment on the compound black market.

I walked over to the new dog run that we had altered to accommodate the latest arrival.

AK's bite marks were healing nicely, and although it had taken a few days for the small dog's appetite to return, she now shovelled the food away just like the others.

Once she had seemed strong enough to walk around the vicinity of the courtyard area we decided to move her in with the rest of our pack. Immediately there was a mass sniffing frenzy, smelling at each other excitedly until Jena got bored and strolled away.

RPG and AK then continued to play with each other until AK tired herself out and collapsed, panting heavily, curled up in a corner. It didn't take her long to recover though and they were soon resuming their play-fighting again.

I think RPG was just happy to have somebody to play with that he could beat for a change. Nowzad just seemed content to watch from his cushion.

Dave hadn't believed me when I told him that I hadn't brought her in from outside, but he had taken a shine to her anyway. Little AK would race to the bars whenever Dave came over to feed her.

'Come here and let me check out your neck, AK,' Dave would call and she would happily trot over and curl up by his feet as he carefully felt around the wound on her neck. We didn't need to discuss it. AK had just joined our growing dog family.

Within a day or so, it was obvious that we would have to move and redesign the run to house three separate fenced areas, each of which would have unique access to a small storeroom.

Nowzad needed his own run as he didn't take too well to RPG and AK constantly tussling away together. 'Words' had been exchanged between Nowzad and RPG already, so we had decided it was best to keep them separated. Despite the fact that he and RPG used to be big buddies he seemed quite happy to be on the other side of the HESCO fencing, able to prowl his own little space.

It also meant I didn't have to stand guard when I fed him. Now I just opened the small hinged gate and shoved the bowl of food through.

I had toyed with the idea of trying to make them all sit before I gave the food out, but that meant taking out the time to train them all and time was the one thing I didn't have.

Jena was definitely the mum of the group and sat in her own little space watching over the proceedings. I had looked up puppy breeding on the web during R & R and now knew that she needed her own space to have her puppies in. She didn't seem to mind being on the other side of the gridded fence.

All the occupants looked up at me expectantly as I rooted through the stack of old rations for today's delights.

I was quite chuffed with the segregated runs. I was not sure why I hadn't used this old building before. Nowzad now had his own favourite spot lying against the fence on top of two old sandbags where he could keep an eye on the single entrance to the run enclosure and the antics of his next-door neighbours. He would lie there barking occasionally when RPG and AK got carried away chasing each other, as if telling them to keep the noise down.

I had just finished cleaning out all three runs when I heard the familiar sound of a mortar round arcing across the sky.

'Here we go again, guys,' I said to the dogs as I ran out the gate. But they had already disappeared into the dark shadows of their respective bolt-holes. I doubted they would make an appearance again in a hurry.

I spent the next two hours in the northern sangar while we took on the Taliban, who seemed hell-bent on dropping a mortar into the DC. A small cheer went up as an American attack helicopter joined the fray, letting loose with two hell-fire missiles on to the enemy position. The joy didn't last long as the Taliban managed to put a few rounds through the weapon pylon of the helicopter with some form of anti-aircraft gun. That decided things there and then and the call was made to bring in the big boys, in this case a B1 bomber that was tasked with dropping a 7,000-pounder on to the Taliban firing point.

I knew what was coming as we all listened to the 30-second countdown over the radio. I also knew the dogs hiding in the dark of the small disused storerooms had no idea of the impending impact. But there was nothing I could do about that.

Even though I was expecting it, the blast wave from the impact zone just over 1,000 metres distant still took me by surprise. I hated to think how panicked the dogs must have been in that second as the explosion echoed across the valley floor and into the mountains.

As the mushroom cloud rose slowly into the damp afternoon air, I didn't spare a thought for the Taliban fighters who had probably been caught in the blast. As far as I was concerned they had sealed their fates when they had ambushed Marine Watson.

These constant exchanges with the Taliban had left us running seriously low on ammunition; a large-scale resupply was the only option.

It would have needed around ten helo lifts to carry all the supplies we needed, but that just wasn't going to happen with the limited air resources available. So a C130 Hercules transport plane had been tasked with dropping the pallets over the desert outside Now Zad. The boss had given me the job of heading out into the desert, arranging the drop zone and then signalling the pilot that it was secured and open.

I didn't get to see the dogs again until around 8 p.m. and even then it was only for a few minutes. I desperately needed to close my eyes. After I had fed them all I climbed in Nowzad's run with him and sat down with my back against the cold, clay wall. Nowzad trotted over and sat next to me. As I rubbed his stumpy ears, he leant into my hand, encouraging me to rub harder. I obliged for a few minutes more. I had set my watch alarm to go off in 20 minutes' time and before I knew it I had nodded off. When I woke up shivering it felt like I'd been out for ten seconds, not 20 minutes. Nowzad was still by my side. Reluctantly I stood up, my sleepiness still trying to pull me back into its grip. I knew it was going to be a long night.

It was one minute after midnight on Christmas morning and the pilot had timed his approach to perfection. The second I hit the button to fire up the infra-red strobe lights I had used to mark out the run, the low hum of the incoming Hercules transport plane filled the sky over the drop zone. The hum quickly became a roar as the dark form of the mighty transport plane passed overhead – surprisingly low overhead, in fact.

As the loadmaster released the heavily laden pallets out into the void of the night sky, I realised the C130 was much closer to the ground than I'd thought.

It might have been a comical moment anywhere else, but suddenly it clicked that we were in the middle of the drop zone – a really bad place to be when 14 wooden pallets laden with ammunition were rapidly descending to earth, supported only by a piece of flimsy parachute silk.

'Oh shit, run,' I shouted to John.

In the dim glow of the early-morning moon it was too difficult to judge how high the chutes were above the ground. But I figured we had only a few seconds before the first pallet-laden parachute crashed to earth. Each one would probably weigh around two tonnes and I had no plan to be under one when it touched down.

My boots were struggling to find a grip on the slippery wet mud wall of a *wadi* as the first impact resounded behind us.

John stood sucking it in next to me, both of us bent over with our hands on our knees. Between us we sounded like we had just rowed in the Olympics.

'Bloody hell, I didn't realise they were going to be that close,' I said.

As I sucked in deep gulps of cold air I saw that the closest pallet had landed only 100 feet away.

As we let our heart rates drop back down to something resembling normal, I pressed the transmit button on my radio.

'0 this is 20C. Santa's sleigh has touched down, over.'

'0, roger go collecting. Out.'

Silence had once more fallen around the darkened

mountains. It was actually fairly peaceful. It definitely didn't feel like the early hours of a Christmas morning.

'Let's go and see what Santa has bought us then, John,' I said as I dropped back down the side of the *wadi*.

The next hour or two passed slowly as along with the lads not on sentry we located the various pallets across a vast section of the desert. We then began the process of removing the straps and cables that secured the enormous parachute, before destacking the ammunition tins ready to be loaded on to the engineers' wagon.

Nobody in the DC was sleeping while this operation was under way. Anybody who wasn't on guard duty was either out here helping with the task in the desert or waiting back in the compound to unload the truck as quickly as possible so that it could turn around and head back out for the next load.

Those in the compound were left with the job of breaking the ammunition down, counting it and then storing it away in the various locations around the compound.

The guys on the hill were our eyes and ears, constantly scanning for the slightest hint that the Taliban were interested in our early-Christmas morning antics.

'Happy Christmas, Sergeant,' a tired gentle Welsh twang called out as I approached the darkened stack of ammunition currently being stripped down.

Taff, who was second in command of one of my sections, was attempting to cut through one of the thick straps. One of his lads was caught up underneath the hulking parachute as he tried desperately to fold it away on his own. The parachutes weighed 20 stone or more. Three people would normally struggle to lift one on to the back of the flat-bed truck; one person was a non-starter.

'Merry Christmas to you, too,' I replied. 'I bet there are some disappointed young ladies back in Merthyr tonight, seeing as you aren't out partying in the valleys, eh?'

'You best believe it, Sarge,' he replied as he finally cut

through the strap, jumping to the side as the ammo tins were released.

'How many pallets is that so far then?' he asked.

'Eleven; still got to find another three,' I answered, as I continued scanning the flat expanse of the Now Zad desert with my night sight. 'I think the last three must have landed away in a *wadi* over there,' I said, pointing vaguely in the dark. 'I'll be buggered if I can see them though.'

'Oh great,' Taff said as he stepped over to the parachute-clad figure, who was now pretending to be a ghost.

'Stop fucking around, Mike, and get out of here,' Taff said with a quick clip around the silk-clad head to reinforce the message.

'Ow, Taff, that hurts,' the voice from under the parachute replied, waving two arms from under the silk to prevent any more blows that might be directed his way.

'Mike, just do as you are told, idiot boy.'

'Give us a call on the radio in about ten minutes. Hopefully I will have found those other pallets by then,' I said to Taff.

I couldn't see his face but I knew there was a sarcastic expression staring back at me in the gloom.

'Can't wait,' he said.

The early-morning sun was just starting to break over the eastern mountain ridges. They were awash with shades of reds and orange as the daylight slowly greeted an Afghanistan Christmas Day.

I needed to get the lads moving again; we had been out here now nearly seven hours collecting ammunition; I couldn't believe the Taliban had left us alone this long.

The last pallet had drifted nearly 200 metres out into the barren desert. Taff's team were on their way over to my location. I was hidden from view down the side of a steep dirt bank. It wouldn't be a lot of fun dragging the ammunition up and over the side of that, I thought to myself.

I started cutting the heavy-duty buckles and straps that had held the ammunition boxes in place then jumped sideways as half the stack of ammunition boxes fell towards me as the last strap was released.

Some foam padding that had been hidden from view in the middle of the pallet stack suddenly caught my eye. I stepped over the tumbled ammo boxes and reached into the padding. It came away easily to reveal a large cardboard box. I carefully lifted the box up from its precarious position among the stacked mortar bombs and opened the cardboard lid.

As the early-morning light infiltrated the box I smiled to myself as I realised it was a traditional, square, white-iced Christmas cake with the words 'Merry Xmas' in blue icing across the top of it. A small white envelope had been carefully laid on top.

Inside the card there was a picture of a rather rotund Santa stuck in a chimney pot, his Christmas sack bulging with brightly wrapped presents. Inside it read:

> To the lads in Now Zad DC,
> Have a safe Christmas
> From the lads of the Royal Air Force

'Nice one, Brylcreem boys,' I grinned.

It was just what our early-morning exertions required. The cake would go down nicely over a cup of tea, whenever we finally made it back to the compound.

The morning sky that had looked so promising was now clouding over, which made the damp air feel quite warm. By the time I was dragging the last of the bloody parachutes through the sticky mud of the desert I was sweating.

It wasn't far off eight o'clock as we entered the compound with the final tins of ammunition. The Christmas cake box had sat securely in my lap for the brief journey.

Wearily we manhandled the last of the hastily folded

parachutes into the metal ISO container that we used for storage.

Eventually the 'chutes would be loaded back to Bastion for another day.

'Meet up round by the vehicles, lads – it's cake time,' I called out as I wiped the dirt and sweat from my eyes.

The cake went in a flash as mud-stained hands snatched it up. The steaming hot mug of sweet tea washed the cake down a treat as we worked out the sentry roster for the remainder of the day. With no operations planned, unless the Taliban had a Christmas surprise of their own, it should be a quiet day.

I quickly heated up some water using the old ammo box that served as our hot water tank and filled the shower bag. Five minutes later I had shaved and dressed in fresh underpants and clean socks. I still wore the same pair of trousers that I had worn for the last week; I had no choice there as my other pair was still trying to dry from the wash two days ago. I had brought back from R & R a bright red barbecue shirt that came out only on special occasions. Lisa hated it, which, of course, encouraged me to wear it more.

Watching it being packed into my day sack for the return to Afghanistan Lisa had suggested I leave it behind for the Taliban when I came home for good.

My mother had sent me some Christmas reindeer antlers and a flashing red bow tie. They finished off my Christmas Day outfit quite nicely. I pulled out the variety box of chocolate biscuits from under my bunk that had also come back from R & R and, in body armour, wandered off to check on the lads manning the sentry positions. Everybody looked tired as I did the rounds, but we had no choice except to keep plugging away at it. We couldn't very well stand the sangars down just because it was Christmas.

By the time I finished my rounds the biscuit box was empty and I felt quite stuffed. I had managed to munch a sickly chocolate biscuit in every sangar. I couldn't let the lads eat on their own, could I?

As I walked back to the galley, Dutchy was already clad in his apron, peeling potatoes into the cooking pot. I walked through the doorway and then stopped and reversed back out into the muddy yard.

'Wow, when did they do that?' I said, staring in disbelief at the home-made oven the Gurkhas had knocked up and which was now placed tight against the outer wall of the little kitchen.

'While you were out jollying around the desert,' Dutchy said, looking at my outfit with a shake of his head. 'Their corporal heard about the problem with the turkey and offered his services.'

It was certainly an impressive piece of engineering. The oven was made from an old discarded oil drum that had been cleaned out and propped on top of two old bricks and packed tightly against the wall with sandbags. The Gurkhas had cut a small A4-size hole in the front that they hinged on one side. Inside they had welded on four brackets that acted as rails for the two baking trays they had fashioned.

The whole drum had been caked in about two inches of wet mud. I could see a rubber gas hose snaking through the wet mud, which disappeared under the oven. I took two steps back and peered around the corner. The rubber hose was connected directly to the six-foot gas cylinder that was propped there.

'How the hell have they connected the gas?' I asked, slightly bewildered.

'Don't ask,' Dutchy replied. 'Just get your arse in here and give me a hand.'

It is a long-running tradition that the lower ranks are served their Christmas dinner by their sergeants and officers. Dutchy and I were perhaps taking it a little far by actually cooking the food as well.

For the next two hours, with help from the engineers officer, we prepared and cooked as much of the Christmas goodies as we could on the hob and in the home-made oven.

The Gurkhas' oven produced a surprisingly hot blast of air every time we opened the door to check on the slowly roasting turkeys inside. We had to use a cleaned metal piquet to move the turkeys round as we had no oven tongs.

The smell of the turkeys as we carved up was enough to stir the hordes. They were soon rapidly flocking to the serving tables. The company second in command came over and duly served and wished the lads Merry Christmas as they filed past.

'No way, look – there is even bacon wrapped around the sausages,' said one marine as they drooled over the steaming plate in front of them. The rain had held off, thankfully, but the queue that had formed in the ankle-deep mud resembled a picture from a music festival.

'Quite proud of those bacon-wrapped sausages,' Dutchy whispered to me.

'Yeah, not bad mate, although I think they like the fried potatoes I prepared better,' I replied with a grin. I was still wearing the stupid antlers and the bright red shirt.

The CSM wandered over to get his share of the food. 'Good effort, fellas. I'll be recommending a change of careers when we get back.'

'Bugger off,' Dutchy shot back through a mouthful of turkey hot off the carving plate.

'Between the two of you, sort the lads out so we can have one troop at a time in the HQ building for two o'clock and then at three, all right?' he said.

'What's happening?'

'Santa's coming,' he replied as he walked off.

I looked at Dutchy, who just looked back at me with a confused expression. We were none the wiser.

As I entered the HQ building with my lads shortly after 2 p.m. I couldn't help but burst out laughing. The company second in command and the CSM had decorated the room with left-over decorations and laid out the welfare Christmas

Day parcels that had slowly been arriving over the last few weeks.

The Royal Marine Association, especially the Tavistock branch, had been doing us proud with the shoeboxes packed with goodies they had been sending. They had been filled with things like razors, toothpaste and sweets, items the military didn't supply. But that wasn't the reason I was laughing along with the other lads.

There, sat in the middle of the carpeted area on a chair, was Father Christmas – drinking a can of beer.

Of course it wasn't the real Father Christmas but 'Scouse', our medical assistant. Being a member of the Royal Navy he had been allowed to grow a beard. And a fine one he'd grown too. It now formed a black bushy clump covering his lower jaw up to his ears. Not quite Father Christmas grade, but good enough. Combined with the red Santa outfit he was wearing, *voilà* – a Santa Claus of sorts had arrived in Now Zad.

'Yo ho ho,' he shouted, unable to hide his strong Liverpool accent. 'Come and sit on my lap, little boys, and tell Santa what you want.'

'I'd rather not, if you don't mind Santa,' I shouted back, 'but Tim will.'

I volunteered the youngest member of our troop and without protest Tim walked over and plonked himself down on Santa's lap.

'Bloody hell,' Scouse Santa groaned as Tim's body armour dug in. 'Have you been a good boy?' he asked as he reached down to a large box just behind his chair.

'Certainly have,' Tim replied, smiling as he played along. Well, I hoped he was playing along and didn't really think it was Santa.

'In that case, have a beer on me,' Santa said as he held out a can of cold beer that he had just retrieved from the box.

'I've changed my mind – me next, Santa,' I shouted as I led the charge to form a queue for Scouse's lap.

*

Santa was also issuing the red military Christmas Day boxes. It didn't matter where in the world you were serving at Christmas: if you were deployed on operations on land or at sea, then as a member of the British Forces you would receive a small Christmas box. We sat with Santa savouring the lager while we rooted through the collection of miniature Christmas puddings, Santa hats, catapults and assorted other bits and pieces inside.

We had asked the Gurkha section to join us as a thank-you for their extreme hard work to make life more comfortable for us all. They giggled away like small children as they entered the room to loud cheers and a shouted rendition of 'We wish you a Merry Christmas'. Their thrilled faces said it all. They couldn't stop grinning and talking excitedly in Nepalese as they each took it in turn to receive their beer and goody box – while sat on Santa's lap, of course.

The small room soon became a hubbub of noisy laughter and high-pitched screams as another victim of the catapults was hit by bits of Christmas cake. In another corner there was lots more excitement as some of the lads were challenging each other with the small plastic racing snails they'd found in their boxes.

Wearing your Santa hat was compulsory, as was a salute to the Queen, who looked out from the small gilt-framed pictures that were found at the bottom of every box.

We all stood up and saluted our pictures before sitting back down in fits of giggles among the crumpled paper, discarded boxes and wrappers.

I looked across and saw two of the lads attempting to cram as many of the small Christmas puddings as they could into their mouths all at once. Instead of telling them how stupid they were being some lads were eagerly donating their own puddings to encourage the record-breaking attempt. It ended with both competitors choking and spraying dried Christmas pudding over all those in range.

We enjoyed a good hour of jovial banter. It was a unique moment. No one really spoke of what they were missing back home; they hadn't been expecting the Christmas dinner and they definitely hadn't been expecting to see Santa bringing beer.

I looked around the room and felt proud of the lads. They didn't complain at being away at Christmas. They just got on with it. And they deserved to have some fun.

The day had been non-stop; I hadn't really been able to see the dogs much except to feed them quickly in the morning. I had sat in the sangars for a few hours in the late afternoon to give a few of the lads an extra hour's downtime; it had passed slowly and I felt the lack of sleep for the last 24 hours taking its toll. I had my down jacket pulled up tight, but the cold wind felt extremely bitter as it pushed through the open gun port of the sangar. There wasn't a cloud in the sky, which meant that it would drop well below freezing again as the night drew in. Through the binoculars the view was the same as it had been since we had arrived. The cold was beginning to bite and the locals had obviously retreated to the warmth of their fires.

I let my mind drift to thoughts of Lisa back home and what she would be up to. I had left a present hidden under our bed, which I would tell her about when I called later that night. As a couple we weren't that keen on Christmas Day but it would still have been good to be back with her.

I was surprised that the Taliban hadn't hit us; maybe they had given a time out as they were respecting the fact it was Christmas Day, but I doubted it. More likely they had suffered a serious setback in yesterday's encounter, at least I very much hoped so.

As it was getting dark I walked back over to feed the dogs. I carried with me four thin slices of turkey that I had carved from one of the joints. It was Christmas, after all.

I could hear all four going crazy as I entered the run area, barking and jumping up and down. As usual Jena was rooted to the spot closest to the door, her high-pitched whines echoing around the little courtyard as she shivered with excitement.

Dave had beaten me to it and was preparing some food, squeezing it from the packet into the bowls. The Christmas tinsel that we had tied along the tops of the fencing was looking battered and had lost its dazzle.

'Just finished sentry, thought you was busy,' Dave said as he carried on dishing out the pork and dumplings.

'Yeah I was, just finished in the northern sangar,' I replied, adding the cuts of turkey to the bowls.

'They will love that, but better not tell the lads, eh?' Dave said.

'Yeah, probably not.'

'Better give Jena the bigger portion, I think she is going to need it,' Dave said, nodding towards her.

I could see what he meant. Her belly was vastly swollen now. It probably wasn't going to be long before those pups of hers would be making an appearance.

'Happy Christmas, dogs,' I said to the patiently waiting audience of four as we finished serving up the food and stepped away from the bowls.

The hounds of Now Zad were soon hungrily tucking into their first Christmas dinner.

CHAPTER FIFTEEN

No More

Duchy and I were back in the galley, cooking a Boxing Day dinner of pasta with chicken and white wine sauce when there was a sudden, thunderous explosion.

'0 to all stations. What the hell was that, over?'

'0 this is Sangar 1. A bloody rocket just missed my position. Over,' a shocked voice shouted back over the radio.

'0 this is Hill. Roger that. That sounded like it was a rocket. Over.'

Oh shit, what are they up to now? I thought to myself.

The Taliban had learnt to fire 107 rockets, which were old artillery shells adapted to fire from a home-made wooden launching ramp. This made them quick and extremely easy to hide once the rockets were fired, but the improvised weapon's range and accuracy left a lot to be desired, unless, of course, the Taliban firing team got lucky.

The 'stand to' shout went up around the compound as Dutchy turned the gas off in the galley. The pot of boiling pasta would have to wait.

Running to the sangars I was shocked to see the all too familiar rising plume of smoke was coming from just the other side of the outer compound wall by the gate.

'That was too close,' Dutchy yelled as we went our separate ways.

The roar of another rocket flying overhead had me

ducking as I ran, but this time it was nowhere near the compound. Instead I watched as it arced skywards towards the hill. Luckily again, the unguided missile exploded harmlessly in a ploughed field away to the south.

I climbed the metal ladder as fast as I could and threw myself into the safety of the sangar's sandbags. Hutch was already bringing the gunners on to a position far out towards Taliban central.

'Making up for having Christmas off,' he shouted over, raw adrenalin glinting in his eyes as he scanned the distance and called corrections for the young gun team.

Apart from Christmas Day the Taliban had now attacked us every single day since I'd returned from R & R. And they were getting closer. It wouldn't be long now before they scored a direct hit on the compound.

As December struggled to a close I had almost lost all track of real time. My days had been blurring into one big repetitive, Groundhog Day routine. Every 24-hour cycle consisted of quick dog feeds, morning meetings, visits to the sangars, patrols, stints sitting uncomfortably in the sangars while the Taliban attacked, cleaning weapons, cooking for the troops, feeding the dogs again, sleeping when time allowed and taking a duty on the radio before starting the whole process all over again.

Keeping an eye on the dogs was becoming even more of a diversion. RPG would keep me amused by chasing AK around the run for most of the day. By contrast, Jena was getting so big and heavy that she just sat waiting for me to make a fuss of her.

The dogs had almost eaten the entire stockpile of unwanted pork casserole and dumplings. Luckily, during his daily water drop-off John had come across three large boxes of unused halal rice and chicken packets that had been delivered for the ANA. They'd headed back to Bastion just before Christmas and not been replaced. The brown rice and stodgy-looking chicken pieces tasted incredibly bland.

'None of our lot will eat this,' Dave said.

'Roger that,' I replied, pulling a face as I chewed on the last mouthfuls. 'Well, why waste it?'

That evening we watched happily as all four dogs devoured their new dish. As John and I cleared away the bowls I remembered what I had been meaning to ask him all afternoon.

'Did you see that white dog today?'

'What dog?' he said.

'I was walking across from the north sangar to the HQ building when this skinny mad little dog ran out of the shadows by the ammunition containers,' I explained. 'It ran around my legs a couple of times before running off like an idiot through a small gap between the gate and the wall. No idea how it managed to squeeze through the gap though; it had to be no more than five inches wide. I stuck a piece of wood in there to stop it coming back in. I think we have enough dogs, don't you?'

'No, I haven't seen it,' John replied, 'and we definitely don't need any more.'

Jena was going to give birth any day now. I had no idea what we were going to do when her puppies arrived and I was still none the wiser about getting the dogs to the rescue.

The emails and phone calls had dried up. Lisa had had no joy trying to get hold of the rescue for quite a few days now.

I could hardly complain of a lack of customer service from the rescue centre. Sometimes in my frustration I forgot that it wasn't a real rescue but a few Afghans who were willing to look after the dogs and other animals that found their way there.

They were prepared to treat the waifs and strays with a kindness that was hard to find elsewhere in this part of the world. They didn't have a dedicated office and almost certainly weren't paid very well for their time, if at all. Most importantly of all they were putting their lives on the line by associating with Western agencies.

As I walked back over towards the galley, the air was still and calm but the temperature was dropping fast like the sun. I needed to get my down jacket on. It was going to be cold one again.

The sudden thud of the explosion as a mortar landed somewhere nearby shook me. From the way the sound was reverberating around the compound wall I could tell it had been close, really close.

The radio burst into life immediately.

'0 this is Sangar 4. A fucking mortar just landed next to my fucking sangar, over.' The animated Liverpudlian accent was instantly recognisable. Scouse was the only lad from Liverpool that we had in the company.

'Sangar 4 this is 0, are you okay? Over.'

'Eh. Only fucking just, yeah. It landed right next to my fucking sangar. Over,' he repeated in a fast babble of words, clearly alarmed at just how close the mortar had landed.

'Eh, eh Sangar 4. This is 0. Eh, just calm down, eh,' came the reply in a mock Scouse accent.

It turned out that Scouse had been extremely lucky. The torrential downpours of the past weeks had softened the flat mud-roofed buildings around his south-west-facing sentry post. Even though it had landed just four feet away from his position, the explosive head of the mortar had punched straight through the sodden roof without detonating, exploding instead when it hit the hard floor below. As a result, the full impact of the explosion had been contained inside the empty building and its thick mud walls.

If it had exploded on the roof Scouse would not have been playing Father Christmas again.

It had been close, too close.

As I climbed the ladder into the sangar ready for another dose of Taliban entertainment I couldn't help thinking about the dogs once more. Things were getting quite crazy and at times scary although we didn't admit it to one another. I hoped the dogs were well hidden away in their small storerooms.

For them there was no running away from the constant soundtrack of battle; it was always Guy Fawkes Day. And, no doubt, it was even more frightening for them than it was for us. At least we knew what was causing these big bangs even if we did have no control over them.

A few days earlier I had watched Nowzad's reaction when a fast jet had flown overhead as a show of strength to the Taliban. The noise of the plane directly over the run had sent him running for cover in the cardboard box inside the old storeroom. No amount of offered biscuits had been able to persuade him to venture out while the noise of the plane raged overhead. Curled tight in a small ball with what was left of his ears pinned back, his wide eyes had stared out at me as I tried for all I was worth to tell him it was okay and not to worry. But nothing I could say reassured him. He looked like he was on the edge, which perhaps wasn't surprising given that most of us in the compound were as well.

The night was quiet and lit by a brilliant moon so I decided to take Nowzad out for what was becoming a regular afterdark walk around the compound.

I'd become a bit worried about him over the past few days. Nowzad had nobody to play with now that he was in a run on his own. This arrangement made it easier for me to feed him and it also kept the other dogs safe in case he decided to turn nasty, especially at feeding times. But I had a feeling it wasn't good for him to be isolated like this.

I knew he needed exercise otherwise he would spend the entire day lying out on his cushion, getting up only to go for a wee. But as he was getting so unpredictable around more or less everyone in the compound, I could only take him out safely at night.

It was frustrating. It wasn't that he was naturally a vicious dog; it was just the training and the treatment he'd been given in his previous life. I hadn't had the time to retrain him, but I couldn't risk him biting someone so I had to keep him on a tight leash, literally.

I'd made a thick strap I'd cut from one of the ripped resupply parachutes as a lead. Even with it around his neck he would still lurch forward and attempt to rear up at strangers. It was so dispiriting. It didn't matter what I said to him or how firm I was, he just wouldn't stop with the evil guttural growl and the snarling teeth whenever anyone walked within ten feet of us.

I understood what was at the root of his aggression: he wanted to protect me. I knew I could cure that. It would just take time. Time I didn't have.

Of all the dogs, Nowzad was the one whose future most worried me. Even if I got him safely to the rescue, I guessed that nobody would choose to take him as a pet. The result would be that the rescue staff there would unfairly be lumbered with a fighting dog that was set in his ways. They would then probably be left with only one option.

That didn't bear thinking about.

John was at the water pump, topping up the jerry cans. I turned to walk towards him; even though he was a young lad we got on well and I enjoyed passing a few minutes while we chatted about whatever was on our minds. It dawned on me that I had never asked him where he was from or even how old he was. Now seemed as good a time as any.

'All right, Nowzad?' he said, turning off the tap as he turned to face us approaching.

Suddenly, without warning, Nowzad lunged at John's legs and let loose his most evil-sounding bark. Luckily John was too quick and moved away before Nowzad could sink his teeth in. If he hadn't been so sharp, he would almost certainly have been badly bitten.

'Bugger, what the hell was that about?' John shouted.

He couldn't understand it and neither could I. It wasn't as if he was a stranger; John fed Nowzad occasionally, for Pete's sake.

Somewhere deep inside me a switch flipped. The frustration of being target practice for the Taliban, the days and months of sleep deprivation, burst to the surface. I had had enough.

'*Nowzad!* That's it! No more,' I shouted as I yanked back hard on the improvised lead, almost forcing him back on his haunches with the force of the pull. I then dragged him towards the gate. 'Nobody will want you at the rescue; you're a total pain in the arse,' I yelled.

John stood there slightly shocked before heading back to the well.

As soon as I got the gate open wide enough I pushed Nowzad's thickset body out through the gap. He tried to resist at first by digging in with his front paws, but I had the upper hand. He wasn't making a noise at all. I think he was in a state of shock as I shoved him out into the night.

The moon was particularly bright, and the frost-covered ground sparkled as I watched Nowzad wander away from the gate, heading off across to the far corner of the next compound and the open spaces on the east side of town.

As he reached the corner he stopped and turned to look back towards me for a split second before disappearing into the night.

I took two deep breaths and realised what had just happened. After all we'd been through together, I'd kicked Nowzad out. It was over.

I felt a pang of guilt. But there was nothing I could do now. It was done.

I walked back across to my bed, the now useless lead in my hand. I needed to sleep. I felt tired.

I had been beaten. The last two months, all the time I had spent desperately trying to convince myself that I could look after an Afghan fighting dog, had been a waste. It wasn't

Nowzad's fault; it was just the way it was. Again I told myself I had done the right thing. I sat down on my bed in the ice-cold room and removed my boots. I couldn't be bothered with getting undressed. I had only three hours' sleep before I was on watch again.

I tried not to think of Nowzad as I drifted off to a better world.

I woke to the sound of my alarm piercing the darkness. I had ten minutes until it was my turn to man the ops room and the radio. Almost three in the morning and all was well.

Well, not quite all, I thought to myself as I quickly laced up my cold boots and stamped my feet around to get some warmth while I slipped on my down jacket and hat.

I walked outside. The moon was still crystal-clear and everything was laced in an icy sheen. The ground crunched softly as I made my way over towards the ops room.

It was then that I heard the sound quietly floating on the still early-morning air.

It wasn't a howl or the werewolves' cry of the movies, just a low, whimpering cry for help, a dog's cry.

I knew who it was.

I had a few minutes to spare and I could always pretend I had overslept so I headed for the home-made wooden ladder that leant against the wall, then climbed up and popped my head over the top so that I was looking down into the open space immediately to the front of the gate.

'Oh shit.'

I felt numb inside.

There was Nowzad propped against the gate, looking lost and rejected. He was waiting to come in, waiting to come back to what he regarded as his home. The home I had created for him.

'Don't do it,' I scolded myself climbing down. 'He'll get tired soon. He'll find shelter soon enough; just leave him be. There is no other way.'

I had to fight against myself to keep walking towards the ops room.

I drifted through the handover. It was the same shit as before, just as it had been for the last two months.

As the minutes on the clock painfully ticked by I sat and stared at the wall decorated with maps in front of me. The line drawings of the buildings and alleys seemed to blur into one swirling black blob.

I kept seeing the image of Nowzad, sitting against the fence, howling. If dogs felt loneliness and fear then that's what Nowzad was going through now.

'Shut up, Farthing,' I told myself. 'Nowzad had his chance. Just let it go.'

I looked at the clock again. The minute hand seemed suspended in space.

I punched the desk.

'Fuck it!'

Slim the signaller shot up in his seat. If I didn't know better, I might have said I'd just woken him up.

'What's up?' he spluttered as he got his bearings.

'Nothing,' I replied as I stood up. 'I need a swamp, back in three minutes.'

I was already out the door and running.

I climbed the ladder again and looked over the wall. Nearly an hour had gone by since I'd spotted him by the gate. Nowzad wasn't there.

I didn't know if I was relieved or not.

But then, as I went to take a step back down the ladder, I caught sight of a curled-up figure at the foot of the gate. It was huddled up in the lengthening shadows.

Nowzad was curled up as tightly as possible, his head buried under his rear legs for warmth. I could now see why. His coat was camouflaged with the glistening frost. No wonder I hadn't seen him the first time I'd looked. He had blended into the lengthening shadows as if he wasn't there.

I almost slid down the ladder. My pulse raced.

In the dead of the night, the noise of the huge metal bar being lifted and the rear gate opening made me wince. It sounded like I was banging on the hull of the *Titanic*.

I opened it just enough to stick my head through. Nowzad had lifted his head up but had not moved.

'Nowzad, it's me, come on, dog,' I whispered.

As he recognised my voice Nowzad pushed clumsily to his feet. I felt as guilty as sin. His stumpy tail wagged uncontrollably as I gave his coat a good brushing down, the ice crystals sparkling as they fell to earth.

I rubbed his head. 'Sorry bud, let's not do that again, eh?'

As I stood up Nowzad pawed my foot in his excitement at being back in. I danced around with him by the gate feeling just as happy to see him as I believe he was to see me.

CHAPTER SIXTEEN

The Laughing Policemen

As the dust cleared and I stared at the huddled group of shapes on the desert floor my first feeling was disbelief. Even though a thin layer of dust covered the half dozen or so kneeling figures, I could clearly distinguish the dull blue clothing and the distinctively shaped muzzles of the AK-47 assault rifles they were carrying on their backs. ANP policemen.

'Did they just get off the helo?' I asked myself.

It was a dumb question – there was nowhere else they could have come from. But it would have been nice if someone had told us we were getting a new ANP police unit.

The previous unit had left in a hurry, a few days earlier. Their departure had caught us all by surprise. During our time together I realised that we had probably completely misunderstood them and they us. Our two totally diverse cultures and beliefs clashed appallingly, with neither side prepared to compromise. During the past month or so they had carried out a few more so-called patrols into the local area, occasionally coming back with supplies, but that was it. But then just before they had left, they suddenly called on Harry the terp to inform us that they were heading for Lashkar Gar. Before anybody knew it we heard the familiar sound of their old 4x4 truck coughing out fumes as the engine roared to life.

We stood there and watched them go. The commander was at the wheel as they sped out the back gate heading south and leaving wet tyre tracks in the damp earth. The younger members of the contingent, their AK-47s poised and ready, were riding high among the stacked bags and bundles in the back of the flat bed as they bounced along the makeshift track. As they disappeared into the badlands, the hill kept 0 informed of their progress southwards.

'How the hell are they going to get past all the Taliban checkpoints?' John asked as we stood in mild shock at their sudden departure.

'Guess they are happy to take their chances,' was all I could say as we trudged over to shut the gate they had been in too much of a hurry to secure.

I looked at John and then back at the six new ANP who were dusting themselves off and chatting excitedly to each other as the Chinook became a black dot in the cold evening sky. They appeared a right motley crew, their blue uniforms covered in dirt from where they had lain on the ground as they were blasted from the helo. Immediately I could see there was a vast range of ages. One looked no more than 13 while the eldest looked around my age, in his late thirties, I guessed.

Standing next to them was just one British marine, covered in mud himself, slowly picking up his belongings from the midst of the huddle of blue mail sacks. The ANP seemed to be lacking any equipment of their own.

'Let's see what this lot are like then,' I said to John as we walked towards them from our hiding place behind the side of the 4x4. The side of the truck was becoming extremely dented and chipped as it took a hammering every time we positioned it to protect us from the blast of the helo. I was glad I didn't own it.

A tallish dark-skinned Afghan with a well-trimmed full-face beard stepped forward. His bushy curled hair was layered with sand and grime from the helo cloud.

'*Salaamu alaikum*,' I offered as I held my right hand up over my heart.

He smiled and replied in kind and then just stood there staring at me as if waiting for me to crack on in Pashtu, his piercing stare making me feel slightly uneasy.

'Okay then, buddy, that's my Pashtu, all gone,' I said, giving John a 'what do we do now?' look.

Silence as all six Afghanis just stared back at me, their faces still beaming from the jolly of what I assumed was their first ever helicopter trip.

'Okay, get in the wagon,' I said, pointing to the back of the pickup truck. They took a quick glance towards the truck then turned back to me and nodded enthusiastically before walking off towards it.

'All right, mate.' I turned my attention to the lone marine. 'Welcome to Now Zad.'

'Smashing fella,' he replied.

I immediately recognised the voice. 'Steve, am I glad to see you!'

The first time I had met Steve he had smacked the back of my hand with a spatula as I attempted to sneak an extra sausage from the hot plate at breakfast time during our brief stay in Gereshk. He was only a corporal but I forgave him, especially now. Steve was a chef, a fairly good chef at that. Not that I would have let him know that as I'd never hear the end of it. Dutchy and I were saved.

Steve could come across as slightly brash, someone who ruled the kitchen with a rod of iron and set high standards. But he had a heart of gold and would bend over backwards to help anybody, whatever they needed. He also had let me have that second sausage.

'Heard that some sergeants can't even boil eggs properly and need a grown-up's help,' he said, trying to wind me up.

'Hey, mate, not sure why they sent you as I'm told that chef's training is the hardest course in the world to pass ...'

He finished the gag before I could, 'Yeah, yeah and you've

never met a chef who has passed it yet. Ho ho ho, just show me the kitchen, loser,' he smiled as we shook hands.

'With joy my friend, with joy.'

As always it was a short drive back into the compound. The new ANP party chattered away happily among themselves as we drove in. I was taken aback slightly as the ANP jumped down from the back of the vehicle into the soft mud of the yard almost before we had pulled to a stop.

They seemed to know where the ANP accommodation was situated and before we could grab Harry to explain the rules of living in our compound they had disappeared off to root around.

'I guess they have been here before,' I said to John as we sat in the front cab and watched them walk off.

I would have to introduce them to the boss later.

Steve was itching to see our galley but he had to sit through the CSM's welcome brief first before Dutchy and I took him on a tour of the kitchen.

Steve mockingly ran his finger along what I thought was a reasonably clean gas hob, under the circumstances. 'Tut tut,' he muttered as he held up an index finger now smeared with dirty grease. 'Don't worry, boys: a professional is here now to save you all.'

'Hey, I thought we were doing okay,' I said, feigning mock hurt.

As far as we were concerned Steve could have the bloody kitchen; I was well chuffed that we were rid of it.

Neither of us would ever admit it to Steve, but he was definitely a better chef than either me or Dutchy. Not that we were bothered in the slightest.

RPG was the latest to confirm it. Within a couple of days of Steve taking over RPG would somehow squeeze through a small gap in the run gate and casually trot over to join the hungry lads in the breakfast queue. He would sit on the sand-filled cardboard boxes that we'd placed along the back wall of the compound, waiting patiently for the queue to disappear so he could get stuck in to the leftovers.

Steve would always save him a sausage, which RPG would gobble down faster than you could say frankfurter.

The other new arrivals were changing the atmosphere in the compound as well.

Our new ANP contingent was proving to be more outgoing and laid-back than their predecessors. Often they would sit on plastic chairs in the middle of their garden area, which was basically a trimmed square strip of grass, bordered on three sides by a mixture of small shrubs and weird-looking tall flowers.

They were gathered there again today as Dave and I strolled back after another frenzied feeding time at the zoo. We couldn't help smiling at their antics.

Four of them were seated, clapping to an imaginary tune while puffing away on what I imagined were home-made smokes, their weapons abandoned haphazardly on the ground.

Two younger policemen were attempting a slow-motion, high-stepping dance. Their shoes were throwing up small globs of mud as the clapping encouraged them to dance more and more wildly.

As we passed by, Dave and I both waved and said hello. I thought that was the least we could do. They couldn't be any worse than the last lot.

One of the police was a slightly more rounded character than the rest, his chubby tanned features framed by a short trimmed beard that covered the lower portion of his face. He was probably as old as the one who had spoken to me on the LS. He had apparently taken to hanging around the open door of the galley, chatting away happily in Pashtu, which had somewhat annoyed Steve as he sought to get to grips with our simple but demanding galley routine.

The Afghan now stood up and bounded over to us as the

two lads in the middle continued their dance uninterrupted. '*Salaamu alaikum*,' he said, holding out his hand.

His eyes shone as his big face formed itself into an enormous grin. His smile was infectious and we both grinned inanely back, shaking his hand back and greeting him in our best Pashtu.

Encompassing us in his enormous arms he pulled us towards the chairs. The commander, who had come forward at the LS, remained seated wearing an impassive grin as we reluctantly went along with our new chubby policeman friend.

'We're not dancing,' I said, even though I knew he had no idea what I was saying.

As he playfully led us into the garden he barked at two of the younger lads sat on the chairs. They immediately jumped up and dusted down the seats to make way for us.

'Thank you,' we said, although we weren't sure that they understood us.

After receiving directions from the commander, the younger boy, who looked no more than 13 or 14 years old, disappeared. Dave and I sat in silence while the rest of the policemen continued clapping for the two lads who were still performing their dance routine in the middle of the circle. Both were dressed in their long blue uniforms. I guessed they were both in their early twenties. As they threw themselves about in what I figured was a well-known traditional routine, their wild, curly jet-black hair bounced out from underneath their dress caps.

I really hoped they didn't have any intentions to get us to attempt the dance.

The larger-than-life character who had dragged us over now stood in front of us jabbering away in fast-flowing Pashtu.

'We don't know what you are saying,' I said once more, looking at Dave for help but he just shrugged his shoulders.

It would have been useful if Harry the terp had been

walking by right now, but there was no sign of him. We shrugged again as the jolly policeman stood in front of us obviously waiting for an answer.

Luckily at that moment the young lad returned carrying a tray of chai tea, accompanied by cups and a large bowl of boiled sweets.

'Ah, tea – marvellous,' I said as the dancing stopped and we all gathered around the tray.

The commander, who still had not moved, was served first. The silver pot was then placed down in front of us as the young lad proceeded to pour the decidedly murky light brown tea into a pair of see-through cups.

I was wary about the origins of the water but I didn't want to offend our hosts on our first real meeting, especially as we had never even got this close to talking with a group of ANP before.

'Cheers,' I said as I raised my filthy cup and then sipped the tea. 'Actually, it's not bad,' I said to Dave, knowing they couldn't understand me. If anything it tasted vaguely of mint.

'Thank you, sir.'

I almost spat my tea out as I realised the young Afghan boy had answered.

'You speak English?'

'Small English. I learn at school before police,' he smiled.

Mentally I powered back through all the conversations we'd had while we'd been in the vicinity of the ANP since they had arrived. None of us had thought that any of them could understand us. I couldn't think of anything too sensitive or secret we might have let slip.

The commander spoke to the young boy, who replied quickly and then turned to us.

'You commander?' he asked.

I was about to explain that I was a sergeant and take him through how the ranks structure worked in our military but

I quickly realised that would take all day. So instead I held the palm of my hand close to the floor and said: 'A small commander.'

I then stood and pointed over to the HQ building, lifting my hand up higher. 'Big commander.'

'Ahhhh,' the young lad seemed to understand as he translated back to his boss.

As one they nodded their heads as the youngster translated.

Not to be outdone, Dave held his hand even closer to the ground than I had and said: 'Tiny commander,' before pointing to his own chest. They all laughed, indicating they had indeed understood.

The young lad pointed towards the unemotional commander and held his own grimy hand up high. 'Commander.' Then he pointed to the bubbly policeman who had enticed us in for the chai tea and pointed his hand lower to the ground. 'Small commander.'

'We understand,' we said as we both suppressed laughter. We were having a conversation and that was all that mattered.

'What are your names?' I ventured.

The young Afghan boy started with the commander and worked his way around the small circle of seated police.

The commander was called Commander. Which made sense. Dave and I both nodded at him. The chubbier policeman was called 'Rosi'. 'Rosi?' we asked in unison, not quite sure if it was right.

The jolly Afghan policeman beamed and nodded. 'Yes. Yes. Rosi.'

After several minutes of us repeating the names and the ANP nodding enthusiastically we had them all squared away. There was Tin Tin, Jemel and Hussein. Tin Tin and Jemel could have been brothers with their long thin faces and similar whiskery beards. The main difference between them was that Jemel had thick straight hair that was cut in a bob around the top of his ears whereas Tin Tin's mass of curly hair ran wild under his small cap. They both wore the same thick dark blue winter jackets, which they left undone. Hussein was dressed in long flowing blue robes and seemed unaffected by the cold wind.

Finally the young lad pointed to himself and told us his own name. 'Abdul la Tip?' Dave said, double checking we had heard correctly.

'Yes, Abdul la Tip,' the boy nodded happily.

'I am Penny and this is Dave,' I said.

'Penny and Dave,' they repeated as one.

Laughter peeled out around the group as we spent the next few minutes pointing to each other and shouting out each other's names. As the laughter died, the clapping started up again, this time with me and Dave actively joining in.

Tin Tin and Jemel stood up and resumed the dance routine, their scuffed leather slip-on shoes defying gravity and staying firmly on the ends of the feet as they flicked their heels madly to the beat of clapping.

I settled into my chair to enjoy the show while Abdul la Tip poured more tea.

We both had no other pressing engagements and it sure beat Steve moaning at us about lack of a decent kitchen. So we stayed and clapped and drank more tea.

CHAPTER SEVENTEEN

A Tight Squeeze

The foot patrol had been the longest we'd yet undertaken and had been slow, hard work. We had covered a lot of ground but in a very stop-start way. The constant crouching into a fire position and then standing back up again had taken its toll on my back, which was giving me grief.

For the moment, however, the pain was forgotten as I stood looking at a scene as disturbing as anything I had yet seen in Afghanistan.

We had decided to check out the former school compound next to the main Now Zad mosque on our way back through the western part of the town. The school was an enormous open compound with buildings along the north and east walls and housed five or six decent-sized classrooms.

Sadly the Taliban had decided to pay the school a visit long before us.

It wasn't the sandbagged gun emplacements on top of the buildings that had given it away but the level of vandalism within the whitewashed school classrooms.

Anything that could be tipped over and smashed had been. Even the doors and door frames had been ripped out.

What shocked me most, however, was the fact that books of all shapes, sizes and colours were emptied all over the floor in two of the classrooms. The piles of discarded books stood at least a foot high. You couldn't walk across the room without standing on books. I bent down to have a closer look. The top layer of books was sodden from winter rains that had unobstructed access through the open windows. Underneath those most of the soft front covers were curled at the edges; many of the books were now useless as the pages were completely stuck together from the damp.

I picked one up that said 'English' in big bold letters and what I assumed was 'English' written in Pashtu underneath. At the bottom was a text box that stated it had been donated by the people of Canada.

I flicked through a couple of pages; it was mainly pictures of everyday objects such as fruit or household utensils with the English word for them in large capital letters underneath.

I placed it back down and pulled another soft cover from the mess. Its rain-soaked pages were stuck together too. It was a maths textbook donated by an American charity. I threw it back on the pile; it was useless now.

Sifting through the mess we also found some hand-held blackboards and a sodden cardboard box of coloured chalk sticks. The Taliban had even snapped each of the chalk sticks into pieces so they were now too small to hold properly.

Totally at a loss as to why anybody would do this, I backed out of the room. The wanton destruction was mind-boggling.

The other lads checking on the remaining rooms reported the same situation. I walked over to the boss and informed him of what we had found. He too, like me, was at a loss as to why anybody would trash a school like this. Without any form of education, the Taliban were doomed to failure. Even they must have understood that.

Quietly we left the school and started on our route back to the DC.

The streets and alleys were as deserted as ever. The torn and ripped canvas coverings of the empty stalls flapped and fluttered in the winter breeze, along with the permanently closed shops, the only remnants of a once thriving town.

As we patrolled through a wide crossroads of the main thoroughfares of the western part of town, we came across an old Russian T54 tank that had been abandoned smack bang in the middle of the crossroads. It was an extraordinary sight, as if it was some bizarre roundabout ornament.

The rusting metal hull was seemingly undamaged, the long barrel protruding from the turret was pointing away down a side street. The top hatch had long ago rusted open, a permanent reminder to the local people of their hard-fought victory against a force that had outnumbered and outgunned them but had ended up withdrawing painfully.

Like all of the lads on the patrol, I had never seen a Russian tank in real life. After all the many hours we'd once spent poring over foreign tank recognition pictures back in the UK in preparation for a cold war that thankfully had never got warm, it was actually quite satisfying to see one in the flesh.

After what seemed like an eternity of plodding the alleys we arrived back at the compound. I was determined to immediately get out of my body armour and heavily loaded webbing. The pain in my lower back had been getting steadily worse over the last few days of patrols. Guess I wasn't as young as I liked to think I was.

I was standing outside the galley and had just lifted the body armour up and over my head, when Grant, my mortar man, appeared.

'Sergeant, you have got to come and look at this,' he said in his thick Scottish accent, motioning for me to follow him.

'Whoa, what's up?' I asked as I reluctantly struggled to let my body armour slip back down over my head. 'Where we going?'

The wind was a crisp northerly as normal and my

sweat-soaked shirt immediately felt cold as the body armour pressed back down against me.

Grant led me round towards the rear gate where a small crowd of lads had gathered, quietly watching something.

I popped my head round the corner. I had no idea what I was meant to be looking at. It was just the same old gate, closed securely.

'What the hell am I looking at, Grant?' I asked, slightly annoyed.

As we came in from patrols Steve would have fresh brewed flasks of tea waiting on the table outside the galley, a small gesture that was hugely appreciated by the lads. I could have been in the galley having a mug of tea by now.

'Ssh, Sergeant, just wait and see.'

I was about to remind the young lad that he didn't tell me to 'Ssh' when I saw it. All thoughts of giving him a rollicking disappeared instantly.

'What the hell is that?'

A grubby grey brownish blob of fur was being forced through a tiny depression in the mud under the bottom of the metal gate. It looked from this distance like a small cuddly toy.

'I'll be damned!' I said to myself as the realisation of what it was clicked into place.

I was watching a tiny puppy, probably no more than a few days old, being forced awkwardly through the gap.

Along with the other marines, I watched transfixed, as the force pushing the puppy came into view. A dirty snout with a bright pink nose appeared first, followed by a thin mud-streaked head. Soon the lean and haggard-looking form of the scatty white-haired dog I had seen running hell for leather through the compound only a few days ago came into view. Safely through the gap, the dog gave the puppy a quick sniff and a prod, before picking it up tenderly between its teeth. We all watched as it padded over to a small mud cave that had been exposed when the Gurkhas had blown away the back wall of the compound to make room for the gate.

'That's the third time she's been in,' Grant said.

'I've already met her,' I said. 'She was obviously on a scouting mission.'

I looked in the direction of the cave. At least it looked dry and sheltered from the winter winds. I watched as the scruffy white dog carefully placed the newborn puppy down alongside two other small, curled-up bodies. She gave all three the once over by sniffing and licking them before turning back for the gate.

'Looks like the word is out on the street, Sergeant,' Grant smiled. 'All strays welcome.'

'Don't I know it,' I replied.

I stood in mild shock as the desperate mother scurried back under the impossibly small gap, heading off to wherever she had left the remainder of her litter. Within minutes we saw the tell-tale signs of another pup emerging through the hole. This one was completely white, just like the mother. It was soon through the gap and in place alongside its siblings.

I had never seen anything like it. All sorts of questions flooded through my head. How the hell did that dog know to bring its puppies in here? Did it really know that I wouldn't be able to say no?

'I don't think I quite believe this,' was all I could say.

I was all too aware that within days we would have Jena's pups arriving on the scene as well. I wasn't sure I knew what to do.

'Can you go and get Dave for me if he is not on duty?' I asked Grant. 'Cheers, mate.'

While I waited for Dave I watched as the mum collected another two puppies. This seemed to be the last of them and she was soon prodding and pulling her complete litter into a living pile before snuggling up around them.

'You have got to be bloody joking,' Dave said as he arrived

from the galley where he had been having a cup of tea and a sneaky cigarette. 'The mum just carried them all under the gate?'

'Yup,' I replied. 'What do we do with them? We can't leave them there.'

Dave gave me a look that said he knew what I meant.

It may have been a good shelter, but the artificial cave was too close to the gate. As the puppies grew stronger I imagined they would take to wandering around their newfound home. That really wouldn't be a good idea when one of our wagons stormed out in a hurry. A puppy that would fit nicely into my open palm would hardly register to one of the drivers, especially if the Taliban were shooting at the time.

'Shit, we've got to move them,' Dave said, looking at me, slowly shaking his head.

'This is getting bloody ridiculous. If I didn't know better I'd say the dogs are talking to each other out there,' I sighed.

Dave didn't answer.

'Best get some food. That dog looks like it could do with it anyway,' I said as we backed away.

'And a box big enough for half a dozen puppies,' Dave added.

Two minutes later, armed with food and an empty cardboard ration box, we approached the cramped cave. The white-haired dog raised her head towards us but stayed put. She must have been beat after finding what she thought was a safe new home.

The puppies were lying on top of one another suckling from her as best they could.

The mother looked like she had seen better days but then so did most dogs in Afghanistan. Her long coat was a dirty dull white from her time spent lying in the open mud-covered ground. She desperately needed to eat; her skinny body was being worn out by the constant demands of feeding her six puppies.

The smell of the open pork and dumplings packet soon got her attention. I gingerly pushed the open packet in towards her.

'Don't worry, we're the good guys,' I said, trying to reassure her as she sniffed the food-scented air as the packet slid towards her. As soon as the exposed foodstuff was within reach the white dog wasted no time in getting stuck in to the gooey mixture. It wasn't long before she had devoured the lot and was contentedly licking clean the insides of the silver packet, the hair around her mouth stained a reddish brown from the contents of the sachet.

The box Dave had borrowed was large enough to carry all of the puppies, but not the mother.

'She'll follow us, don't worry,' Dave reassured me as I expressed concerns about the mum running off and leaving us with six puppies to contend with.

I gently reached into the cave and prised one of the puppies from its cherished position by its mother's belly. The little thing was as cute as you like, its tiny face still screwed up firmly, its eyes closed tight. It easily fitted into my hand as I placed it down in the box, the mum not moving. She just looked at me. As I reached for the next one she struggled to get up. I pulled my hand back thinking I was about to get bitten, but she just crawled around to the box to lick the first puppy I had placed there.

I made the most of the opportunity. While she was distracted I gathered together her remaining pups and arranged them in the box as the mother dog watched wide-eyed, not knowing whether to protect the last puppy or to try and snatch the others back out of the box.

Before she had a chance to attempt the latter, Dave lifted the box high into the air.

'Time to go, mum,' I said as Dave moved in the direction of our dog run.

The white dog darted around between our legs, obviously slightly panicked by the removal of her pups, as I am sure any dog would have been.

'It's all right, we aren't going to hurt them, okay?' I tried to reassure her.

We had already quickly arranged a small piece of HESCO fencing next to the dog compound. It was tall enough to stop the puppies from venturing out, but allowed the mother dog to come and go as she pleased. We had nowhere else to put her. We had destroyed Nowzad's original run, which would have been ideal.

John had already placed another open packet of pork and dumplings in the enclosed space as a tempting distraction. This worked a treat, occupying the mum as we carefully set the box of puppies down on its side. The puppies hadn't really moved. They were too busy cuddling together for warmth.

With the sun now slowly dipping down under the rim of the mountains to the west it wouldn't be long before the night freeze was upon us again. Nowzad, RPG, AK and Jena were all squashed up against their respective fences, vying for positions, so they could get a glimpse of the new arrival. Jena was making little whining noises, as she wasn't the centre of attention in our dog world at the moment.

When the new mum had licked clean the open packet she scurried over to the box and somehow managed to squeeze herself into a curled position towards the back behind them. Immediately the puppies scampered around to get a decent position in the feeding queue.

'What are we going do now?' John asked as we backed away to give the mum and her pups some space.

It was a fair question. Including this new dog and her six puppies, we now had 11 dogs in the compound. When Jena finally gave birth, that number was going to rise even higher.

I looked at Dave and then at John.

'I have no fucking idea,' I said. And I really didn't.

*

The scatty white dog had been easy to name. It was a fore-gone conclusion really: Taliban, or Tali for short. She'd crawled in under the gate and left us to deal with six little booby traps.

Tali didn't answer to her name. Even if she had, she was too busy running off around the compound. But she would always climb back into the small fenced area and lie down so the puppies could feed. They were getting bigger by the day. And she had to be more resourceful in keeping herself strong enough to feed them.

Unbelievably I discovered that she had been climbing the only tree in the compound that still had green leaves on it, coming down with a few random feathers hanging out of her now bloodstained mouth. I knew she was quick on the ground, but I hadn't realised she was quick enough to catch one of the many small sparrow-like birds that hopped around on the gangly branches.

If I visited the run while Tali was off exploring I could spend hours mesmerised as the puppies slowly woke up, the small living mass of tiny paws scrabbling over each other. They would all then slowly peel away and explore their surroundings, looking for whatever puppies looked for, probably the familiar warmth of their mum.

One little dark brown and white fella was decidedly smaller than the others, his wrinkled face giving him the look of a little old man. I decided he was definitely the runt of the family. But could he move or what? He reminded me of Fizz Dog the first day we had seen her at the breeders when she had been no older than this. Lisa and I had watched her running buoyantly around the litter, always being forced out of the feeding queue by her bigger siblings.

I carefully lifted each puppy in turn so I could check them over. I had no idea what I was looking for but they all seemed okay, clinging to my hand as I rolled them over in my palm. Most were a mixture of tan or dark browns. Only one was a single colour and that was the biggest pup of the litter. She was perfectly white and looked like a miniature polar bear.

CHAPTER EIGHTEEN

In with the New

'O this is 20C. Nothing to report yet. Over.'
   '0, roger. Out.'

I clicked off the radio and walked away from the run again, trying to generate some warmth. It was bloody freezing. My watch had recorded −12 centigrade the last time I could be bothered to take my glove off to have a look. I didn't need to check the temperature to know it was not a good night to be giving birth to puppies.

As the cold weather had really started to bite during the past few days, Jena had retreated into the box we had provided for her. She had not come out since; she just lay there panting heavily.

The bottom of the box was lined with old clothes and I had covered her over with an old towel, but it was still freezing. It was New Year's Eve: out with the old and in with the new.

If tonight was indeed the night that Jena became a new mum then it was also going to be the night that I really would start to panic.

The lads who were on duty in the sangars had asked to be kept informed. They were having a torrid time in the sub-zero conditions.

After leaving Jena, I took a brisk walk around to visit all of the sangars to check that the lads were doing okay and to wish them Happy New Year.

I had to muffle my laughter when I arrived at the sangar that Taff was manning. I thought he had looked an odd shape as I first glimpsed his silhouette against the crystal-clear night sky through the open gun port of the sangar. He was wearing two down jackets, one on top of the other.

'A bowl of those chips would go down nicely now, eh Taff?' I asked as I climbed into the sentry position next to him.

'Bloody not wrong,' he replied in his deep Welsh twang as we both remembered the moment.

A week or so ago I had been checking on the limited supply of fresh rations that we held in one of the empty ISO containers. The containers had been used to bring the initial supplies out to the compound in Now Zad well before we had ever arrived here.

As I wandered around the 20-foot-high metal containers I had caught a scent in the air that I couldn't quite place.

I moved around to the back of the containers where their positioning had created a hidden, secluded area no bigger than a small room. To my surprise I found a figure crouched over a fair-sized pot on an open flame, occasionally stirring the contents with a spoon. There was an open newspaper and a tin of salt on the ground next to him.

'So what's going on here, then?' I barked.

The marine shot up immediately and spun in the air. His face was a picture as he recognised he had been caught red-handed. It was Taff.

'Oh Jesus, you sacred the living crap out of me,' he said, holding his hand over his chest as if feigning a heart attack.

I stooped over the pot and noticed the potato peel lying on the ground. The smell made sense now. Taff was cooking chips.

I smiled at him. 'And we are doing what, exactly?'

I was extremely curious to see how he was going to talk himself out of this. Taff was known as a master of waffle.

'Missing home,' was all he said as he continued to give the pan a stir. The small cooking pot contained probably four potatoes' worth of cut chips gently bubbling away in the cooking oil that I knew we kept hidden in the back of the container along with the remainder of the fresh rations. Including the potatoes.

I sat down next to him. 'Stealing fresh rations, I see then, Corporal?' I teased him as he used the spoon to fish out a couple of neatly cut deep-fried chips and placed them down on an open sheet of the newspaper. He did it a few more times so there was a nicely draining pile of about ten thick-cut crispy brown chips. He picked up the salt container and lightly coated the chips before handing me a few.

'Want to make yourself an accessory to theft?' he asked.

I grinned back and accepted the bribe. No way was I able to resist.

'Just don't let Steve know you have been in his store, all right?' I winked at him as I picked out a chip and slowly let my tastebuds enjoy themselves. 'Oh yeah, these are good,' I said as I closed my eyes and imagined I was back home on the beach. A pint of lager popped into the picture as well.

Taff added a handful of freshly cut potato to the pan. We sat there quietly, each wrapped in our own thoughts, while the next batch gradually cooked.

The memory fled my mind as the northerly wind that was whistling in through the narrow open slit of the gun port maximised the wind chill. It was probably the equivalent of −19 degrees centigrade at the moment.

'How bloody cold is it?' Taff asked.

Nothing that I could see was moving out there. Strangely, even the dog pack was quiet. I couldn't see or hear any of them out in the open ground that they normally roamed and played in. It really was cold.

'Cold enough to freeze your skinny arse off,' I replied sarcastically.

'I lost all feeling in my feet hours ago,' he shot back. 'I

should be tucked up with a good woman. There should be a law against sitting out here on New Year's Eve.'

'Taff, there are no good women who would sleep with you, not even drunk ones, so don't kid yourself.' I giggled away at my own joke as Taff gave me the finger.

'Happy New Year,' I said as I climbed back out of the sangar and walked around to the next one.

There were no fireworks to signal the turning of the year, just the quiet whistling of the cold wind and the crunching of the crisp covering of frost underfoot as I walked around the compound, blowing crystallised clouds of warm air into the freezing moonlight. But it didn't really matter here; Afghanistan wasn't a place much interested in this kind of ceremony.

When I had completed my New Year call on all the sangars I checked in to the ops room. Even the signaller manning the radio was wrapped up tight in all the warm clothing he could lay his hands on. In his thick woollen mitts he was struggling to turn over the pages of the book he was reading.

'All right, Pen?' Jimmy asked as I quickly checked the log. The doctor was next to him engrossed in writing a letter while wearing thick gloves. 'Any sign yet?'

'Not yet, mate. I'm going back to check again a bit later on,' I replied.

After making a cup of tea, I headed back out in the empty quiet night. The wind, if anything, had picked up as I tried to walk over the frozen ground as quietly as possible.

'You picked the night all right, Jena,' I said to myself as I pulled the zip on my jacket even further up around my neck. It was bloody freezing.

The dog runs were perfectly quiet. If I hadn't known better I would have said there weren't any dogs living there any more. I called out Nowzad's name and waited. But he didn't appear from the darkened storeroom and the semi-cosy warmth of his cardboard box. 'Fair enough, I wouldn't come out either,' I said into the darkness.

I carefully untied the gate fencing and slid into the run we had given to Jena. I removed my gloves so I could untie the fiddly string that held it shut. The metalled gate was icy cold to the touch.

I crept like a mouse into the small storeroom. If anything it felt even colder inside than it did out. My head torch cut a swathe of light through the gloom. I wasn't going to step on any newborn puppies.

I had placed the cardboard box down on top of an old piece of carpet we had scavenged from one of the older buildings. We had lined the base of the box with newspaper and then filled the rest of it up with scrunched-up paper for extra insulation. I had no idea whether that was what dogs about to give birth needed or not. I was making it up as I went along; there wasn't much else I could do.

I knelt down and shone the torch into the box.

'Way to go Jena,' I said quietly as the beam revealed two small newborn puppies snuggled together next to Jena's belly. I placed the torch down so that the beam filled the box and Jena could see it was me. I reached in and stroked her head. She licked my hand before nudging the two puppies and slowly licking each in turn just as if she was showing them off.

I held half of a broken biscuit, one of Jena's favourites, military-grade cardboard flavour. She reached for it and took it gently from my outstretched hand and nibbled away.

'Good girl. Can I have a closer look?' I asked her before reaching in and ever so carefully scooping up the closest small soft black pup.

Jena just carried on munching away on the biscuit as I lifted the little pup out through the opening. I held it in my hand and gave it the once over. It was hardly moving and its little eyes were scrunched up tight. I had heard somewhere a puppy wouldn't open its eyes for a few days; I would have to check on that with Lisa next time I called.

The puppy was tiny; it was no longer than the palm of my hand, its tiny black-haired body felt velvety and warm as I gave its belly a few gentle rubs.

Carefully placing it back down next to the other one I nudged both puppies back towards each other and they both slowly wriggled in closer to Jena's belly.

I covered them with a piece of an old T-shirt that we had put in the box. Judging by the size of Jena's still swollen body, there were a few more deliveries on their way.

I rubbed her head again and then stood up.

'0, this is 20C. We have two new mouths to feed so far, over.'

The radio static hissed for a second before: '20C, roger. Any more on the way? Over.'

'20C, definitely. Over.'

'20C, this is the Hill. Let me know when it's five puppies, over.'

'20C, roger. Out.'

Some of the lads had started a sweepstake on the number of puppies Jena would have. There was about £30 in the pot.

I had about an hour until I was on duty in the ops room myself. That meant I could spend just under an hour in the time accelerator. I couldn't wait.

The crisp morning air took my breath away as I headed over to see Jena; I had left her alone now for nearly three hours. I was eager to see how many more puppies she'd had.

I had rifled a packet of pork stew from the ration store. I reckoned she could do with it; after just the two puppies she had looked thoroughly knackered.

As I knelt down and looked in the box, Jena was lying with her eyes closed. Her belly was nowhere near as swollen as before. The smell of crap and blood was pretty bad. I lifted the box up from around her.

'Good effort, Jena,' I said quietly as I counted the tiny

different-coloured figures lying by her belly. All told we had eight new additions to our compound.

The task I had set myself in rescuing the compound's population of dogs had been daunting enough. The odds seemed even more ridiculous now that our small compound contained five adult dogs: Nowzad, RPG, Tali, Jena and AK, plus 14 newborn puppies. I didn't want to admit it but I had a serious problem. Rescuing them all was going to be a tall order.

I ditched the bloodstained paper and screwed up a few fresh sheets to cover the puppies, who were vying for the best position near Jena's teats. I used a bit of the torn material to give Jena a bit of a clean. She opened her eyes as I worked but didn't lift her head up. I gently stroked her head and offered her the open packet of food. She didn't want it. Instead she slowly closed her eyes again.

'No worries. I'll leave it there for later, all right girl?'

I placed the box back over the huddled mass and backed out of the room. The sweepstake money would be added to the rescue fund that I was slowly putting together. Nobody had guessed that Jena would deliver a monster litter of eight puppies.

I had called Lisa to tell her the news. The silence on the other end of the phone had signalled that she was doing the mental arithmetic in her head.

'That's fourteen puppies.'

'Yes, honey, I know,' I replied, trying not to sound sarcastic.

'How the hell are we going to get fourteen puppies to the rescue?'

'Actually, it's fourteen puppies and five adult dogs,' I reminded her. 'Can you speak to the rescue and make sure they are prepared for what we are sending them?'

'Yeah, I will call them tomorrow. Any ideas on when you are leaving yet?' Lisa asked.

'Maybe a week after my mother's birthday,' I replied. We

couldn't openly discuss dates and places on the phone but we could use a little code. Even if they were listening, the Taliban would have no idea when my mum's birthday was.

'What about transport, have you spoken to anybody yet?' she asked. I think she was now becoming as concerned as I was.

'No, we haven't seen any truck drivers to ask. I don't know what we are going to do if I don't find one.'

'Oh yes, talking of your mum, she has put a little piece in your local paper about the dogs,' Lisa said.

'What?' I asked, slightly worried about what might have been printed. I already had the military telling me not to rescue the dogs. Putting a story in the paper might not have been in my best interests.

'No, it's good; it says that you are trying to save some stray dogs that live in the compound and besides, your mum got it printed not you.'

'Yeah, I suppose it can't do any harm, can it?' I replied.

CHAPTER NINETEEN

Patrol Dogs

The compound had been a hub of activity since long before sun-up. The R & R and lack of replacements had severely affected our manpower. With the company short of numbers, more or less every available member had been recruited for today's patrol into the south-east quarter of the town.

Steve gave me the thumbs up as I took up my position among the lads in the patrol that was forming up prior to departing.

'Ready?'

'Born ready, bring 'em on,' Steve replied, his excitement at taking part in the patrol rather than spend another morning frying sausages in the galley plain to see.

'Just keep an eye on me, all right?'

'All right, Sarge,' he replied as he flicked me a salute and lifted the heavy patrol pack on to his back. Given our lack of men I had commandeered Steve to patrol alongside me, which freed up one of my younger lads to join one of the sections that would be roving more freely.

'0 this 0A leaving now, out.'

The signal was given and we all ran out of the open gate and straight into the myriad of deserted and crumbling alleyways that surrounded our compound to the east.

We'd barely travelled a few yards when I heard Steve calling. 'Pen. Have you been training a new recruit?'

I looked behind and saw that he was pointing forward and to my right. I did a double take.

A large white dog was patrolling along next to one of the lads. Every time the lad stopped and dropped to the ground then so would the dog. It was like he had been trained to patrol with us.

I looked back at Steve and shook my head.

Steve just laughed.

'Am I watching your back, Dushka, or are you watching mine?'

I'd noticed Dushka first a few evenings earlier. A solidly built young white-and-tan dog with dark patches around his eyes, he had taken to hanging around near the back gate when Steve was serving up the evening meal.

Steve and I had started giving leftovers to the dogs outside in the streets of Now Zad. The sound of the creaking hinges would be the signal to the strays camped outside that a possible feeding time was at hand.

The white-and-tan dog would spring easily up on to his long powerful legs and run away about 30 yards from the gate. He would then wait patiently while I scooped the food into several old plates and placed it out evenly around the back gate. As soon as I took a step back he would trot over cautiously, sniffing what was on offer, always keeping an eye on me.

His ears had suffered the same fate as Nowzad's; there were tufts of hair sticking out from where they should have been. His slight stump of a tail would wag madly from side to side as he ate.

I had been in the sangar overlooking the gate when I glimpsed him, playing along with a small white dog that was the spitting image of Tali. The white dog stood only as high as the larger dog's belly but that didn't faze it. The pair were play-fighting with each other as they tussled on the muddy ground. Every now and again the white dog would stand up.

When he did so his coat looked like a patchwork quilt of dried mud stains and white hair.

They were the friendliest of the dogs that still gathered outside the gate, but I had no intention of adding them to the dog pound. We had more than enough to contend with. But I thought it wouldn't hurt to name them. So, the big beast dog became Dushka, which was the next size up in Russian weaponry after RPG and AK. Predictably I called the other one Patches.

With Dushka still moving along with us like a professional marine, we had patrolled a few hundred yards from the compound.

Most of the alleys and buildings around us were beyond repair. Those that remained standing were just broken shells, shadows of their former glory.

I signalled to Steve to look in the direction I was pointing. Just one house stood untouched. With its white painted walls, it looked like a high-quality piece of construction, for this area, anyway. Where the wall had been chipped by shrapnel there was solid brickwork underneath. The metal-rimmed windows and second-floor balcony suggested somebody with money and influence had once lived there. But as I carefully patrolled along the small low fence that marked the property's boundary it soon became clear that the front of the building was just an illusion.

The rear of the house was no longer there. In its place sat a crater surrounded by large chunks of mud, which had landed in random clumps in an ever-increasing circle from the centre of the impact.

I shook my head at Steve and he just hunched his shoulders back at me. The chaos and destruction that an aerial bombardment can cause was numbing.

This must have been the scene of a significant fight as the further we moved along the patrol line eastwards towards Taliban central, the more craters and ruined buildings we found. Windows, where there had been any in the first place, were just shattered frames. Along with our patrolling dog we were walking through a ghost town.

The boss called a halt over the radio so I took the opportunity to look into the nearest building. The door was missing and the mud wall was peppered with bullet holes. I turned and looked 180 degrees away from the building. Standing proud and defiant was the top of the hill. Somebody had obviously had reason to place some well-aimed shots towards this building. From the size of the holes it looked like rounds from a sniper's rifle.

We were trying to build up a picture of the Taliban's recent movements so every now and again we stopped the patrol to check buildings for the tell-tale spent bullet cartridges scattered by open windows with a view towards the compound or the hill.

With the lads on watch outside the building I ventured slowly inside what was left of a single-storey building, the muzzle of my gun leading the way through the door; the butt of the rifle sitting firmly in my shoulder. Self-preservation was all I had on my mind.

The whitewashed room was almost bare. An upturned chair lay over by the far corner. Strangely a picture of a beautiful wooden Swiss villa high in an Alpine pasture hung on the wall, a slight tear in one corner. Looking closer I saw that it was an official poster advert for the Swiss tourist board.

It wasn't the first time I had seen this. We'd come across several former shops and residences that displayed similar pictures. I made a mental note to ask Harry what was the fascination with Swiss mountain chalets.

I progressed through the building, stepping around a pile of rubble from the rear outer wall that had collapsed inwards. There was no sign that anybody had been here since it was abandoned.

I entered a room towards the rear of the bombed building; the walls had been painted an immaculate white. A large brightly coloured carpet covered the floor. A table with a red tablecloth stood along the back wall. The only ornament was a small two-inch-high vibrantly decorated case sat squarely in the heart of the table. Curious to see what it was but wary of booby traps I cautiously approached the table. It struck me that it looked as if it was a makeshift altar of some description. I carefully lifted the red cloth to check under the table but it was just a hiding place for several flat square red cushions, the sort you would kneel on in church.

I stood upright and carefully lifted the square lid of the case. Inside was a plain hardbound red-jacketed book. It was a copy of the Koran. I delicately lifted the cover of the book and flicked through a few pages. I had no idea what I was looking at – the swirling lettering made no sense to me – but I had no doubt as to what it was. Why else would anybody have left it?

It belonged to this house.

I carefully closed the book and the protective case. I hoped the owners of this house would one day be able to return.

As the patrol moved further away from the DC we entered the habitable areas. Steve had yet to experience the delights of the hordes of maddening children as they demanded pens, sweets and anything else that wasn't secured to your person.

'We must be able to give them something?' he yelled back as we turned a corner through a rickety old wooden gate where three youngsters stood watching our progress. The older girl was dressed in long blue trousers and a flowing blue top, her head and shoulders covered by a bright pink shawl. The young lad's hair was cropped short and in his faded off-white baggy shirt he held his hand out towards Steve in what had become a familiar gesture.

I threw Steve some boiled sweets. 'Give them those and walk away quickly.'

I knew what Steve was feeling; we had all been there. It

was that powerless feeling you got when confronted by a group of totally innocent kids of not being able to do more. A group of kids that hadn't asked to grow up in the midst of a war they knew nothing about.

I looked across at a group of older men who were stood watching our progress. They were laughing.

'Harry, can you ask them what is so funny, please?'

Harry stopped and turned to look at the men, who were all dressed in long blue robes and had full black beards that nestled on to the top of their chests.

'I don't need to ask,' he replied. 'They are laughing at our new friend.'

Harry had turned the opposite way and was pointing at Dushka, who was sat on his rear legs waiting patiently for the marine next to him to start moving again.

I had forgotten Dushka was still casually trotting along-side us. I imagined for the local people it was indeed a funny sight.

We turned on to a larger street that even had the odd battered 4x4 truck parked haphazardly along its side.

From behind us I could hear the noise of an approaching truck. We had orders to stop and search all vehicles, which for me was an added bonus. I had another motive, of course.

Over the net I informed the boss of my intention to carry out a search. The patrol went to ground and held position while we blocked the road as the truck lurched into our street. The driver had no choice but to come to a reluctant stop as he faced several heavily armed marines.

By the state of the truck I assumed we had just stopped the Afghan equivalent of a UK boy racer. The truck had a single front cab that had been painted with pictures of what appeared to be a brightly decorated mosque set among imaginary mountains.

From the bumper hung hundreds of shiny metal heart-shaped discs on chains and, to cap it off, the driver's name was printed on the bottom of the windscreen. It was a safe guess that this driver was fiercely proud of his vehicle.

As Harry talked with the driver two of my lads checked out the cargo bed of the truck. There among neatly stacked household furniture were two skinny goats tied loosely to the side of the truck by rotten string.

'Where is he going, Harry?' I asked as I walked back around to the front of the vehicle.

'He says he is moving his family to Lashkar Gar,' Harry replied.

'Why is that?'

After a quick exchange Harry replied, 'Too dangerous here with British and the Taliban.'

'Has he seen any Talibs?' I asked, even though I knew the answer would be no.

'Harry, please ask him if he wants to work for me for one trip. I will pay well.'

Harry translated to the driver, but again I had figured out the answer before he responded from the raised shoulders and waved arms.

'No, Penny Dai, he says it will be too dangerous.'

I had been asking the drivers – and there hadn't been many of them – whom we had seen over the last few patrols and it was the same answer all the time. Nobody was willing to help me, even if I was paying in American dollars.

I waved the driver goodbye as we continued with the patrol, feeling slightly deflated. There had to be somebody who would drive the dogs to Kandahar for me.

CHAPTER TWENTY

Down the Drain

'Well, where the hell are they?' I shouted across at Dave as he double-checked the small run.

'I don't bloody know,' he replied in desperation.

We had casually walked over to feed the dogs after breakfast. For once we had loads of time on our hands and we'd been looking forward to being greeted by an eagerly waiting Tali and her pups. To our horror we'd arrived to find the filthy box that should have been home to six puppies was empty.

'Oh shit.'

Nowzad and the rest of the gang were barking and jumping up against the HESCO fencing in anticipation of feeding time. They were going to be disappointed. We had to find these puppies first.

'Reckon the ANP took them?' I said as we both ran back to the gate that Tali had crawled under over two weeks ago.

The earth was undisturbed where I had filled in the gap from her burrowing. If she had left the compound it had not been that way.

'No, they wouldn't have done,' Dave said, looking at me questioningly. 'Would they?'

The truth was I didn't know for sure. I didn't think the new ANP crew would get involved in something like this. They seemed to be fitting in well and knew from our talks over tea that I was looking after the dogs. I hoped they hadn't betrayed my trust.

As I tried to clear my head it struck me that Tali might have just wanted some peace. So many of the lads had been coming over to see her and Jena and the two sets of puppies that maybe she'd decided she'd had enough. So she had gone off to find somewhere quiet. But where?

'Where the hell would she have gone?' I asked out loud as Dave and I both jogged back around to the living areas.

The dogs were tolerated within the compound because they were out of sight and out of mind. I couldn't have Tali popping up under the boss's feet.

'Tom, have you seen Tali?' I asked as we passed him on his short walk to take up his watch.

'No, sorry,' he replied as he continued on his way.

'Crap.'

The story was the same when we asked around the compound.

It was beginning to become clear to me. Tali and her puppies were gone. For a moment a wave of slight relief washed over me; maybe it was better this way. After all, we had our hands full looking after Nowzad, RPG, AK, Jena and her eight puppies. Maybe it was for the best that Tali had decided to leave.

'Maybe we will find her later?' Dave said. 'We still have to feed the others.'

'Yeah, you're right. Come on,' I replied.

As we turned to walk back across the slowly thawing compound, we passed Harry chatting away happily to Rosi outside the ANP sleeping room. It was still too early and cold for the other members of the ANP to be up.

'Have you seen Tali, the white dog, the one with the puppies, Harry?' I asked hopefully.

'No, I haven't see the dogs,' he replied.

Without me having to ask, Harry turned and spoke to Rosi, whose face immediately lit up, his big beaming smile just too infectious for us not to smile back.

'Yes, yes,' he said excitedly as he pointed to a small mud tunnel that disappeared under the track across the ANP garden, no more than ten feet from where we stood.

'What?' I asked as Dave and I moved towards the darkened hole.

'Rosi says that he saw the mother taking her puppies in there this morning,' Harry translated after consulting Rosi.

'Really?'

I bent down to look at the tunnel properly. It was no more than half a foot in diameter, but within a few inches the tunnel was shrouded in darkness. The path was over eight feet wide and I quickly moved over to the other side where in theory the tunnel should reappear. I could only assume it was used as drainage for the area of the ANP accommodation which flooded every time we had a downpour. The tunnel would allow the water to drain away into the garden.

Except that where I should be seeing a tunnel exit I could only see a sea of solid mud that had blocked the hole a long time ago. It explained why the immediate area outside the ANP building flooded every time it rained.

'Better come and have a look at this, Pen,' Dave said. He was by now kneeling in the wet mud by the tunnel entrance. 'Tali, you stupid dog, what are you doing in there?' He lifted his head up, his torch firmly in his right hand.

'No, don't tell me she really is in there?' I said, but I knew she was.

'Yup, probably about four feet in as well.'

That put her somewhere firmly in the middle underneath the stone and mud path.

Rosi was grinning like a Cheshire cat. He was happy that he had been able to help us. We would never have thought to look in the partially hidden tunnel in a million years.

I looked north towards the snow-capped mountains. The dark rain clouds were gathering pace again. We had been forecast rain and they normally didn't disappoint.

'Looks like all the puppies, too,' Dave said grimly. 'You know it is going to rain don't you?'

'Yeah and this area will flood again.'

I was about to turn and get some help from the lads who were off duty, but Rosi was already stood in front of us with a shovel he had obviously borrowed from the ANP garden. 'Yes,' he said smiling.

I smiled back. 'Yes.'

I looked at Dave, who was smiling at Rosi too. 'Yes,' I repeated. It was time to do some digging.

We knew that we could entice Tali to leave the tunnel. A simple open packet of pork and dumplings would do the trick, but it wouldn't get the puppies out. They were too far towards the back of the tunnel to be reached even by lying on the ground and extending our arms in as far as they would go. Tali had well and truly hidden them.

My earlier thought that she had moved her pups because she was fed up with the constant attention that came her way as one and all in the compound attempted to see the new arrivals had turned out to be correct.

The sight of me and Rosi taking turns in slowly digging at the sealed end of the tunnel started to draw attention from the lads as they came on and off sentry duty. Those who were going on rest immediately volunteered their services to help with the dig. It was not a straightforward case of just digging a hole and pulling the puppies out. We didn't know exactly where they were in the tunnel under the path. As we were standing on the path, we had to be careful not to collapse the tunnel, thereby burying the puppies alive. So we started at the sealed end and were slowly and very carefully working our way back towards where the puppies were.

The earth was still soft from the constant rains, which made the digging fairly simple. However, I was still glad when I had finished my brief spell on the shovel and the digging tool was snatched from my hand by the young Abdulla Tip. I wasn't quite sure whether he was a volunteer himself or had been volunteered by the commander, who now seemed to be officiating from the comfort of the mattress that had been laid out on one of the metal beds by the doorway.

I had to smile.

Even with an open packet of pork dumplings wafting down from the drainage entrance Tali was refusing to come out. The lads were trying to dig as carefully as possible but Tali was obviously still spooked. She must have been if food wasn't getting her to take the bait.

'We're through,' John shouted.

In the gathering gloom he was already on his hands and knees shining his torch into the fist-sized hole he'd dug.

Everybody stood back as John stretched his arm into the hole up to the shoulder.

'Got one,' he yelled.

As he stood up the grey-white puppy appeared in his hand. While John took the puppy over to the box that Abdul was carefully holding I knelt down to retrieve the next one. I looked inside the darkened tunnel and could just make out the white form of Tali huddled against the remaining five puppies. It was reminiscent of when I had first seen her in the cave by the gate.

I reached in and carefully grabbed the large white fluffy pup. I thought Tali might bite me as I stole her puppy away but she left me be and I pulled the still sleeping pup from the tunnel.

Rosi wanted a turn. He clumsily dropped to his knees and reached in the hole, pressing his head to the ground so he could get in far enough. I smiled as he removed the small runt-like pup, carefully placing it in the waiting box with the other rescued but still dozing pups.

As the last of the litter was pulled out safely by John, Tali appeared out of the tunnel as if by magic. She followed us as we took the box back to the puppy run, dancing madly around our legs as we walked.

'Better stick her in a run of some type I guess,' Dave suggested as we walked. 'Otherwise she will only move the pups again.'

'Yeah, I think you're right,' I replied. 'What have you got planned for the next hour or so?' I asked as the first drops of rain splattered on the almost dried desert floor.

CHAPTER TWENTY-ONE

A Dinner Invitation

Our relationship with the ANP was growing more and more comfortable.

Most afternoons, if we had no pressing tasks, Dave and John and I would sit with the blue-shirted policemen for an hour, either in the garden or around the entrance to their living quarters. We would sit there, drinking chai tea and generally talking about everything and anything, as long as Harry was with us to do the translation honours (Abdul la Tip's English wasn't quite as good as his). Luckily Harry liked his tea as much as we did.

As the tea flowed one afternoon we all watched amused as John, holding himself in a press-up position, tried to demonstrate to Tin Tin just how exactly it was meant to be done. The ANP lads couldn't grasp why we took part in physical exercise during our downtime. John's demonstration wasn't making it any clearer.

Through Harry they kept asking: 'Why? Why?'

As this had been going on I noticed Jena quietly trotting along behind the row of closely planted trees on the far side of the small garden. She was on her way to the galley. Since having her pups she was becoming a master, or was that mistress, of escapism. We should have renamed her Houdini. Somehow, and we still didn't know how she had done it, within days of giving birth she had moved all of her puppies into the next-door run occupied by RPG and AK.

At first it had taken us a while to figure out where she had gone. We had feared a rerun of the storm drain episode. But as we'd looked in to see RPG we discovered a happy Jena staring out from RPG's cardboard box surrounded by her six puppies. RPG and AK were curled up together in the remaining box.

'How the...?' Dave had asked as we looked on in disbelief.

'Don't ask, I don't know,' I replied as we just stood there. Some things were best left a mystery.

I excused myself from the tea and jumped up shouting after her. Moving quickly I managed to intercept her and take her back to the run.

As I walked by the ANP garden with a bemused-looking Jena in my arms, the Afghans were all staring and laughing.

'What's up, Harry?' Dave asked, looking bewildered.

'They are laughing at Pen and the dog,' Harry smiled.

'Why's that?' I asked too as I detoured over to the garden and put Jena down, leaving her to start sniffing the tall plants along the border.

Rosi spoke to Harry who then translated for us, a big grin on his face.

'You name the dog and chase it like it is people,' Harry explained.

'Yeah, I suppose I do,' I replied. 'Don't Afghans name their dogs, then?'

Harry turned and spoke to the commander and Rosi. They listened intently before bursting out with laughter.

'No,' Harry said, 'they call a dog a dog.'

He then started laughing too.

I turned to John and Dave; they were both stifling laughs. We couldn't hold it in. We all burst out laughing along with the ANP.

I stood up again and grabbed Jena.

'Come on dog, let's go.'

*

The air felt cold and dank as we were led towards the low glow of light somewhere inside the ANP building. The beams of our head torches cut through the darkness to reveal plain grey walls. As we moved sideways we were careful to avoid banging into several cold metal bare beds that were stacked on top of each other and had been shoved to one side to allow access.

Eventually Abdul la Tip stopped by a basic wooden door and knocked politely, obviously waiting for permission to bring us in.

A gruff voice answered on the other side.

I looked down by the floor and noticed four pairs of neatly stacked scuffed leather shoes. I turned to Dave and John.

'Boots off, fellas.'

We bent down to start untying our long bootlaces but Abdul la Tip immediately grabbed my arm.

'No no, Penny Dai, it is good.'

'We will take them off, Abdul; this is your house, my friend,' I said.

Abdul la Tip backed off and waited patiently for us to ditch our boots unceremoniously by the dark leather shoes.

As the door was pushed open we found ourselves in a room that was flooded with bright light. Having been in the dark of the winter night for the last hour or so, it was a shock to the system and my eyes winced.

It was as they focused again that I noticed what was left of the goat hanging from the wall behind us. Bloodstains formed a large heart shape down the dirty wall, where the gutted carcass had been suspended from the soft mud wall by a hook. Not that health and safety played a large part in life out here but they had killed the goat nearly a week ago.

'Don't look at the back wall guys, it might put you off your dinner,' I motioned in the direction of the goat.

'Euuurrgg,' was John's only comment.

Abdul la Tip held the door open for us as we entered the

extremely cosy room. The difference in temperature between the draughty outer room and this was astonishing. I immediately noticed the gas-powered fan heater that was blasting out hot air from the far corner.

The commander and Rosi were waiting to greet us. We all shook hands warmly as if we hadn't seen each other for years, which was a little bizarre as we had spoken only a few hours ago.

Harry had been invited, otherwise it would have been an extremely quiet meal and besides I think he was striking up a fair repartee with a couple of the ANP.

'The commander would like to welcome you to his house and wishes that you enjoy the meal he presents you,' Harry said, standing between us.

'Thank you, Commander, we feel very honoured that you have invited us,' I replied.

It had started as a simple question over tea a few afternoons previously. We had asked what they normally ate for a meal. We hadn't realised that it would turn into a full-blown dinner invitation.

We sat down on the carpeted floor, each choosing one of the oversized cushions that had been laid out around the outer edges of the room.

The walls were neatly painted in two colours, grey on the lower half with a dull yellow orange on the upper half. The thick padded blue jackets that constituted the uniform of the ANP hung along the wall using the same type of hook that was used to hang the goat outside.

It was slightly amusing to see their AK-47 assault rifles hung on the walls as well, the muzzles pointing down towards the floor. Jemel with his basin-style haircut and his wispy trimmed beard entered the room with a bowl of water and a cloth. He bent down towards us offering the bowl.

'To wash your hands,' Harry said, recognising the uncertainty in our faces and chuckling along with the police.

Sporting embarrassed grins we took the opportunity to

rinse our hands as Jemel moved around the room. Abdul followed him with a tray of just washed cups and a scalding hot silver pot of chai tea. A bag of British-looking sugar had found its way on to the tray.

Abdul la Tip served the commander first before moving round to us.

I had John on one side and Harry on my other. Dave sat next to Harry with an even more bubbly than usual Rosi to his left. The remainder of the ANP sat either side of the commander who remained quietly staring at the three of us.

No matter how hard I tried I just couldn't figure out how old the commander was. He was a hard one to read.

His tanned face gave little away; his eyes were the only source of emotion. He clicked his fingers at Adbul la Tip who was waiting patiently by the door. We still hadn't seen Tin Tin, who was obviously tonight's cook.

Abdul la Tip disappeared out of the doorway, detailed to chase up the meal I imagined.

The commander spoke to Harry. The three of us waited politely to discover what they were talking about.

'The commander would like to know how long you have been a soldier,' Harry translated after he had finished nodding to the commander.

'I have been a Royal Marine for seventeen years,' I replied. The commander on hearing the translation nodded his approval.

'And he asks where have you fought?'

'Before we came to Now Zad we fought in Gereshk, before that we have all been to Iraq,' I replied. Again the commander nodded his approval, I guessed.

'And how many Taliban have you killed he would like to know?'

I looked at Dave, who just shrugged his shoulders back at me.

'Tell him I do not know as we have only heard the Taliban go quiet on the radio after we have attacked them.

I can only hope they will not be around to fight another day,' I replied.

This caused an exchange between the commander and Rosi but before I could ask Harry what they were saying Dave piped up with a question of his own.

'Harry, please can you ask Rosi how many Taliban he has killed?'

Harry spoke to Rosi and immediately Rosi let out a war-like cry and waved his arms in the air as he excitedly described what I assumed were his numerous battles.

'He says he has killed many, many Taliban. He says they fear him when he is on patrol and run away.'

The ANP in the room all burst out laughing as they gave Rosi a round of applause. The three of us couldn't help but laugh with them and started to clap as Rosi continued to wave his arms around and shout in the air.

With all the chatter and laughter the room was becoming extremely warm. We would definitely feel the cold when it was time to venture outside again.

Abdul la Tip and Tin Tin came through the door followed by a blast of cooler air from the outer rooms. Both Afghans were carrying a large plastic tray that they placed down on the floor in the middle of the room to more clapping.

On one tray were two full bowls of white rice and about ten large flat breads. The other tray contained two large steaming bowls of ropey-looking meat chunks that floated in a watery sauce and a jug of thick white liquid.

I snuck a quick glance at Dave. We had thought long and hard about accepting the invitation for the meal. We were extremely touched that they had asked us. The problem wasn't that we were ungrateful, but we knew how and where they prepared their food. I had watched the younger members of the ANP making the flat bread and cooking their evening meal out on the hot stones near the rear gate.

The dough for the bread was mixed in two large mixing bowls before being laid out on an enormous flat charred metal plate. The rice, which they seemed to eat every day, was cooked in a large thick pot that was baked black from the naked flames along the outside. But the problem lay at the end of the cooking. When they had finished with the pots and bowls they would be left out during the night to be washed in the morning before breakfast. Maybe it was too dark and cold for them by then? But what I did know was that at night I would sometimes see the compound's stray cats having a field day licking the pots, glasses and bowls clean. I had even chased RPG and Nowzad away from the stacked pile of dirty utensils during the early days when I had attempted to give them a nightly leg stretch.

The ANP version of washing up in the morning would involve cold water along with the palms of their hands. It was their way of life and I assumed their stomachs could take it. But I doubted ours could or would.

For the last two and a half months we had religiously wiped our hands with an alcohol-based gel before handling any food. Any pots or pans that were used for preparing meals were washed in hot soapy water almost immediately. We couldn't afford to get ill, not with the vital jobs we had to do. Running to the toilet pit every ten minutes, especially when the Taliban were attacking, would not be fun.

I was probably doing the ANP a total disservice but I had only to think back to the time I served on board RFA *Sir Galahad* during a deployment to Egypt. Over 90 per cent of the ship's company had gone down with diarrhoea and vomiting at the same time. The experience of being in a cramped environment during an outbreak like that was not something I wanted to repeat.

It was too late to back out now. We had decided it was a once-in-a-lifetime opportunity to experience a meal with the ANP. Just to be on the safe side, however, the three of us had each stockpiled a tidy stash of toilet roll.

The commander indicated that we were to help ourselves. I looked around for the serving spoon but I couldn't see one.

'Use your fingers, Penny,' Harry laughed as he mimed scooping up rice with his right hand.

Fingers it was then. I reached for the bowl of rice and lifted two large clumps of soft rice on to the plate that had been placed before me on the floor. I then passed the rice to John.

I scooped two pieces of the goat out on to my plate as Harry used a large ladle to scoop up some of the thick white liquid, which he then passed to me.

'What is it Harry?' I asked.

'Milk of the sheep,' he replied.

'You mean goat's milk,' I corrected him.

'No,' he replied. 'It is milk from a sheep.'

Dave chuckled away as I took a sip from the ladle. I tried my best not to curl my lips as the bitter-tasting milk hit my tastebuds. I didn't do a very good job. The police had been watching intently and one burst out laughing. I handed the ladle back. Harry dipped it into the jug and took a mouthful of the milk. He didn't pull any faces.

'I am sure Dave would like to try this,' I said.

Dave shot me an 'I'll kill you later' look.

The meat was chewy and fatty but it tasted like it had been cooked in onion gravy. We were all wary of dropping bits of rice on to the carpeted floor. The police seemed to be shovelling the food away without dropping any scraps.

As the plates became empty Abdul la Tip served out the remainder from the large serving bowls. He seemed to be favouring us as he shared it out. I felt guilty having seconds but the commander insisted.

As the plates were cleared away, the faithful tea was poured and we started to talk. The commander wanted to know more about England and how long we would spend there when not in Afghanistan. The police all chatted excitedly when they discovered I was married to a Wren. The commander could not understand how a woman was almost as senior as I was and could tell men what to do. It took several minutes for the discussions to die down.

In the last few days I had thought about how the ANP would patrol out of the compound without us. It had given me an idea.

'Harry, can you ask the commander if he stops and searches trucks or cars when he patrols?'

Harry duly asked the commander and then nodded as he said that the commander did.

'Can you ask him if he could find a vehicle for me?' I asked as I sipped on the third cup of tea in less than half an hour. Abdul la Tip made sure it was never empty.

'The commander asks why,' Harry said.

'I would like to transport the dogs that I look after to Kandahar.'

This caused much discussion between Rosi, the commander and Harry. Finally they looked at me and just like that Harry said what I had waited nearly three months to hear: 'The commander will make it happen.'

I closed my eyes. I couldn't believe someone had finally agreed to move the dogs for me. Not only that but someone who I felt could deliver on his promise.

The next half an hour was spent discussing details and payments. It was going to cost US$400. We were as excited as the police. The plan was simple. The commander would hire a vehicle that would drive from Now Zad to Lashkar Gar; once there another vehicle would transport the dogs to Kandahar and meet up with Lisa's waiting rescue wagon.

I shook hands with the commander. It all sounded so simple. Why had I not thought of this before? But I guess the 400 dollars had probably made the difference.

'We are going to celebrate,' Harry announced as Abdul la Tip was sent from the room. He returned within seconds carrying a pack of playing cards.

'But we don't have any money,' Dave admitted as we looked at each other.

'No, no, Dave, we do not play for money, only for the fun of winning.'

Again we looked at each other.

'I will teach you,' said Harry.

We should have spent the next two hours sleeping but we whiled away the time playing Afghan cards. The idea of the game was to 'out-trump' your opponent, although with Harry having to watch our three hands and his own it was normally Rosi who was triumphant at the end of each game.

Finally, as we ate the last of the oranges that had been produced during the fourth or fifth game it was time to say goodnight.

We shook hands and bade the policemen farewell. As we walked out into the cold night I felt something I'd not felt since arriving here in Helmand. I finally had a sense that I'd formed a bond with the people I had come to Afghanistan to help.

And maybe, just maybe, I had at last found a way to rescue the dogs of Now Zad.

CHAPTER TWENTY-TWO

Lewanay

I had fed the dogs and missed breakfast to join John on the early-morning run out into the desert to meet the incoming resupply flight.

Normally, the drive out to the LS was a cautious one as we kept an eye out for any nasty surprises. Today, however, it was one of the more amusing trips I'd made. We had company.

As we drove under the watchful eye of the hill, Dushka and Patches were trotting happily alongside us.

The sight was clearly entertaining the lads on the hill.

'20C, this is Hill, are you fitness training the dogs now, over?'

'Hill, this is 20C, just watch for the Taliban, out.'

With ranks still going on R & R, including the CSM, I was now standing up to take on the role of the company sergeant major. On its own, it wouldn't have been too much of a problem, but right now I really didn't want the extra responsibility. As Dutchy was on R & R as well, I had to manage both our troops. Juggling all these hats was going to be a test. Not that I could say anything, but I was also conscious of the fact that it would leave me even less time to look after the hounds. I would just have to manage my time even more efficiently.

We drove into our defensive position and stopped to wait

for the incoming helicopter. The dogs were panting heavily after their brisk trot but seemed quite happy to sit next to the disembarked lads.

Dushka sat tall and proud as one of the marines roughed his head.

'What are we going to do when the helo comes in?' John asked, looking across towards the dogs.

'I hope they'll run off,' I said as I looked southward, just making out two black dots in the light blue sky.

'Get your gear ready,' I yelled as I lobbed a smoke grenade out into the desert to indicate where the helo was to land. The other was just dropping off an under-slung pallet of stores for us.

Dushka and Patches broke off from their pampering session and looked across in the direction of the cloud of smoke. Watching the dogs as I walked back towards the safety of the 4x4, I could see them reacting to the low hum of the approaching aircraft.

As the noise steadily built it was too much for them. The two dogs ran just like a pair of startled gazelles.

John and I were hunched down, leaning against each other as the helicopter pilot completely ignored my smoke grenade and landed face on to us. I swore under my breath as we were pelted by stones and lumps of soft desert mud. Once again I was really glad that the 4x4 wasn't mine. Between us and the helo pilots we were doing a grand job in trashing it.

When the dust settled and the helos disappeared back to the safety of Bastion, I stood looking in mild disbelief at the pallet lying on the desert floor in front of me.

'John,' I yelled as he loaded the postal sacks into the back of the 4x4. He hadn't looked at the pallet yet.

'What's up?' he yelled back as he continued throwing the sacks on to the flat bed.

'How's your electrical wiring skills?'

'What are you on about?' John had stopped throwing the

sacks now and was stood looking at the pallet with a confused expression.

'Strip lighting.' I turned to face John. 'Why have they sent us a pallet of strip lighting? There isn't even any electricity here.'

We both turned and looked in the direction of the departed Chinook. The pilot had obviously been given the wrong load. The fresh rations and ammunition that we really needed were obviously still sat on the pan at Bastion, or worse, at another out station.

As we drove back to the DC, still cursing whoever it was who had cocked up, we kept a lookout for Dushka and Patches. But like our rations and ammunition, they were nowhere to be seen.

'I think you will find there are two Ps in happy, Cheffy Boy,' I said to Steve as innocently as I could while sipping my warming cup of tea.

'Oh shit, I haven't, have I?' he said, looking horrified and stopping what he was doing at the stove.

Somehow Steve had found the ingredients to rustle up a birthday cake for one of the lads. He'd done a grand job, decorating it with blue icing he'd laid on through a rolled-up newspaper and finishing it off with a large Happy Birthday in thick red creamy letters.

Steve was reading the writing for the second time when the penny dropped and he realised I had got him. 'Bugger off, Sarge, and go and do something useful like burn the shit,' he said.

'Too late, Chef. Already burnt it as we came in this morning while you were still snoozing away.'

I drained my tea and headed off clutching the mail that had come in the resupply. Unusually among the mail from Lisa and my mum were several letters from people whose writing I didn't recognise. I selected one and ripped open the envelope. I pulled out a card. It had a Christmas scene on the front. There was a Labrador and her two young puppies sitting looking at a snow-covered church. There were three kittens in the picture, too.

I read the neatly written message inside:

To you all,

Thank you lads for the great job you do, also for finding the time to help the abandoned dogs. Cheque enclosed.

All the very best
From
Colchester

As I lifted the card a cheque fell on to my lap. It was made out in my name for £20.

I quickly opened the other hand-written letters; all were along the same lines.

I counted the cheques; in all I now had donations totalling nearly £100.

My mum's story to the local paper had attracted some attention after all.

As the warmest place in the compound, the galley had become a magnet for everyone during the cold weather, including the ANP.

Rosi in particular would hang around the door attempting unconvincingly to 'borrow' ingredients while Steve's back was turned. Every time he got caught red-handed he would throw his hands up innocently, provoking gusts of laughter from the lads.

I had tried to pressure Rosi for news of how the commander was getting along arranging the vehicle for the dogs, but always he would point at the sky and shake his head. I didn't know what he was really trying to say but the gist of it was easy to glean. He wasn't having much luck. Which didn't help me as everything now rested on the commander coming good on his promise.

By now Jena's pups had begun scampering around the run, annoying the hell out of RPG in particular as they bit his long ears while he was lying in the sun. Nowzad and AK on the other hand never minded being bothered by the pups. Nowzad would let them paw at him through the fencing grille while AK didn't react at all when they tried to clamber all over her. It was as if she was practising for motherhood of her own. I hoped she and RPG hadn't been getting it on too well. We didn't need any more puppies roaming the compound.

Tali's pups were older and much more interested in trying to explore the outside world. We had moved them into the old building and sealed the door, barricading it up with rocks and wooden supports. Tali could easily jump up to the open window to come and go as she pleased but importantly we didn't have to worry about the pups escaping.

In the morning I would open the door to the room and enjoy watching the comic ritual as the little pups slowly stumbled towards the open doorway, sniffing quietly at the sudden rush of new smells bursting in.

The step leading into the room was probably at least six inches high. They would balance precariously on the edge, all six pups lining up as if waiting for somebody to help them down. But as they all pushed and jostled forwards, their leader, the polar bear puppy, would usually lose her balance and perform a quick head over heels tumble to the desert floor. Immediately she would jump to her feet before giving the 'come on, it's clear' sign to the rest of the litter so they could all follow.

They would then 'bomb burst' in every direction, sending me rushing madly after them as Tali sat unimpressed in the corner watching it all. The whole performance never failed to put a smile on my face.

*

I had told Lisa the good news about the potential help the ANP were going to give us.

'Thank God for that,' she had replied, the relief clearly evident in her voice. 'The rescue truck is ready and waiting to collect the dogs from Kandahar.'

'As soon as I know when I'll be calling you,' I had replied.

But I knew we weren't out of the woods yet. The ANP commander had to fulfil his side of the deal.

It had now been almost a week since the meal and still Rosi shook his head at me when I questioned him about that elusive truck.

Rosi was a real character. Most days he would come to the doorway of the galley and talk for what seemed like hours, attempting to copy our English. We would carry on talking as if he fully understood us, much to everyone's amusement.

'How are you today, Rosi?' we would ask as he arrived at the galley door.

'Yes,' was his emphatic reply as he stood sockless in his scuffed black leather shoes, his dirty blanket pulled tightly around his head and shoulders.

We all enjoyed watching Rosi, with his sunbeaten face screwed up into a beaming smile, his large chubby hands gesturing wildly in front of him as he tried to communicate with us.

'We hate the rain,' I would say to him.

'Yes,' he would reply, raising his eyebrows as high as he could.

'What about you, Rosi – do you like the rain?' Dave would ask.

'Yes,' he'd say. There would then be a pause. 'No.'

Then Rosi would point to the overcast sky and say a word that to us sounded like 'barram'. Together we would repeat it, sending Rosi into a fit of mad clapping and laughter.

'I think we just learned the Pashtu for rain,' I would say.

Rosi had the ability to keep everyone amused most of the

time with his comical antics. It was especially funny watching him chase a flighty chicken around the compound that he had accidentally let loose from the dinner pot. Seeing his light blue robes flowing behind him like a superhero cape as he tried desperately to lunge for the poor chicken was utterly hilarious.

'What is the Pashtu for crazy?' I asked Harry, who was stood laughing with us.

'*Lewanay*,' was his reply.

The compound was soon echoing to a chorus of *lewanay* as Rosi tripped over a bush in the pursuit of his dinner.

When he finally cornered the chicken in a mud alcove, Rosi held the chicken above his head like the captain of a team winning the World Cup. He marched back to the ANP quarters shouting '*lewanay*' all the way.

We all enjoyed Rosi's company. Already I had started to wonder what was going to become of him when we had left.

With less than six days until our planned handover of the compound the boss had called a meeting of the senior ranks to discuss what we could achieve in the last week. The room had fallen silent so I had done what I normally do and spoken up.

'Boss, if we go back to the trashed school in Now Zad we could salvage those schoolbooks that are still usable and deliver them to the Barakzai school,' I said.

I could hear a few heavy huffs from those who weren't thinking along the same lines.

'Why?' the boss asked, sensing my keenness for the idea.

'The Barakzai kids were practically begging us to get their school up and running; we haven't exactly managed to do anything else to reconstruct the town,' I replied, being careful not to overstep the mark.

The boss conferred with the company 2IC before nodding, 'It's all yours, let me have your plan tonight.'

Well chuffed with myself I stayed in the small briefing room and worked out a plan, first to get into the Now Zad school then to get the books back to the compound and on to Barakzai.

I knew it would have to be quick. I didn't want to put anybody in harm's way unnecessarily. It was to be a snatch-and-grab op.

All the usual suspects had volunteered for the patrol, including Steve the chef. I think he had been particularly keen to do something for the children of the area after seeing their lives up close during the previous patrol.

As the advanced group secured the perimeter of the school, my team drove straight into the school compound as if on a bank raid.

'Five minutes, team,' I had yelled. 'Grab what you can!'

With the back of the truck full of books we returned from the patrol to the safety of our compound and immediately began the process of sorting out what we had bagged.

Within half an hour we had several piles of undamaged books covering a range of subjects mainly aimed at primary school kids, including books about animals, maths, English/Pashtu dictionaries and, strangely, some covering the geography of America.

We were soon setting off to deliver the books to the village school in Barakzai. As we headed out, I felt good, like I was finally doing something positive. But that feeling soon dissipated.

Arriving at the village we headed for the elder we'd spoken to during the previous patrol. With Harry translating, he told me how the Taliban had come in to see him after our last visit. In no uncertain terms, they threatened them with violence if he accepted any support or help from us.

He told us that the only sensible thing he could do to protect his people was to reject the books. Unless, that was, we stayed there to protect them.

As Harry translated his words for me I had a terrible sinking feeling.

Again I had been fooled into thinking everything would be so simple and fit nicely into place. Afghanistan had proved me wrong again.

As we headed back to our vehicles, Harry was walking slowly in front of me. I grabbed his arm. He stopped and turned to face me; his usual smile was missing.

The wind had picked up and it felt much fresher again now that we were out of the village and on our way back to the compound.

I looked directly at him as I spoke.

'I am sorry Harry.' I paused. 'We have been here three months and achieved nothing for you or your people, have we?'

He held my gaze. 'No, Pen, you have not been here three months.'

I looked at him, confused; his English was normally perfect.

'Yes, it is three months,' I replied. I didn't want to get in an argument.

He continued looking directly at me. 'No. You have been here five years and still the people are scared.'

I looked away; I didn't know what to say.

We hadn't gone into Afghanistan because of the atrocities of the Taliban originally. We'd gone in because of one man and his orders to massacre thousands of innocent lives with the destruction of the Twin Towers. Now the mission had changed and it was about the people of Afghanistan and the suffering they were enduring. Taming the wild lands of Afghanistan would take time; everybody knew that. But maybe the international community was not pulling its weight as much as it should be.

I desperately wanted to promise Harry that one day the nightmare that was the Taliban would be gone, but right at that moment I couldn't. I couldn't promise anything that involved any politician from whatever country keeping their resolve. That was well above my pay scale.

'Sorry,' was all I could muster.

I turned and continued the chilly walk across the desert.

As we patrolled back towards the compound along a track that divided two ploughed fields I was acutely aware that it would be the last time I ever set foot outside the town of Now Zad. Even if I did ever come back to Afghanistan, I doubted very much that I would find myself based back in the compound.

Today's failed patrol just about summed up our wasted three months here, but I wasn't looking at the bigger picture, I supposed. The benefits of our holding the compound at Now Zad wouldn't really be seen for another two years when, thanks to our success in clearing the Taliban away from the Sangin valley, the turbines of the strategically vital Kajacki Dam would be installed in the summer of 2008.

But right now the refusal of the Barakzai schoolteacher to accept the teaching supplies felt like a kick in the teeth.

I sat looking south-west across the dried mud tops of the buildings, enjoying the last glimpses of the late-afternoon sun as it descended behind the distant mountains.

I didn't even register the barbed wire no more than two feet in front of me. Instead I was walking on those mountain ridges with Nowzad happily strolling by my side as we explored the uncharted Afghan peaks. Every now and again we would stop to stare at the glorious views laid out before us, I would reach down and pat him as he quizzically cocked his head to one side as a new smell or noise caught on the wind.

He was a good dog – he would have been totally misunderstood back in the UK. His scarred and pitted face with his grossly chopped ears would have frightened even the hardiest of dog lovers. But if you looked beyond that at the brown-tinted eyes you would see a dog that was happy just being by your side.

'Penny Dai, Penny Dai,' the calling from below me in the compound caught me by surprise.

'I am up here, Rosi,' I called back.

He spoke fast and with much waving of his arms. I had no idea what he was saying.

Over the last weeks of talking with Rosi the only worthwhile bits of Pashtu I had picked up were 'hello' and 'thank you'. I guessed that what Rosi meant was he still had not found a vehicle. The look of shame in his eyes was plain to see. I shook my head in sympathy with his plight.

'I know, Rosi,' I said, patting him on the arm. I knew he had no idea what I was saying but I felt he needed to hear me say something in return.

'You can't find a truck for me – all the money in the world won't get the dogs to Kandahar.'

Whether that's what he was saying or not, I knew it was true. With just days to go now I had resigned myself to the fact that the dogs were not going to the rescue. I felt so hopeless. Rosi sat down next to me obviously satisfied with my answer. Neither of us needed to say anything.

In silence we looked west again to the distant hills, the sun now an orange faded memory behind the darkened mountainside. I tried to picture myself and Nowzad back up on the ridge line but this time the image just wouldn't come.

My moment of hopeful reflection had passed.

CHAPTER TWENTY-THREE

The Taxi

Dushka looked at me with a puzzled expression, his head held at a slightly skew-whiff angle, his hacked-off ears pulled back.

I think I understood his confusion. This was probably the first time anybody had made a real fuss of him.

I had tried my best to ignore him. Leaving Nowzad, RPG, Tali, Jena or AK was going to be heart-wrenching enough. I didn't need to get attached to another dog in the days before leaving. But of course it wasn't that easy.

Often I'd seen Dushka curled up next to Patches outside the compound wall at night. I'd look at both dogs lying out in the open waste ground, a thin layer of frost coating their thick coats as they slept, knowing there was nothing I could do for them.

But as I fed him some scraps tonight I couldn't help but make a fuss of him.

Dushka responded to my playful rubbing of his head by pushing his head into the folds of my jacket. I responded by whispering quietly in his missing right ear. Dushka had to be the biggest dog I had ever encountered this close, but he was also the softest dog too. Even Beamer boy would trail a poor second behind Dushka in the softness stakes.

I couldn't imagine the life these dogs had endured. But as I gave him what was probably the first bit of compassion he'd ever been shown I wondered whether I'd done the right thing for him and the other dogs. I'd given them a totally unfounded trust in humans. When I was gone that might not be the best thing for them.

The following morning dawned grey and overcast, a light drizzle complementing the bitterly cold easterly wind. After the morning meeting I walked to the galley to collect the leftovers from the night before. I was greeted by the usual sight of an escaped Jena waiting patiently at the head of the breakfast queue. I shook my head, made a fuss of her then reminded her that she breakfasted over in her run.

'You are meant to be a responsible parent these days,' I said.

She happily followed me and the smell of yesterday's sausages back to the run. The others were waiting in their respective kennels, all unusually subdued, probably due to the dramatic drop in morning temperature. Jena was a persistent offender at escaping and we had now become accustomed to her doing the Houdini thing every day.

I fed the dogs their breakfast and tried to make a fuss of each in turn. For some of the dogs, this would be the last time I would ever feed them.

I reluctantly left the dog runs to grab Dave and John; we had one thing left to do.

'This compound will have to do, ' I said as I surveyed the abandoned old compound we were stood in one more time.

I kicked the desert floor in frustration. I was in agony emotionally. I looked across at Dave and John. Their faces were drawn and tired. I knew they felt the same as me.

Time had run out and had left us with no other option.

Our time in Now Zad had come to a close. In just under two hours Lima Company of 42 Commando would relieve us. The boss had turned a blind eye to our small dog-welfare operation. I couldn't count on the incoming officer to be as accommodating. And besides, I didn't know anybody in the arriving group who was even remotely interested in dogs.

Even if there was, I wouldn't be in the compound during the handover operation. I would be out in the desert arranging the positioning of the escorting convoy that would be taking us overland back to Bastion.

Dave and John too would have their own responsibilities during the handover, so there would be nobody to look after the dogs. The dogs would have to leave the Now Zad compound when we did.

'What about water?' Dave asked.

'There are some buckets over there,' John said, pointing to a few old rotten buckets that had been discarded in one corner of the compound next to a long ago disused diesel generator.

I slowly turned through 360 degrees and surveyed the 100-foot-square compound.

The 15-foot-high mud walls that made up the four sides of the compound were cracked and crumbling slowly from the bottom up. Just a lone metalled double gate in the north wall provided access in and out.

Just one corner sprouted a small patch of dried grass and the remainder was barren desert mud. Except for the generator there was nothing else to be seen. What it had been used for would remain a mystery.

I walked over towards the corner furthest from where I had been standing; a piece of dull metal had caught my eye in the sun.

'Oh, fantastic,' I called over to the other two who were carrying out a check of the other barren corners.

Lying on the floor, no more than a foot in front of me, was the brownish green warhead of a foot-long rocket-propelled grenade. It had failed to explode.

'Some unexploded ordnance over here,' I said as the other two strolled over.

'Nice,' Dave said, recognising the weatherbeaten casing immediately.

I knelt down and studied the ground around the warhead. I could clearly see the indent in the softened mud where the grenade had impacted.

Cautiously I reached down and picked it up by the safe end. Dave and John automatically took a step back each.

'And where are you putting that?' they said as I turned and carefully walked towards the open gate.

'We can't have the engineers blowing anything up if the dogs are in here, can we?' I said as I studied the ground in front of me. The last thing I wanted to do was trip over with an RPG in my hand to break my fall.

Our only option was to move both sets of puppies along with Jena and Tali into this deserted compound that lay across from our occupied one. We had never seen anybody using it since we had arrived.

As the ANP detachment was staying in the DC for at least another month I had brokered a deal with Rosi to feed the puppies for the remainder of his stay.

I had already put a pile of ration packs to one side for him to use. I had to trust him; he had promised that he would not let any locals take the puppies. When the time came to leave he would leave the compound gate open. I knew it wouldn't be long before they succumbed to starvation, but at least this way they would have a chance to put on a bit of weight and have a fighting chance to fend for themselves in the streets and alleys of Now Zad.

Nowzad, RPG and AK would find it the hardest. I knew they would try and get back in; hell, I had fed them two meals a day, more or less, for the last three months. For them it would be a hard habit to break. I realised now that I should have kicked them out earlier. Leaving it until the last minute was a big mistake.

For days now I had sat and anguished over this situation,

delaying the inevitable until the last moment. Until now I had truly believed that the ANP commander was going to fulfil his side of the bargain. He had arranged a truck to take the dogs from Lashkar Gar to Kandahar, but he just could not find anybody to take the dogs on the first part of the journey of just 60 kilometres.

I knew the journey would be through some of the most loyal of Taliban areas, but I had, probably foolishly, clung to the hope that we could still find a driver. After all we'd been through, I really should have known better.

I walked out the open gate and waved the unexploded grenade at the nearest sangar. The marine on watch just waved back. I warily placed it well away from the compound entrance and walked back in. I could tell the engineers about it later.

'It will have to do, fellas; we don't have time for anything else,' I shouted over to Dave and John, who were stood talking quietly to each other, their rifles hanging limply by their sides. I recognised the look of calm resignation on their faces. 'We can use that old corrugated iron to make a shelter for each set of puppies in opposite corners,' I added.

I looked around the completely empty square compound one more time. 'Come on, let's go get Tali and Jena; we don't have much time left.'

At least the compound would shelter the pups from the worst of the bitter wind and rain – not that I could draw any comfort from that thought.

I waited for Dave and John to walk over to me and then turned for the gate.

The sound of Tin Tin shouting excitedly caught us all by surprise. We looked up to see his silhouetted figure balancing on top of the compound wall looking down on us. He was shouting something but I didn't know what.

'What's up, Tin Tin?' I shouted back.

I knew he couldn't understand me.

'Listen.' Dave motioned for us to shut up.

It was then we realised that he was repeating just one word over and over.

'Taxi.'

'Is that a bullet hole?' I asked Dave, still slightly out of breath from the sprint around to the gate. We were with an extremely happy-looking Rosi.

'Yeah, that looks like a bullet hole to me, all right,' he replied as we stared at the dirt-splattered windscreen of the battered white minivan. The van had suddenly arrived at the compound gate accompanied by the ANP commander and Abdul la Tip.

It was being driven by a poorly dressed middle-aged local. The dashboard of the van was decorated with sun-faded plastic flowers and the front bumper was dented and broken from less than careful driving. The driver's dark eyes were nervously darting from one marine to another as he drove along the uneven track into the compound. He was clearly uneasy and I suppose I couldn't really blame him.

The commander gave me his best smile as he approached me. Abdul la Tip was close behind as the commander spoke to me while clasping my right hand with both of his.

'The commander has got you a taxi my friend,' Abdul la Tip translated.

'I am eternally grateful, Commander,' I replied, smiling like the Cheshire cat from *Alice in Wonderland*, 'very last-minute but very grateful.'

Klaus, our resident Dutch reconstruction adviser, and Harry the Terp had strolled over to see all the commotion. The grins on their faces told me they both realised what was happening. They both knew how much it meant to us to be able to get the dogs to safety.

I grabbed Harry's hand as we both smiled like small kids.

'Harry, can you tell the driver that we will get the dogs travel crates?' I didn't wait for the reply but along with Dave and John darted off to grab the crates that we had built a long time ago for this very moment.

I didn't hear the brief exchange but as I arrived back with RPG and AK's crate I twigged that something was not right. Harry, the driver and the commander were all engaged in a heated debate. Finally they broke off and Harry turned to face me.

'The driver will not take the crates. It is too dangerous for him. If he is stopped the Taliban will know it is for Westerners. He will only take the dogs as we would carry them.'

'You mean, just free in the back?' I asked.

'No, Penny Dai, the dogs must be tied up,' Harry replied.

I looked at the driver and then at the still unemotional eyes of the commander. There was no time for debate.

'John: go find some heavy-duty string from the store and Dave, can you go and get that tin box by the living compound? We can use it to put Tali's pups in.'

'We will need to rig something up to stop them scampering out,' Dave shouted as he turned and ran off.

'Harry, can you ask the commander for the birdcage that I know he has?'

I didn't have time to be polite about it. I had spotted it during our brief peek in the ANP quarters when we had first arrived over three months ago.

'Yes, but you must hurry; the driver does not like being here.'

'Tell him I am hurrying.'

I knew the journey would take several days. The plan had always been that a local would get the dogs to Lash and then the police would assist in transporting the dogs to a meeting point nearer Kandahar. I couldn't do anything about the fact that there would be two different change-over points, both run potentially by Afghans who didn't actually like dogs.

With the dogs not being in cages I had no idea how they would handle them. And what about Nowzad? He didn't really like anybody else apart from me and then I still had to be careful. Hell, he still gave Dave and John the evil eye.

As we carried on with the preparations to put the dogs in the van, an even bigger problem was beginning to form in my head. Looking at the cramped van, I could see that there simply wasn't room for all the male dogs.

I would have to make a choice. There was no way Dushka and Nowzad or even Patches could all go in the same small six-seat wagon. It would be carnage. Two of them would have to be left behind.

Instinctively I knew immediately it would have to be Dushka and Patches. Even though deep down I knew Dushka was more sociable with people, I knew that I could not leave Nowzad to remain here now. Not after the last three months.

Time didn't allow me the luxury of pondering it any further. I would be able to do that later during the seven- or eight-hour drive back to Bastion.

Already, however, I could see that if this worked maybe I could get the driver to do the journey again and to collect Dushka and Patches later. It was a big if, I knew.

We had to get the other dogs ready for the taxi; I wasn't about to let this opportunity slip through my fingers. John arrived with the string and coaxed Tali over. She had no idea what was about to happen and with her tail wagging she crawled over to us expecting a fuss.

'Sorry, Tali, but it is for the best, okay?' I said as I lifted and rolled her on to her back. She didn't resist and meekly gave in as we bound her front and rear legs together.

I carefully picked her up and carried her to the waiting van. I placed her down on the front rear seat. She casually propped herself up and stared at me with a puzzled look. I rubbed her ears.

Dave had arrived back with the old metal Afghan suitcase that had been outside the living area for months. He had ripped the lid off and using some old flexible metal wire had quickly fashioned a covering that would stop the puppies getting out.

Carefully he placed Tali's pups one by one into the metal box before gently pushing their heads down as he secured the wire to criss-cross the top. Immediately the large light brown puppy with the darker colouring along the top of its nose poked its head up through the mesh. Dave gently pushed it back down and pulled the wire even tighter.

He placed the suitcase on to the floor of the minivan as Tali looked on.

As I was tying Jena, Tin Tin returned with the commander's old wooden birdcage. The delicately made top part of the hand-crafted cage was connected to the wooden base by three small catches. It easily came apart so we could carefully place Jena's eight pups on to the base before replacing the frame. I secured it with the string as well, as I doubted very much that it had been built for the weight it now carried.

Luckily the pups were still in the clingy puppy stage of life and I hoped they weren't going to be too bothered about being stuck in a birdcage. The only problem I could see was that they would not be able to feed until they eventually made it to the rescue.

There was nothing I could do about that. Our original dog crates would have allowed Tali and Jena to travel with their respective pups but obviously we hadn't contemplated Taliban interference.

I placed the wooden birdcage with its fragile cargo down next to the suitcase containing Tali's puppies.

RPG knew something was up and it took me and Dave a few minutes to corner him in his run as he ducked and dived as we went to grab him. Once caught though he gave in like Tali and Jena and let us tie his paws together.

We didn't need to talk about it. I knew from the look on Dave and John's faces that they were as unhappy about tying up the dogs as I was but it was a means to an end. Either we did this or we threw them out on the streets of Now Zad to face a bleak future. There was no choice.

We put RPG, Jena and AK on the back seat of the van. All three huddled uncomfortably together. It hurt to see the total confusion in their eyes as I closed the rear door. But I didn't have time to make a fuss of them and it hadn't really sunk in that I would probably never see them again. I was working on automatic pilot. The constant sound of the countdown clock echoed in my mind as I quickly jogged round to the run to get Nowzad.

I wondered briefly what the driver thought of dogs sitting on his plastic-covered passenger seats but he didn't protest. I guessed the ANP commander was paying him enough for the journey.

'Come on, then, Dave, give me a hand with Nowzad,' I urged him as I untied the gate to Nowzad's run.

'Get real; he doesn't like me at the best of times. You tie him up,' Dave said, standing outside the fence with John.

'Don't be soft,' I replied as I turned and looked at Nowzad as he bounded over to see me, his tail stump in a constant state of motion.

I felt guilty at what I was about to do.

'All right buddy, it is time to go.'

I quickly fed him two biscuits and made him sit as I tied his front legs together. He was too big and heavy to roll over and I knew he would put up a fight. We knew each other but not that well.

I tied his rear legs together and forced him to hobble over to the gate. He was as happy to be getting out of the run as I was that we had found finally found a vehicle.

As I struggled around the corner carrying a tied-up Nowzad, the driver began shouting and pointing at Nowzad, sheer terror in his eyes.

'What is he saying, Harry?' I asked.

'Fighting dog no good,' Harry replied.

'Tell him it is okay. I will tie his mouth shut, okay?'

Harry and the driver carried on debating the matter for another minute before the driver eventually backed down and agreed. The piercing looks he was being given by the ANP commander may have played their part in persuading him.

I hated myself for doing it and I knew I wouldn't be winning any RSPCA prizes for animal welfare, but I slipped a strip of black masking tape around Nowzad's muzzle, leaving it loose enough so that he could breathe and drink water. If anybody bothered to offer him some on the long journey, that was.

'Sorry, Nowzad,' I said, as I carefully lifted him into the rear of the van and placed him alone on the middle seats. I made a loose-fitting collar from the remainder of the string and secured it to the rail inside the minivan. At least he would not be able to bound over the seats and go for the driver.

'Please hurry, Penny Dai,' Harry said, tapping me on the shoulder. 'The driver wants to leave now.'

'Okay.'

I looked at the dogs one more time, all of them bizarrely staring out the windows like something out of a Walt Disney kids' cartoon about animals on a bus ride.

'Tell him to look after the dogs. Do not leave the doors open if he stops. They will escape if he does,' I told Harry.

To reinforce this, the commander jumped in with his own orders for the driver. The commander knew that I wouldn't pay until the driver had delivered the dogs. I got the impression he was making this clear to the driver, just in case he had any other ideas.

I stood with John and Dave as the driver slammed the side door shut and jumped in behind the steering wheel. A cloud of diesel fumes exploded from the exhaust of the van as he turned the ignition.

The van lurched its way out of the compound as the commander led the driver out through the gates. Through the mud-spattered rear window I could just make out the narrow head of RPG darting from side to side as I am sure he wondered what the hell was going on.

In all it had taken just 20 minutes to load all the dogs onboard.

I turned to face the two lads who for the last three months had given up their time and energy to help me.

'Am I dreaming or did that just happen?' I said, offering my hand first to Dave and then John.

'Talk about cutting it fine,' Dave replied, smiling a big stupid grin of relief at what had just taken place.

'You reckon they will make it?' John asked.

'They have to after all this,' I said.

'We need to pull the runs apart; I don't want the ANP or anybody putting any more dogs in there,' I said. I knew it would make an ideal place to keep a fighting dog in once we were gone. 'Can you two start on that while I speak to Klaus a minute please?'

Klaus was putting away his camera. He had been snapping away while we had tied the dogs. 'You are happy – yes?' he said as I approached.

'Oh yes, indeed,' I replied. 'Can you do me a favour, please?'

I knew that Klaus was staying for another two weeks when we had gone with the new company that was taking over.

'If and when the dogs make it to the rescue, can you pay the commander for me?'

I took the $400 in crumpled notes from my pocket and offered them to him. 'I will get a message to you over the radio net.'

'It is a good thing you have done,' he smiled as he slipped the money into his top pocket.

'Thank you, it feels good that we have done something good here,' I replied as I looked upwards towards the clear Afghan sky. I didn't want to think about the wasted trip to the Barakzai school.

'If this trip works can you put Dushka and Patches in the taxi for the next run?'

I hoped I wasn't asking too much of him.

'Of course I can; he won't bite me will he?' Klaus chuckled as we shook hands.

'Not unless you poke him in the eye.'

The first swirl of smoke filled the air as Dave set alight the blankets and boxes that had once housed the dogs of Now Zad.

The next hour flew by as we saw to the last-minute preparations for the arrival of Lima Company.

Harry for once was quiet as I handed him the present that we had arranged to be sent out. It was a proper cricket bat signed by all the lads. Harry just nodded and shook our hands, a big smile on his face.

With minutes to spare we had said goodbye to the ANP lads, posing together for a group photograph. We had swapped weapons, the three of us kneeling in front of a seated ANP. We had all shaken hands and embraced as we stood up. We all knew we would never see each other again.

As darkness fell and I walked out of the compound gate that been my home for the last three months, I looked for Dushka and Patches.

They weren't there; maybe there were still off playing.

I didn't look back. There were too many memories, too many emotions tied up in those mud walls.

CHAPTER TWENTY-FOUR

Over and Out

'Here we go again,' somebody yelled as we all looked towards the sky. 'Incoming.'

All thoughts of drying out our wet uniforms in the early-morning February sun were instantly forgotten as we scrambled for the safety of the closest building.

'Why the hell have we run inside this one to hide?' Hutch yelled over the noise of the hideously close-sounding 107mm rocket.

It was a valid question. The building's location, at the source of the Helmand River at the base of the Kajacki Dam, was undoubtedly spectacular. It was also within a compound that, apparently, had at one time served as a retreat for the Afghan royal family.

The problem was that it was also where we had stored nearly a month's worth of ammunition. One direct hit and there would be no more royal holiday villa and, more importantly, no more Kilo Company.

The Taliban were firing at us from over eight kilometres away, well out of range for our mortars to be able to strike back. We had no option but to sit it out, waiting for the fast air to arrive while hoping at the same time that the Taliban didn't get lucky.

The air around us vibrated as noise filled the compound, the boom echoing off the surrounding mountains.

'Shit, that sounded like it was in the compound,' Taff shouted, confirming what everybody hunched low against the walls had already gathered.

For some reason, I suddenly found myself thinking about the compound's two resident stray camels. I wondered what they did while all this was going on.

I didn't have time to consider their plight for long. The shriek of another rocket heading our way forced me to flatten myself even closer to the cold concrete floor.

Another 11 rockets landed nearby before the fast jets finally did their thing and we were given the all clear.

As things returned to normality, I stood up carefully. My right ankle was killing me, the throbbing building as the latest batch of painkillers wore off. There was no getting away from it. I would have to see the compound doctor.

It had now been 36 hours since I had gone over on my ankle during an operation to clear the deserted villages that surrounded the dam. I'd known something was badly wrong when I'd tripped as we ran across a hand-ploughed field in the dark. With the ludicrous weight of the kit I was carrying I had clearly heard the snap of something in my ankle as I hit the soft mud, face first.

Thanks to some quick strapping, a few very strong pain-killers and Grant my mortar man's kind offer to lighten my load, the pain had been bearable for a while. But the long operation that followed had overspilled into the night, which was the last thing I'd needed.

On our journey back towards the dam, the latest torrential rain had turned the dry *wadi* we had passed through on our way out into an almost waist-deep flood. Dave and I had spent almost four hours ferrying our heavy equipment back across the *wadi* to our temporary compound. We'd used the company's quad bikes to do the job, leaving the rest of the lads to carry the ammunition by hand back across the *wadi* and back to the former royal retreat.

I had not had a chance to get my boot off during the

entire operation. Which had probably been for the best. I doubted very much that I would have been able to put it back on afterwards.

I found the doctor sitting on the steps to the makeshift surgery. He was actually probably one of the fittest blokes in the unit, but, his being in the Navy, we weren't ever going to tell him that.

'Need you to take a look at my foot please, Boss,' I said.

I had to remove the laces completely just to be able to pull the boot off. Without even removing my sock we could both see my foot was swollen big time. The doctor prodded and poked it, coming extremely close to being punched in the process.

'Nasty,' the doc said.

I bloody knew that; it was my foot.

'Probably broken, I'd say,' he said, prodding the puffed-up ankle some more. 'Yup, Sergeant, you need an X-ray.'

'When?' I asked, although I knew the answer.

'As soon as possible; back to Bastion for you I'm afraid.'

There was an eerie silence as I sat on the LS waiting for the helicopter.

Apart from the sound of the light breeze rustling the row of trees along the nearby dirt track, all you could hear was the gently flowing waters of the Helmand River. In the background the jagged cliffs of the surrounding mountains soared into the grey-blue sky. I could have been taking two minutes out from a chilled walking holiday.

The reality, of course, was that I was still in the middle of a war zone. And I had no choice but to leave my lads in the thick of it.

I had just about managed to say goodbye to most of them as I hobbled around the compound. Putting my boot back on had been extremely painful but I wasn't going to be carried to the LS.

Dave had been still hanging his kit out to dry when I had found him.

'Hear you have got an appointment with some nurses,' he said before I could say anything.

News travelled fast.

'I may have,' I offered, smiling.

'Well you're married so give 'em my number,' he said as we shook hands.

'Keep your stupid big head down, all right?' I told him. 'I'll see you when we get back for a beer.'

'Roger that.'

I hadn't seen John; he was around the compound some-where doing his thing. I had asked Dave to say goodbye for me.

Most of my lads were around in the sangars on duty and would probably find out I had left during the evening meal, I guessed. As always time was short. I had to hobble to the LS.

As I sat against my rucksack I felt my eyelids growing heavy as the tension and stress of the last few days faded. For some reason the image that filled my head was of RPG, sitting on the sand-filled boxes waiting for his breakfast; I smiled to myself as it brought back happy memories.

I thought about the last few days; they had gone by in a blur. It was now six days since we'd left Now Zad, six days since we'd put the dogs in the taxi. There had been no news.

I'd managed to have a good talk with Lisa when we'd arrived at Bastion. It was good to hear her voice again but she had heard nothing from Afghanistan either. It was going to take at least three to four days to get to the north of the country. There were going to be changes of car and three drivers in all. In reality the dogs had only just begun their long journey.

Within two days of landing at Bastion we had been turned around and redeployed here to Kajacki. We had been given just enough time to grab our cleaned washing from the laundry, pack our bags and form up for the departure for this operation. But within days I was already on my way back, perhaps for good.

At least my trip back to the hospital at Bastion would give me a chance to find an Internet terminal. I figured that I might be able to find out any updates on the dogs' progress. I kept my fingers crossed.

As the sound of the river filled the air, that was my last thought as I drifted off. I have no idea how long I had been dozing when the roar of the helo landing woke me up.

As Lisa read me the email for the second time, it seemed even more brief and to the point than it had been the first time.

'It says: "Hi, we have two brown dogs and a white dog with 13 puppies from Helmand."'

'That's definitely all it says?' I asked again.

'Yes, there was nothing else attached to the email. I told you,' Lisa said, the impatience in her voice clear.

Communications between the UK and Afghanistan were never great. I had got used to it, just about.

As I said goodbye to Lisa and absorbed the raw information within the email a million questions were flying around my head.

The white dog, without doubt, that was Tali. She was the only white dog that we had tied up and placed in the taxi. But which dogs were the brown dogs?

Nowzad, RPG, Jena and AK were all a shade of brown in colour. That meant two of them had made it. And two of them hadn't.

The email hadn't said which litter the missing puppy had been from. I figured I probably wouldn't find out either.

As Lisa's words sunk in I felt a mix of emotions brewing up inside me. I wanted to shout for joy and cry all at the same time.

In the week since we'd left Now Zad I'd played the possible scenarios a million times over and over in my mind. What if they all made it? Could the rescue centre cope with them all?

What if none of them had made it? What would happen to Nowzad if he did make it?

Now with the snippet of info that Lisa had given me I was really still none the wiser. I'd rather still be totally in the dark. At least I wouldn't have to agonise over struggling to work out which dogs were safe and which weren't. Before, ignorance had actually been bliss.

It was funny how things had worked out, I thought to myself. The one dog I knew was safe was Tali, the dog I knew the least. She'd been one of the last to arrive in the compound and had spent most of her time going off on her little hunting excursions. The dogs that I was closest to, RPG, AK, Jena and, most of all, Nowzad, were still effectively unaccounted for.

I guess deep down I knew one of the ones that hadn't made it would turn out to be Nowzad. If any of the three drivers had been forced to ditch a dog I knew it would have been him. He wasn't exactly the most tolerant of dogs to be transporting around.

Maybe I should have left him to his own fate in the alleys of Now Zad; at least he would have been at home.

I couldn't work out why there were only 13 puppies. We had parcelled 14 up that day back in Now Zad. What had happened to the puppy that hadn't made it? I hated to think.

As I waited for the results of my X-ray, the lack of information was killing me. Hobbling around Bastion on crutches, feeling a total fraud for having an injury just because I tripped over, was bad enough. But the gut-wrenching image of two of the dogs being abandoned to starve on the side of the road was tearing me apart. Especially when I didn't know which dogs they were.

The military surgeon sat me down in the medical centre at Bastion. I had been chatting away to the marine in the bed next to me on the ward. He had driven over a landmine but had had a lucky escape as he only suffered a broken leg. His passenger had not been so lucky and had sustained more serious injuries that had required an immediate flight back to Britain.

Both of us were slightly bemused to be lying opposite Afghan civilians who needed medical treatment. We were both fairly laid-back about the situation but I knew some marines who would not have been.

The surgeon's chat had been brief and to the point. I assumed he was having a busy day and I was just a minor blip he had to deal with.

'It is not a bad break, six to eight weeks to heal, tops,' he said matter-of-factly. 'If you do as you are told and don't run around like an idiot,' he added.

'Great,' was all I could reply.

'I have booked you on a flight back to the UK in two days' time. Nothing more you are going to do here.'

I didn't argue with him; there was no point. We were meant to be going home in six weeks anyway. I wouldn't be able to carry any form of weight on my back until then. My tour in Afghanistan was over.

I sat and stared at the flickering computer screen in the so-called Bastion Internet café, which was cunningly disguised as a Portakabin.

There were three emailed pictures in front of me, three very familiar-looking dogs staring at me from the screen.

The email attached to the pictures simply read:

Dear friends of the Helmand dogs and pups,

Fahran send us two female dogs and one male dog, one of the females dog is white with five puppies and the second female dog is dark brown skinny with eight puppies and the male is with no ears and no tail.

Thank you very much for saving them.
Best regards
Koshan

So that was it, in black and white. The agonising wait was over.

Tali, Nowzad and Jena had made it to the rescue.

RPG and AK hadn't.

I closed down the email and limped out into the heat of the day to find a quiet spot. My head was, once more, filled with a mixture of thoughts, some good, some not so good.

I looked away over the outer perimeter wall and towards the far distant mountains in the direction of the town of Now Zad. Somewhere out there were RPG and little AK.

We knew that if any of the dogs was going to take the chance to escape if offered it, RPG was the one who would make a run for it. I tried to imagine what must have happened. Perhaps the driver had hoped the dogs would follow him to the next van?

The puppies would have been carried in their containers, so Tali and Jena would have instinctively followed. Nowzad would have been attached still to the makeshift lead and wouldn't have had a chance to break away.

But RPG and AK were a different matter. If the driver had left the vehicle door open even for a second they would have done their familiar 'bomb burst'. They certainly would not have followed him.

I could only hope they had chewed the rope from around their paws so that they could run freely and escape.

The nightmare image of them abandoned on the side of the road still tied up filled my head. I tried desperately to shut it out.

I tried to console myself with the thoughts that at least the other dogs looked fairly well in the digital pictures.

In her photo Jena was sitting bolt upright in front of a wire fence and staring straight at the camera; she had a smart green collar around her neck. She looked confused more than anything.

An unknown rubber-gloved hand held a white puppy close

to her. From the size of the puppy I guessed it was one of hers.

Tali was looking her normal self but this time sat looking chilled on top of a wooden kennel.

Nowzad didn't look particularly happy in his photo. I wasn't surprised. He was chained to a wall. The image left me feeling confused and disillusioned again. I'd freed him to what I thought would be a better life. But was it really any better? And what sort of future had I given him? Probably not much of one at all.

Realistically he was not going to go to an Afghan home. And I didn't think there was much chance of him leaving the country to be taken to a more dog-friendly society.

I doubted he would survive for long in his new environment.

I closed my eyes and let the warming rays of the sun heat my face. 'At least Nowzad is alive,' I said.

I knew that maybe – just maybe – RPG and AK were running around happy out there somewhere still.

I knew, though, that the same couldn't be said for the dogs I had left behind in Now Zad.

The day before I had made a call to Klaus back in the compound.

I had told him to pay the ANP commander and I wanted to make sure that had happened. I also wanted to know how the remaining dogs were doing.

It was then that he had told me about Dushka.

As soon as he said it I knew it had been my fault.

One of the new Army Engineers to the compound had gone to the rear gate in the evening to take the rubbish out to the burns pit.

Of course, as soon as he had opened the rear gate Dushka had bounded over, probably thinking it was me bringing out some left-over food. After all hadn't I encouraged him to come over to me so I could make a fuss of him?

The young lad had panicked at the sight of a large fighting dog running towards him.

Without waiting he had shot Dushka.

The gentle giant fell to the ground and died by the rear gate.

On hearing the shot Klaus had raced to the rear entrance but when he got there it was all over. There was nothing he could do except drag Dushka to the burns pit.

Klaus hadn't seen Patches since then. I imagined he was still off roaming the alleys, trying to find his friend.

Out of pure emotional frustration and anger I had shouted at Klaus, asking for the lad's name. I wanted to kill him.

Luckily for both our sakes Klaus had refused.

The heavy drone of the C130 transport plane as it rose steeply into the cold blue air of the Helmand desert had an instant calming effect. Squashed into a canvas seat, I looked around at the weary faces staring vacantly back at me.

I didn't feel like talking; besides, even if we had wanted to the engines were too noisy.

I imagined we were now flying high above the mountains I had spent so much time daydreaming about. I knew I wouldn't be opening that adventure business among the Afghan people any time soon.

I thought about all that had happened over the last five months. A phrase that we marines use popped into my head. 'At the end of the day it gets dark,' I said to myself. 'At the end of the day it always gets dark.'

There was nothing you could do about that.

There was nothing I could do about what had happened in Afghanistan.

I closed my eyes. All that mattered now was the fact that for this tour, I was going home for good.

CHAPTER TWENTY-FIVE

Homecomings

As we ground to a halt on the motorway, I quickly wound the window down to get some air into the car. The shimmering heat was reflecting off the black tarmac.

Lisa had the right idea. She was snoozing, her head back against the headrest in the passenger seat.

I seemed to have picked a busy day to be driving towards London.

Everybody in the country seemed to be on the move. Or not, as in our case.

Today was a special day. Even more so than the outings with Fizz and Beamer that had remained our end-of-week focus, the escape that let us unwind from the stress of work.

Living with dogs had become a part of our lives, so much in fact that we'd decided to take on a couple more. We'd spoken to Fizz and Beamer about it and they didn't seem to have any objections to us expanding our canine family, especially as we had plied them with biscuits when we had asked.

Which was why, despite the slow-moving traffic on this baking hot June afternoon, we were on our way to visit an animal quarantine centre on the outskirts of London.

To say the four months since I'd arrived back from Afghanistan had been an emotional rollercoaster ride would have been the understatement of all time. So much had happened in such a short time.

Readjusting to life back home had at times been difficult. When I'd arrived back at RAF Brize Norton, Lisa had collected me so I didn't have to get the ambulance home.

Fizz and Beamer of course came along to greet me. It had taken a few minutes to calm the pair of them down in the back of the car before we could drive off.

I'd celebrated my arrival back at the house with a beer before heading out for a steak in the pub and a few more pints. I was soon strutting my stuff on one foot around the floor of our local like a man possessed, trying desperately to avoid knocking my strapped ankle against any of the bar stools.

I had been given sick leave but there were a few lads already back home with injuries far worse than mine. I made use of my time by helping them to arrange transport and welfare visits. It also kept me around camp in case there was any news from the lads still out in Afghanistan. But normally there was nothing new to hear.

Until, that was, I got an unexpected call to go and see the CSM. As soon as he welcomed me into his office and asked me to sit down I knew something was wrong.

'You were in Kilo Company weren't you?' he asked.

'Yeah, why?' I said, cautiously.

There was no beating around the bush, there was no point.

'Marine Ben Reddy was killed yesterday. The company were caught in the open by a Taliban ambush. Several other lads were injured,' the CSM said.

I just sat there. Immediately I pictured Ben's big smiling face. The lads good-humouredly compared him to Silas, the assassin albino monk in *The Da Vinci Code*. Ben hadn't minded the likeness; at least he had been given a nickname that was associated with a hard-man – unlike mine, which came from being related to a Victorian bike, although most of the lads wouldn't know what a Penny Farthing looked like.

Ben had been a true Royal Marine who had wanted nothing more than to muck in with the rest of the lads no matter what task they had been given.

In Now Zad, Ben had been one of the lads who'd taken an interest in the dogs. He'd been over to say hello to Nowzad, RPG, AK and the rest many times. He'd also kept an eye on the stray cats that roamed the compound. I hadn't known it at the time but he had asked his mum to send small packets of cat food through the post to Afghanistan so he could feed them.

He was only a young lad in his early twenties who had been determined to serve his country. He had paid for that determination by making the ultimate sacrifice.

'His coffin will be arriving at Brize Norton in a few days; we have a Bearer Party already sorted,' the CSM said, dragging me back into the room.

I knew that. They had already carried out the sombre duty for our unit three times before during this deployment.

'I'll do it,' I said without hesitation.

'What about your ankle?'

'What about it?' I replied, perhaps a little curtly.

I might not be able to carry his coffin but I could lead the young lads who would. It would be our honour to carry him back on to UK soil.

Carrying Ben from the C130 transport plane and out on to the tarmac at Brize Norton was one of the most important roles of my time as a Royal Marine. The day had been overcast and the eeriness as Brize Norton fell silent just added to the poignancy of the moment.

Meeting Ben's parents Liz and Phil after the repatriation ceremony was emotional; I just didn't know what to say. It took every ounce of strength not to choke up. Our small Bearer Party just tried to be strong for them in that moment.

The turnout for Ben's funeral in Ascot where he had

grown up was fantastic. Present and past marines made the trip. Even Prince Philip was seated in the church. I took great comfort from the fact that there were too many people to fit in, such was the level of support for Ben's family. I hope it helped them deal with their grief.

In the true spirit of Her Majesty's Royal Marine Commandos, we made sure that evening that we toasted a marine who had been killed in the service of Queen and Country.

The drinking went on into the dark hours. Those with the sorest heads the following morning claimed to have toasted him the most.

Within weeks the rest of the unit started to return home from Afghanistan as the army took over their duties in Helmand. For a while everything that had happened on the other side of the world was forgotten as marines and families were reunited. As the company was reunited too, drinking far too much became the order of the day.

The Royal Marines' contribution to the campaign in Afghanistan was soon being recognised. The OC was awarded an MBE for our time in the isolated Now Zad compound.

Yet despite the fact that the company were back on British soil, I didn't quite feel that I could just leave it all behind. There was a part of me that was still in Afghanistan and I had a feeling always would be.

It was just as hot still as we pulled into the gravel car park of the animal quarantine. Lisa had timed her snooze to perfection and was just waking up.

The high metal galvanised fences made the place look like a prison, which I suppose in a way it was.

The quarantine manager Rebecca introduced herself as we entered through the large gate.

'How are they doing?' I asked.

'Great, I don't know why you were worried,' she replied.

'I wasn't really,' I lied, smiling.

It had taken a lot of paperwork to get this far. We had learnt fast and had come across a few stumbling blocks, but eventually, with Rebecca's help, we had overcome them.

As Rebecca led us through the six different locked doors to get to the quarantine area, the sense of being in a jail got even stronger. Neither Lisa nor I could get back out without a member of staff accompanying us.

'You can visit when you want,' Rebecca said as we walked along the final corridor. The glass sealed doors at regular intervals all housed excited barking dogs from all corners of the world. The noise was almost deafening as they pawed against the plastic viewing slots.

Rebecca stopped at the first of the two doors that we had come to see.

I turned to Lisa. 'Ready?'

'Ready,' she replied. Even if she wasn't it was too late. There was no going back now.

Rebecca opened the door and I slipped inside.

He was curled up in the far end of the small enclosure. He looked skinnier than I remembered him. He wasn't barking like the rest of the dogs in the quarantine. When he heard my voice, however, I saw his stumpy tail beginning to wag itself silly.

'Hey, Nowzad,' I called out as he bounded over to me.

We hadn't seen each other for nearly five months but that didn't matter. He knew who I was.

He had definitely lost loads of weight. I could see his ribs through his sandy coat. He buried his head under my armpit as I rubbed his head.

'What did you think? I'd leave you in Afghanistan? No chance, lofty.'

The way the dogs' story had panned out since I'd left Afghanistan had been another succession of highs and lows.

A month after I had returned from Afghanistan an email

arrived from the rescue telling us that eleven of the puppies we'd sent them had died from an outbreak of parvovirus. All of Jena's litter had died. Only two of Tali's puppies were still alive.

I was gutted. After all they had been through. I felt hopeless inside.

But within days we had been given some good news regarding Jena. The American aid worker who had first set up the rescue, although she had not returned to the shelter, had seen our pictures of Jena. Immediately she had fallen for the homeless 'little chocolate Helmand mom' as the rescue staff called her.

And with that Jena had just started living a pampered pet's life in America.

Lisa and I had celebrated the news with a few pints. It didn't make up for the puppies but it helped.

Closer to home, the other good news was that more local newspapers had run stories on my rescue attempt and we were now being inundated with cheques. The only problem with this was they were all still in my name, which wasn't good. So one night over a pint or two Lisa and I decided to do something that was going to change our lives.

'Why not launch a charity? We've got enough money now to do some good,' I had suggested, testing the water. 'Maybe we could even eventually help fund the rescue centre.'

'Not like we have enough to do already,' Lisa replied sarcastically as she took a sip of her cider.

'It won't be that bad,' I said naively. 'The main thing is that we can get people to send cheques to a proper charity bank account and not to me.'

And so we had spent countless hours poring over applications to form a charity. The name of the charity was the easiest bit of the application.

'Nowzad Dogs, it has to be,' I had said aloud.

The response to the charity was instant and phenomenal.

Soon Lisa and I were spending most of our spare time dealing with emails and the donations that were slowly but surely trickling in.

The security situation in Afghanistan was still not the best and communicating with the rescue at times was frustratingly slow. The centre struggled to get hold of the desperately needed medical supplies. By the time they reached their remote location they were either damaged by the sweltering heat or out of date. That was, of course, if they had made it there at all. A lot of supplies were simply stolen.

The communication problems had also made it hard to keep up with news on the dogs. I was becoming particularly worried about Nowzad. Since seeing that photo of him when I was at Bastion, I had known that he hadn't settled in well at the rescue. They had asked me what I intended to do with the fighting dog; they knew nobody would want to look after him.

I had shown Lisa the email that voiced their concern for Nowzad. I had let her read the email and then looked at her.

She did that mindreading thing again and just gave me her 'whatever' smile back.

We both knew what we had to do.

Nowzad needed someone with huge patience to train him. I doubted there was anyone around who fitted that bill.

Well, apart from me and Lisa, that was.

The problem was that, until Jena, I'd never heard of a dog leaving Afghanistan. The admin that would be involved didn't bear thinking about. I'd learned the hard way that moving dogs around within Afghanistan was next to impossible. Moving them out of the country to the West, with all the red tape involved, was a complete non-starter. But we had to try.

Over the following weeks, with huge help from our

supporters and the Mayhew Animal Home International, we had sorted out the paperwork and the money needed to pay for two animal cargo flights to the UK.

I somehow convinced Lisa that if we were going to take in one dog we might as well take in two.

The words 'You owe me, Farthing' will live with me for ever.

Tali was coming to live with us too.

The two remaining puppies were still too young to travel; I hoped they would be okay left at the rescue for now. We would sort their futures out in due course.

Getting Nowzad and Tali to the UK wasn't cheap. The cost of keeping the two dogs in quarantine for six months was mind-boggling. The operational bonus I'd received on returning from Afghanistan was soon disappearing before my eyes as I wrote out another cheque to support the running costs of the rescue for the time they had housed our dogs.

But to me it was worth it. I had shared so much with the dogs of Now Zad; I had to do everything possible to get them back.

And now they were here.

I'd spent a minute or two playing with Nowzad when Lisa was let into the quarantine run by Rebecca.

We'd agreed that she had to be careful approaching him. He had never liked strangers and was highly likely to react. When he sensed the new arrival in his run, Nowzad broke off to cautiously stroll over to Lisa and sniff her legs.

Lisa rubbed the top of his head.

'See, told you it would be all right,' I said cheerfully.

But without warning Nowzad snapped at her legs. Not too aggressively but enough for Lisa to jump sideways.

'Bugger.' I grabbed him and gave him a stern telling off. '*Nowzad*, remember what happened last time you did that?'

Lisa warily walked back towards him; luckily for both me

and Nowzad it would take a lot more than a snarl to put Lisa off.

'Okay, that was your one chance to impress, nice one, Nowzad,' I berated him.

Suddenly it dawned on us that Lisa, Rebecca and the other female staff here were the first women he'd ever met.

After spending half an hour running around the small enclosure with him it was time to introduce Lisa to our other 'new' dog.

We left Nowzad lying tired out on the concrete floor as we walked the few yards to the next kennel.

We had no idea what the two of them would have been like together so we had made the decision for them to spend the six months' quarantine on their own. Time to socialise them would come later.

The moment I appeared at the plastic viewing grille Tali went completely berserk running around and around in circles. She carried on like this as I walked in until she finally came to rest at Lisa's feet. The two of them hit it off just like that. Tali had found her owner. It was as natural and easy as that.

Lisa's nickname for Tali came easily too. She took one look at the slightly scary way Tali pulled back her lips to reveal her white teeth when she was playing and was immediately reminded of her least favourite movie monster.

'Come here, little Alien,' she smiled.

After spending about an hour with Nowzad and Tali we said our farewells.

Apart from the quarantine requirement, they both needed medical attention including worming. They would also need to go through the slow painstaking process of having the numerous ticks they each carried removed. Any worries I had about leaving them there were lifted by the main keeper, Rebecca, and her staff, however.

I could tell during the following months Tali was going to become the little darling of the quarantine with people fussing over her all the time. Even other owners who had their own dogs in quarantine were already taking time out to see Tali, who didn't mind in the slightest.

Rebecca was an expert at bringing out the friendly side in dogs. She assured me that she would work hard on bringing the best out of Nowzad in the weeks ahead.

As we left the quarantine I was quietly confident that all would work out well. I would travel up to see the two dogs as often as I could. When the BBC had stated an interest in filming the dogs Dave and John had immediately joined me in the long journey to the rescue. Dave had hoped it would improve his profile with the ladies. Me and John had just laughed.

And still they were both scared of Nowzad, feeding him biscuits through the fence while I sat with him.

As I drove home I felt like it was the beginning of a new day. For the past five months or so my head had been filled with thoughts of what might have been if things had been different during my time in Afghanistan. From now on it was going to be about the future, not the past. It was all about what we could achieve now.

* * *

The road to the beach was surprisingly busy for Christmas Day. Cars were streaming out from the town.

'What's going on down here? I thought everybody would be at home opening presents?' I said to Lisa.

As I turned the car on to the main sea front drive we both let out a low 'wow'. There seemed to be thousands of people walking, driving or cycling along the beach road.

'Look at the pub,' I exclaimed as we drove past happily beer-swilling punters spilling out on to the road as they struggled to find room in the outdoor seating area.

'Look at those mad fools,' Lisa shouted. I turned to look down on the beach in the direction she was pointing.

'No way.'

There must have been over 500 crazy idiots stood in swimsuits or bikinis about to make a mad dash into the rough sea. We had our winter coats on. It wasn't that warm out there.

We continued driving slowly along the beach front but the crowds didn't thin out. If anything it was getting busier as we moved further away from the pub and arcade areas.

'This is a bad idea, way too many people,' I told myself.

I had planned on Nowzad having a bit of peace and quiet for his first walk of freedom. I seriously doubted whether this was going to happen today.

Eventually I found an empty parking slot facing the beach. I pulled in and turned the engine off. Right in front of us was a parking meter. It read 'Charges apply 365 days of the year'.

'Miserable bastards,' I said as Lisa and I both rifled through our pockets trying to cuff together the required 85 pence.

There were so many people walking past us I still couldn't believe it. There were mums and dads nervously following their kids as they tottered along the promenade on their new bikes, young couples were strolling along arm in arm, groups playing ball on the damp beach and dogs running wild, lots of dogs running wild.

The one thing that I couldn't see was somebody else getting ready to break in a former Afghan fighting dog with no ears.

'Oh shit, this really is a bad idea,' I said.

'Not one of your better ones, I must admit,' Lisa replied.

We'd collected Nowzad and Tali from the quarantine on Christmas Eve, on the last day of their six months in isolation. The weather had been wet and damp. It had reminded me of Afghanistan the previous Christmas.

It was a busy period for us. We were halfway through

moving to a new house in a new area. Not our choice but sometimes you didn't get much say as far as the military were concerned. It wouldn't be a permanent home, of course. Nothing ever was in the forces. We could be posted elsewhere at a minute's notice.

A pile of boxes, suitcases, rucksacks and plastic bags were sitting in the hallway waiting for us to unpack. When that was going to happen I didn't know, although if Lisa had anything to do with it they wouldn't stay there for very long.

Most of the quarantine staff had come to see Nowzad and Tali go. I thought I even saw a few tears.

It was the first time Nowzad and Tali had been outside for over six months. I don't know who was more excited, us or them. Getting to the car for the drive home took nearly half an hour as both dogs dragged us around the woods outside the quarantine. We let them, as we thought it was only fair. Nowzad, when I thought about it, had been shut in an enclosed space for nearly thirteen months.

Both rummaged and sniffed everything and anything they could find.

Finally Nowzad stopped and stood by my legs. I rubbed his head while he sniffed the air of the quarantine car park.

When the Afghan dogs had met Fizz and Beamer it had been almost a non-event. Both sets of dogs sniffed each other and then lost interest and wandered off. The precaution of having Nowzad wear a muzzle had proven unnecessary.

Fizz and Beamer were with us today. The sight of the beach and the hordes of other dogs running around had them chomping at the bit to get out. I wasn't worried about them running off. My concern was Tali and, in particular, Nowzad.

I looked over the back seat and at Nowzad and Tali in their separate travel crates with Fizz and Beamer between them.

'We are here now, Nowzad, try and behave, buddy,' I said.

Nowzad was sat upright patiently waiting to be let out so he could discover even more smells in this strange, new world.

'Ready?' I asked Lisa.

'No,' she said as she slipped out of the passenger seat and walked to the back door of the car.

As soon as she had opened the door both Beamer and Fizz were straining their necks out of the door, trying to take in the view. Our two foreign dogs were making little whimpering noises as they pawed the mesh flaps of their travel crates.

Nowzad stood quite happily while I attached his full body harness. At least I had some experience of walking him from the compound. Tali had never been walked before. We couldn't risk her running off so she wore a full body harness as well.

The waves crashed against the shoreline, sending the spray flying through the air. I sat on a large boulder that had been worn smooth by the constant motion of the incoming tide.

After a good 30-minute walk along the bottom of the shale cliffs Nowzad had finally stopped pulling on his lead for all he was worth and was now sitting quietly by my side.

He had curled up tight in a ball with just his head held up looking out towards the surf. I imagined he was still trying to work out what the foaming white waves were.

Tali, still on her lead, was running around Lisa as she in turn was chasing Fizz Dog. Beamer was running alongside them further up the beach.

I stroked Nowzad along the back of his head as the wind whistled over the flat sandy beach. He turned his head towards me, his big brown eyes still looking sad but showing no hint of worry about what lay in store for him in this unfamiliar place. I figured he had enough savvy to know it couldn't be any worse than the life he had left behind.

I looked out to sea. There was nothing on the horizon, just the distant tips of breaking waves and the odd seagull swooping low to make a catch.

My mind wandered back to Afghanistan, Now Zad and, for some reason, to the curly-haired, smiling figure of Rosi. For a minute I was back with him on the roof of the galley building talking away about everything and anything without either of us understanding the other in the slightest. Maybe we hadn't needed to. We had been friends. That was enough.

'I wonder what Rosi is up to, eh Nowzad?' I asked Nowzad out loud. But he had already closed his eyes and looked asleep. I couldn't blame him. After all this was the furthest he had walked in nearly 13 months, since he'd first crept into the compound and my life.

The compound. My thoughts drifted back to the mud-walled fortress and a part of my life that was now gone for good. As I shut my eyes and let the sea breeze wash over me, I could see the dogs that had made my six months there bearable. Skinny RPG sat on top of the pillow on the cardboard box near the galley, patiently waiting for his turn in the breakfast queue. Of all the dogs, he had been the one that I thought would be here with me now. He would have loved running free with Beamer on the beach. I just hoped that he had managed to chew loose the bindings on his front legs.

I chuckled to myself as I pictured little AK, that mini-version of RPG. I hoped she had managed to escape with RPG and that, wherever they were, they were having fun, tussling and chasing each other.

We would never know what had happened to the two of them. In truth, I doubted they were both still alive.

I smiled again as I remembered Patches and Dushka trotting along to the LS with us. It had been funny to watch. I fought to control my thoughts. I still had no idea what had happened to Patches. I knew every time I looked at Tali I would see him there, tail wagging.

Maybe I could have saved them but I had made the decision not to. Instead Nowzad was next to me on the beach. That was nearly ten months ago now. Time was flying by. So much had changed, so much had happened.

I stroked Nowzad's head a few more times; his light brown hair was damp from the sea breeze.

'But we got you two guys out, didn't we?' I said aloud.

I doubted anybody else, let alone Nowzad, would blame me for not getting them all out. But I knew I would always blame myself.

Lisa was coming back along the beach towards us, Beamer in the lead as always.

'Come on, Nowzad,' I said, 'time to go home.'

The two of us sat around the table surrounded by our four dogs as we ate our Christmas dinner. I couldn't stop smiling. For the second successive Christmas, Nowzad munched away at his own slice of turkey for his evening meal.

As Lisa and I lazed around on Christmas night, I couldn't help but think back to the previous Christmas Day in the Now Zad DC.

If I had known then what I knew now. Would I have guessed that I would now be running a charity set up specifically to try and help Afghanistan and its people and animals? I doubted it.

I now had an opportunity to do something positive at last. We had plans to use some of the money the charity had received for the only one of the two puppies that had survived from Tali's litter. He was almost a year old and we had named him Helmand.

Thanks to the charity we were beginning to make plans to fly him to the UK in January. We already had a prospective home lined up.

We were also trying to put in place a proposal to train young Afghan vets. There was a desperate shortage of them out there. They would help make a real difference to the welfare of not just the dogs but the farm animals that were desperately needed to support the remote villages.

But the dogs for now were going to be the main focus of our efforts for the next year or so. When I had flown out of Afghanistan I had left behind thousands of stray dogs, many of them living in pitiful conditions or – worse – being abused in dogfights. They'd had no hope. Helmand was going to be the latest in what I hoped would be a long line of dogs that would find a loving home.

I had briefly checked my email as we had got back from the beach. I knew it was Christmas Day but I had just had a feeling there was going to be some news.

Sure enough, as I logged on one email stood out. The subject was direct and to the point: 'Afghan dog'.

The email from a soldier out in Helmand was simple:

I am serving in Afghanistan and have befriended a young stray dog that lives in the military base where I am stationed. Can you help me rescue it? I can't just leave it here to starve.

I smiled as I read it. I now had a new mission in my life and this time it didn't involve being armed to the teeth.

I knew it would probably at times prove to be extremely frustrating but then Afghanistan always was. Anyway, we had already proved that it could be done.

I looked at Nowzad and Tali sleeping quite happily in their new dog beds. I needed to reply quickly. I knew that the soldier would want to know there was somebody else in the world that thought like he did.

I had another dog to rescue.

Fizz Dog

Beamer Boy

On the beach with Lisa, Fizz Dog, Beamer Boy,
Tali and Nowzad.

Tali

Nowzad

Acknowledgements

When I deployed to Afghanistan back in September 2006 never for one moment had I any inkling of what was to come. To be sat here two years later, knowing that my life has changed beyond all recognition because I befriended a few starving and battered stray dogs, is still slightly unbelievable. That I have now written a book about it is even more incredible. Thank you Mary Pachnos and Fiona MacIntyre for realising the potential of the Nowzad Dogs story and to Garry for my 'inner voice'. I'll get the next bottle of red wine ... But mostly I need to say a big thank you to Charlotte Cole at Ebury for putting everything together in the right order and keeping me on track – if only she knew how really chaotic it was in our house while trying to write this book!

A big thank you must go to Joy and Caroline at the Mayhew Animal Home. They were there when we needed them most. And if any stray dogs out there need an angel, then Pam should be their number-one choice. Words cannot express our thanks, Pam.

But most of all I must thank our many supporters who share the same passion as me towards our four-legged friends. It is why Nowzad Dogs has gone from strength to strength. Your support has been fantastic.

And finally to the one person that – without her support – I am not sure where in life I would be. Lisa, without you putting up with me and supporting me in my mad crazy plans none of this would have been possible. Love you always, honey BBCOMB xxxxxxxxxxxxx

PS Fizz Dog and Beamer Boy – I promise not to bring any more strays home ... honest!

nowzad d🐾gs

registered charity in the UK (number 1119185)

Mission statement: To relieve the suffering of animals, predominantly stray and abandoned dogs, in need of care and attention, and to provide and maintain rescue facilities for the care and treatment of such animals, especially the dogs of Afghanistan.

We know that we cannot bring all the stray dogs of Afghanistan back to the UK, but we can help support those soldiers who find themselves trying to look after Afghan strays and aid the vital work of the Afghan rescue centre that helped me. Contributions to the rescue centre help their educational programme for children, their free neutering programme for stray dogs and cats brought into the rescue and further the welfare and local rehoming of rescued animals. We also support Mayhew International's training programme for vets from developing countries who are working to help animals in their local communities.

We have started small but with your help we can only get bigger! Nobody involved with Nowzad Dogs is paid for their time – all the money you donate goes directly towards helping the dogs (and cats) in need while raising awareness of the problems that homeless dogs, wherever they are in the world, can and do face.